chinese

chinese

KATHY MAN

LORENZ BOOKS

First published in 1999 by Lorenz Books
Lorenz Books is an imprint of Anness Publishing Inc.
27 West 20th Street, New York, NY 10011; (800) 354-9657

ISBN 0-7548-0261-2

Publisher Joanna Lorenz
Senior editor Doreen Palamartschuk
Copy editors Linda Doeser & Jenni Fleetwood
Photography William Lingwood, Dave King, Nicki Dowey
Design Wherefore Art?
Styling Clare Louise Hunt & Clare Reynolds
Food for photography Lucy McKelvie, Jennie Shapter, Becky Johnson
Production controller Karina Han

Printed & bound in Singapore
10 9 8 7 6 5 4 3 2 1

Some of the recipes in this book previously appeared in *Low Fat Chinese*.

chinese

introduction

Delicious dishes from this **popular** cuisine, that can be cooked in minutes—what could be better for the **modern cook?** The recipes are a unique and **tempting collection** and a combination of **irresistible** favorites with refreshingly new tastes and **textures. Quick** and **easy** to prepare, these simple dishes capture the **authentic flavors** of this superb cuisine to give **spectacular results** for entertaining and every occasion.

flavorings & spices

CHINESE COOKING IS SO **POPULAR** THAT EVEN SMALL SUPERMARKETS TEND TO **STOCK** AN **EXTENSIVE SELECTION** OF **FLAVORING** INGREDIENTS.

BLACK BEAN SAUCE

This sauce is made from salted fermented soybeans, which have been crushed and mixed to a thick paste with flavorings. Black bean sauce is highly concentrated and is usually added to hot oil at the start of cooking to release the flavor.

YELLOW BEAN SAUCE

A puree of fermented yellow beans combined with salt, flour and sugar. This thick, sweetish, smooth sauce is often used in marinades.

CHILES

A wide variety of these hot members of the capsicum family is available, both fresh and dried. They are mostly used for flavoring, but plump, fresh ones that are relatively mild can be stuffed and served as a vegetable.

CHILI OIL

This reddish vegetable oil owes both its color and spicy flavor to the chiles that have been steeped or marinated in it. Use chili oil sparingly in cooking or as a peppery dipping sauce.

DRIED SHRIMP

Dried, salty shrimp used as a flavoring and also as an ingredient. The shrimp are always soaked in warm water first to remove some of the salt. They have a strong flavor, so should be used sparingly.

FIVE-SPICE POWDER

A finely ground mixture of fennel seeds, star anise, Szechuan peppercorns, cloves and cinnamon. It has a fairly strong taste and a pungent spicy aroma and should be used sparingly. It can be used in both sweet and savory dishes.

GARLIC

This small, aromatic vegetable is one of the most important flavoring ingredients in Chinese cooking. The most common method of preparing garlic is to peel it, then chop it finely or mince it. However, garlic is sometimes simply bruised, or peeled and sliced.

GINGER

Fresh ginger root is an essential flavoring ingredient in Chinese cooking. It is peeled, then sliced, shredded or chopped before use. Dried ginger or ground ginger does not have the same fresh flavor and is not suitable as a substitute. Fresh ginger root freezes well. Keep a well-wrapped, peeled root in the freezer and grate it as required. It will thaw instantly.

HOISIN SAUCE

A thick, rich, dark sauce often used for flavoring meat and poultry before cooking. It is also sometimes used as one of the ingredients in a dipping sauce.

LOTUS LEAVES

The dried leaves of the lotus plant are used as an aromatic wrapping for steamed dishes. Lotus leaves must be soaked in water for 30 minutes to soften them before use.

OYSTER SAUCE

This thick, dark sauce is made from oyster juice, flour, salt and sugar. It is usually added to dishes at the end of cooking.

RICE VINEGAR

A colorless vinegar used to add sharpness to sweet-and-sour dishes. If rice vinegar is not obtainable, white vinegar or cider vinegar can be used as a substitute.

ROCK SUGAR

An aptly-named ingredient that consists of irregular lumps of amber-colored sugar. Derived from sugar cane, rock sugar is mainly used in sweet dishes and has a caramelized flavor.

SESAME OIL

This aromatic oil is made from roasted sesame seeds. Small quantities are used as an accent at the end of cooking to add flavor to a dish.

DARK SOY SAUCE

A rich, dark sauce that is used to add both color and flavor to many sauces and marinades. Dark soy sauce is quite salty and is often used instead of salt to season a dish.

LIGHT SOY SAUCE

A thin, dark sauce used for flavoring many Chinese dishes and also as a table condiment. The flavor is slightly lighter and fresher than dark soy sauce, but it is a little more salty.

STAR ANISE

A strong licorice-tasting spice mainly used to flavor meat and poultry. The whole spice is frequently used in braised dishes so that the flavor can be released and absorbed slowly.

vegetables & mushrooms

AUTHENTIC INGREDIENTS MAKE ALL THE **DIFFERENCE**. LOOK OUT FOR **THESE** AT **ASIAN** MARKETS.

BAMBOO SHOOTS

Crunchy young shoots from the bamboo plant, these have a delicate, but distinctive flavor. They are available in cans, either whole, sliced or cut into thin, matchstick-size shreds.

CHINESE MUSHROOMS

When fresh, they are sold as shiitake mushrooms, but the dried version is more widely used in Chinese cooking. Dried Chinese mushrooms have a more concentrated flavor. Soak in hot water before use.

CLOUD EARS, WOOD EARS

Dried edible fungi that have a crunchy texture; cloud ears have a more delicate flavor than wood ears. Once reconstituted in water they expand to many times their original size.

STRAW MUSHROOMS

These are grown on rice straw and have a slippery, meaty texture with little flavor. At present these mushrooms are only available canned. In Chinese cooking, they are used mainly for their texture.

LOTUS ROOT

A crunchy vegetable with naturally occurring holes, lotus root is occasionally sold fresh, but is more frequently available dried or frozen. When cut and pulled apart, thread-like strands are produced from the cut surfaces. Also known as renkon.

TARO

A starchy tuber used in both savory and sweet dishes. It looks like a hairy rutabaga with white flesh slightly marked by purplish dots. The flavor and texture resemble those of a baking potato.

WATER CHESTNUTS

Once peeled, these black-skinned bulbs reveal a white, crunchy interior with a sweet flavor. Canned, peeled water chestnuts are available in most supermarkets, but the fresh, unpeeled bulb can sometimes be bought in Chinese stores.

beans & bean products

PACKED WITH **PROTEIN**, THESE ARE ESSENTIAL INGREDIENTS THAT **NO SELF-RESPECTING** CHINESE **COOK** SHOULD **BE WITHOUT**.

ADZUKI BEANS

Small red beans used mainly in sweet dishes. As with most pulses, adzuki beans must be soaked in water before use. They should be boiled hard for 10 minutes at the start of cooking, then simmered until soft before use.

TOFU (BEAN CURD)

As its name suggests, this is a product made from soybeans. Fresh tofu is sold covered in water. It has very little flavor of its own, but readily absorbs flavorings. Tofu is used extensively in Chinese cooking and is a good source of protein. There are several different types, including "silken" tofu and smoked tofu, but the firm variety is the one normally used by the Chinese.

DRIED TOFU (BEAN CURD) STICKS

These are sheets of tofu, which have been formed into sticks and dried. They are an important ingredient in Chinese vegetarian dishes. They must be soaked in hot water before being used. Tofu sticks are usually available only in Chinese supermarkets.

A

B

C

A: From top left, bamboo shoots, the large tuber known as taro, lotus root with its naturally occurring holes and water chestnuts.

B: From top left, fresh shiitake mushrooms, canned straw mushrooms, dried cloud ears and Chinese mushrooms.

C: Fresh tofu (bean curd), adzuki beans and dried tofu (bean curd) sticks, protein rich components of many Chinese recipes.

soups & appetizers

tomato & beef soup

FRESH TOMATOES AND **SCALLIONS** GIVE THIS LIGHT BEEF BROTH A **SUPERB** FLAVOR.

method

SERVES 4

1 Cut the beef into thin strips and place it in a saucepan. Pour in boiling water to cover. Cook for 2 minutes, then drain thoroughly and set aside.

2 Bring the stock to a boil in a clean pan. Stir in the tomato paste, then the tomatoes and sugar. Add the beef strips, allow the stock to boil again, then lower the heat and simmer for 2 minutes.

3 Mix the cornstarch to a paste with the water. Add the mixture to the soup, stirring constantly, until it thickens slightly. Lightly beat the egg white in a cup.

4 Pour the egg white into the soup in a steady stream, stirring constantly. As soon as the egg white changes color, add salt and pepper, stir the soup and pour it into heated bowls. Drizzle each portion with a few drops of sesame oil, sprinkle with the scallions and serve.

cook's tip

For the best flavor, use sun-ripened tomatoes for this soup, rather than tomatoes in greenhouse, which lack flavor.

ingredients

3 ounces **round steak,** trimmed of fat
3¾ cups **beef stock**
2 tablespoons **tomato paste**
6 **tomatoes,** halved, seeded and chopped
2 teaspoons **sugar**
1 tablespoon **cornstarch**
1 tablespoon cold **water**
1 **egg white**
½ teaspoon **sesame oil**
2 **scallions,** finely shredded
salt and freshly ground **black pepper**

ingredients

2 ounces **jumbo shrimp**
2 ounces **scallops**
3 ounces skinless **cod** fillet, roughly chopped
1 tablespoon finely chopped **chives**
1 teaspoon **dry sherry**
1 small **egg white**, lightly beaten
½ teaspoon **sesame oil**
¼ teaspoon **salt**
large pinch of freshly ground **white pepper**
3¾ cups **fish stock**
20 **wonton wrappers**
2 Romaine **lettuce leaves,** shredded
cilantro leaves and **garlic chives**, to garnish

cook's tip

The filled wonton wrappers can be made ahead, then frozen for several weeks and cooked straight from the freezer.

seafood wonton soup

THIS IS A **VARIATION** ON THE POPULAR WONTON SOUP WHICH IS **TRADITIONALLY** PREPARED USING **PORK**.

method

SERVES 4

1. Peel and devein the shrimp. Rinse them well, pat them dry on paper towels and cut them into small pieces.

2. Rinse the scallops. Pat them dry, using paper towels. Chop them into small pieces the same size as the shrimp.

3. Place the cod in a food processor and process until a paste is formed. Scrape into a bowl and stir in the shrimp, scallops, chives, sherry, egg white, sesame oil, salt and pepper. Mix thoroughly, cover and set aside in a cool place to marinate for 20 minutes.

4. Heat the fish stock gently in a saucepan. To prepare the wontons, place a teaspoonful of the seafood filling in the center of a wonton wrapper, then bring the corners together to meet at the top. Twist them together to enclose the filling. Fill the remaining wonton wrappers in the same way.

5. Bring a large saucepan of water to a boil. Drop in the wontons. When the water returns to a boil, lower the heat and simmer gently for 5 minutes, or until the wontons float to the surface. Drain the wontons and divide them among four heated soup bowls.

6. Add a portion of lettuce to each bowl. Bring the fish stock to a boil. Ladle it into each bowl, garnish each portion with cilantro leaves and garlic chives and serve immediately.

THIS **SPICY**, WARMING SOUP REALLY **WHETS** THE **APPETITE** AND IS THE PERFECT **INTRODUCTION** TO A CHINESE MEAL.

ingredients

- 1/4 ounce dried **cloud ears**
- 8 fresh **shiitake mushrooms**
- 3 ounces **tofu**
- 1/2 cup sliced, drained, canned **bamboo shoots**
- 3 3/4 cups **vegetable stock**
- 1 tablespoon **sugar**
- 3 tablespoons **rice vinegar**
- 1 tablespoon **light soy sauce**
- 1/4 teaspoon **chili oil**
- 1/2 teaspoon **salt**
- large pinch of freshly ground **white pepper**
- 1 tablespoon **cornstarch**
- 1 tablespoon **cold water**
- 1 **egg white**
- 1 teaspoon **sesame oil**
- 2 **scallions**, cut into fine rings

hot-&-sour soup

method

SERVES 4

1 Soak the cloud ears in a bowl of hot water for 30 minutes, or until soft. Drain, trim off and discard the hard parts from each and chop the cloud ears roughly.

2 Remove and discard the stems from the shiitake mushrooms. Cut the caps into thin strips. Cut the tofu into 1/2-inch cubes and shred the bamboo shoots finely.

3 Place the stock, mushrooms, tofu, bamboo shoots and cloud ears in a large saucepan. Bring the stock to a boil, lower the heat and simmer for about 5 minutes.

4 Stir in the sugar, vinegar, soy sauce, chili oil, salt and pepper. Mix the cornstarch to a paste with the water. Add the mixture to the soup, stirring constantly until it starts to thicken.

5 Lightly beat the egg white, then pour it slowly into the soup in a steady stream, stirring constantly. Cook, stirring, until the egg white changes color.

6 Add the sesame oil just before serving. Ladle into heated bowls and top each portion with scallion rings.

cook's tip

To transform this tasty soup into a nutritious, light meal, simply add extra mushrooms, tofu and bamboo shoots.

crisp turkey balls

TURKEY IS NOT TRADITIONALLY USED IN CHINESE COOKING, BUT IT MAKES A VERY **TASTY ALTERNATIVE** TO CHICKEN.

method

SERVES 4–6

1 Preheat the oven to 250°F. Brush the bread lightly with olive oil and cut it into 1/4-inch cubes. Spread over a baking sheet and bake for 15 minutes, until dry and crisp.

2 Meanwhile, mix together the turkey, water chestnuts and chiles in a food processor. Process until a coarse paste is formed.

3 Add the egg white, cilantro, cornstarch, salt and pepper. Pour in half the soy sauce and process for about 30 seconds. Scrape into a bowl, cover and set aside in a cool place for 20 minutes.

4 Remove the toasted bread from the oven and set aside. Raise the oven temperature to 400°F. With dampened hands, divide the turkey mixture into 12 portions and form into balls.

5 Roughly crush the toasted bread, then transfer to a plate. Roll each ball in turn over the toasted crumbs until coated. Place on a baking sheet and bake for about 20 minutes, or until the coating is brown and the turkey filling has cooked through.

6 In a small bowl, mix the remaining soy sauce with the sugar, rice vinegar and chili oil. Serve the sauce with the turkey balls, garnished with shredded chiles and cilantro sprigs.

ingredients

4 thin slices of **white bread**, crusts removed
1 teaspoon **olive oil**
8 ounces skinless, boneless **turkey**, roughly chopped
1/3 cup drained, canned **water chestnuts**
2 fresh **red chiles**, seeded and roughly chopped
1 **egg white**
1/4 cup **cilantro leaves**
1 teaspoon **cornstarch**
1/2 teaspoon **salt**
1/4 teaspoon freshly ground **white pepper**
2 tablespoons **light soy sauce**
1 teaspoon **sugar**
2 tablespoons **rice vinegar**
1/2 teaspoon **chili oil**
shredded **red chiles** and **cilantro sprigs**, to garnish

variation

Chicken or pork can be used instead of turkey, with equally delicious results.

THIS **HEALTHY** VERSION OF THIS **POPULAR** APPETIZER HAS LOST NONE OF ITS **CLASSIC CRUNCH** AND TASTE.

ingredients

6 slices **white bread**, crusts removed
8 ounces **jumbo shrimp**, peeled and deveined
⅓ cup drained, canned **water chestnuts**
1 **egg white**
1 teaspoon **sesame oil**
½ teaspoon **salt**
2 **scallions,** finely chopped
2 teaspoons **dry sherry**
1 tablespoon **sesame seeds**, toasted (see cook's tip)
shredded **scallion**, to garnish

shrimp toasts with sesame seeds

method

SERVES 4–6

1 Preheat the oven to 250°F. Cut each slice of bread into four triangles. Spread out on a baking sheet and bake for 25 minutes, or until crisp.

2 Meanwhile, put the shrimp in a food processor with the water chestnuts, egg white, sesame oil and salt. Process until a coarse purée is formed.

3 Scrape the mixture into a bowl, stir in the chopped scallions and sherry and marinate for 10 minutes.

4 Remove the toast from the oven and raise the temperature to 400°F. Spread the shrimp mixture on the toast, sprinkle with sesame seeds and bake for 12 minutes. Garnish with scallion and serve hot or warm.

cook's tip

To toast sesame seeds, put them in a dry frying pan and place over medium heat until the seeds change color. Shake the pan constantly to prevent them from burning.

crab spring rolls
& dipping sauce

CHILI AND GINGER ADD A **HINT OF HEAT** TO THESE **SENSATIONAL** TREATS. SERVE THEM AS A STARTER OR **SIDE DISH**.

method

SERVES 4–6

1 Heat a wok briefly, then add the peanut oil and sesame oil. When hot, stir-fry the crushed garlic and chile for 1 minute. Add the vegetables and ginger and stir-fry for 1 minute more.

2 Drizzle the sherry or rice wine and soy sauce over the vegetables. Allow the mixture to bubble up for 1 minute.

3 Using a slotted spoon, transfer the vegetables to a dish. Set aside until cool, then stir in the crabmeat and season with salt and pepper.

4 Soften the spring roll wrappers, following the directions on the package. Place some of the filling on a wrapper, fold over the front edge and the sides and roll up neatly, sealing the edges with a little beaten egg. Repeat with the remaining wrappers and filling.

5 Heat the oil in the wok and fry the spring rolls in batches, turning several times, until brown and crisp. Remove with a slotted spoon, drain on paper towels and keep hot while frying the remainder. Serve immediately and with the sambal kecap, garnished with lime wedges and cilantro.

ingredients

1 tablespoon **peanut oil**
1 teaspoon **sesame oil**
1 **garlic** clove, crushed
1 fresh **red chile**, seeded and finely sliced
1 pound package fresh stir-fry **vegetables**
1-inch piece of fresh **ginger root**, grated
1 tablespoon **dry sherry** or Chinese **rice wine**
1 tablespoon **soy sauce**
12 ounces fresh **crabmeat**
12 **spring roll wrappers**
1 small **egg**, beaten
oil, for deep frying
salt and freshly ground **black pepper**
Indonesian sambal kecap, to serve
lime wedges and **cilantro**, to garnish

cook's tip

Spring roll wrappers are available in many supermarkets as well as Asian grocers. If you are unable to find them, use phyllo pastry instead. Keep the wrappers and filled rolls covered with plastic wrap, as they will dry out if exposed to the air.

mussels in black bean sauce

THE LARGE **GREEN-SHELLED** MUSSELS FROM **NEW ZEALAND** ARE **PERFECT** FOR THIS DELICIOUS DISH. BUY THE **COOKED MUSSELS** ON THE HALF SHELL.

ingredients

1 tablespoon **vegetable oil**
1-inch piece of fresh **ginger root**, finely chopped
2 **garlic** cloves, finely chopped
1 fresh **red chile**, seeded and chopped
1 tablespoon **black bean sauce**
1 tablespoon **dry sherry**
1 teaspoon **sugar**
1 teaspoon **sesame oil**
2 teaspoons **dark soy sauce**
20 cooked **New Zealand green-shelled mussels**
2 **scallions**, 1 shredded and 1 cut into fine rings

method

SERVES 4–6

1 Heat the vegetable oil in a small frying pan. Fry the ginger, garlic and chile with the black bean sauce for a few seconds, then add the sherry and sugar and cook for 30 seconds more.

2 Remove the sauce from heat and stir in the sesame oil and soy sauce. Mix thoroughly.

3 Have ready a saucepan with about 2 inches of boiling water and a heatproof plate that will fit neatly inside it. Place the mussels in a single layer on the plate. Spoon the sauce over the mussels.

4 Sprinkle the scallions over the mussels, cover the plate tightly with aluminum foil and place it in the pan on a metal trivet. Steam over high heat for about 10 minutes, or until the mussels have heated through. Serve immediately.

cook's tip

Large scallops in their shells can be cooked in the same way. Do not overcook the shellfish.

mini phoenix rolls

THESE **ROLLS** ARE AN **EASY APPETIZER** AND CAN BE SERVED **HOT** OR **COLD**.

method

SERVES 4

1 Lightly beat the 2 whole eggs with 3 tablespoons of the water. Heat a 8-inch omelet pan and brush with a little of the oil. Pour in a quarter of the egg mixture, swirling the pan to coat the bottom lightly. Cook the omelet until the top is set. Slide it onto a plate and make three more omelets in the same way.

2 Mix the pork and water chestnuts in a food processor. Add 1 teaspoon of the ginger. Drain the mushrooms, chop the caps roughly and add these to the mixture. Process until smooth.

3 Scrape the pork paste into a bowl. Stir in the egg white, sherry, remaining water and salt and pepper. Mix thoroughly, cover and set aside in a cool place for about 15 minutes.

4 Have ready a saucepan with about 2 inches boiling water and a large heatproof plate that will fit inside it on a metal trivet. Divide the pork mixture among the omelets and spread into a large square shape in the center of each of the omelets.

5 Bring the sides of each omelette over the filling and roll up from the bottom to the top. Arrange the rolls on the plate. Cover the plate tightly with aluminum foil and place it in the pan on the trivet. Steam over a high heat for 15 minutes.

6 Make a dipping sauce by mixing the remaining ginger with the rice vinegar and sugar in a small dish. Cut the rolls diagonally in ½-inch slices, garnish with the cilantro or flat-leaf parsley leaves and serve with the sauce.

ingredients

2 large **eggs**, plus 1 **egg white**
5 tablespoons cold **water**
1 teaspoon **vegetable oil**
6 ounces lean **pork**, diced
½ cup drained, canned **water chestnuts**
2-inch piece of fresh **ginger root**, grated
4 dried **Chinese mushrooms**, soaked in boiling water until soft
1 tablespoon **dry sherry**
¼ teaspoon **salt**
large pinch of freshly ground **white pepper**
2 tablespoons **rice vinegar**
½ teaspoon **sugar**
cilantro or **flat-leaf parsley**, to garnish

cook's tip

These rolls can be prepared a day in advance and then steamed just before serving.

THIS **PRETTY** DISH IS NOT AS **HOT** AND **FIERY** AS YOU MIGHT EXPECT, SO GIVE IT A TRY.

ingredients

- 10 fat fresh green **New Mexico** or **poblano chiles**
- 4 ounces lean **pork**, roughly chopped
- 3 ounces **jumbo shrimp**, peeled and deveined
- ½ cup **cilantro leaves**
- 1 teaspoon **cornstarch**
- 2 teaspoons **dry sherry**
- 2 teaspoons **soy sauce**
- 1 teaspoon **sesame oil**
- ½ teaspoon **salt**
- 1 tablespoon cold **water**
- 1 fresh **red** and 1 fresh **green chile**, seeded and sliced into rings, and cooked **peas**, to garnish

stuffed chiles

method

SERVES 4

1 Cut the chiles in half lengthwise, keeping the stem. Scrape out and discard the seeds and set the chiles aside.

2 Mix together the pork, shrimp and cilantro leaves in a food processor. Process until smooth. Scrape into a bowl and mix in the cornstarch, sherry, soy sauce, sesame oil, salt and water; cover and let marinate for 10 minutes.

3 Fill each half chile with some of the meat mixture. Have ready a saucepan with about 2 inches boiling water and a steamer or heatproof plate that will fit inside it on a trivet.

4 Place the stuffed chiles in the steamer or on a plate, meat-side up, and cover with a lid or aluminum foil. Steam steadily for 15 minutes, or until the meat filling is cooked. Serve immediately, garnished with the chile rings and peas.

cook's tip

If you prefer a slightly hotter taste, stuff fresh hot red chiles as well as the green ones.

chicken & vegetable bundles

THIS **POPULAR** AND DELICIOUS DIM SUM IS **EXTREMELY EASY** TO PREPARE IN YOUR **OWN KITCHEN**.

ingredients

4 skinless, boneless **chicken** thighs
1 teaspoon **cornstarch**
2 teaspoons **dry sherry**
2 tablespoons **light soy sauce**
½ teaspoon **salt**
large pinch of freshly ground **white pepper**
4 fresh **shiitake mushrooms**
1 small **carrot**
1 small **zucchini**
½ cup sliced, drained, canned **bamboo shoots**
1 **leek**, trimmed
¼ teaspoon **sesame oil**

method

SERVES 4

1 Remove any fat from the chicken thighs and cut each lengthwise into eight strips. Place the strips in a bowl.

2 Add the cornstarch, sherry and half the soy sauce to the chicken. Stir in the salt and pepper and mix well. Cover and marinate for 10 minutes.

3 Remove and discard the mushroom stems, then cut each mushroom cap in half (or in slices if very large). Cut the carrot and zucchini into eight sticks, each about 2 inches long, then mix the mushroom halves and bamboo shoots together.

4 Bring a small saucepan of water to a boil. Add the leek and blanch until soft. Drain thoroughly, then slit the leek down its length. Separate each layer to give eight long strips.

5 Divide the marinated chicken into eight portions. Do the same with the vegetables. Wrap each strip of leek around a portion of chicken and vegetables to make eight neat bundles. Have ready a saucepan with about 2 inches boiling water and a steamer or a heatproof plate that will fit inside it on a metal trivet.

6 Place the chicken and vegetable bundles in the steamer or on the plate. Place in the pan, cover and steam over a high heat for 12–15 minutes, or until the filling is cooked. Meanwhile, mix the remaining soy sauce with the sesame oil and use as a sauce for the bundles.

fish & shellfish

ingredients

1¼ cups **fish stock**
12 ounces **jumbo shrimp**, peeled and deveined
1 tablespoon **vegetable oil**
1 **garlic** clove, finely chopped
2 cups **snow peas**
¼ teaspoon **salt**
1 tablespoon dry **sherry**
1 tablespoon **oyster sauce**
1 teaspoon **cornstarch**
1 teaspoon **sugar**
1 tablespoon **water**
¼ teaspoon **sesame oil**

stir-fried shrimp with snow peas

SHRIMP AND **SNOW PEAS** MAKE A PRETTY DISH, WHICH NEEDS NO **EMBELLISHMENT**.

method

SERVES 4

1 Bring the fish stock to a boil in a frying pan. Add the shrimp. Cook gently for 2 minutes, until the shrimp have turned pink, then drain and set aside.

2 Heat the vegetable oil in a frying pan or wok. Add the chopped garlic and cook for a few seconds, then add the snow peas. Sprinkle with the salt. Stir-fry for 1 minute.

3 Add the shrimp and sherry to the pan or wok. Stir-fry for a few seconds, then add the oyster sauce.

4 Mix the cornstarch and sugar to a paste with the water. Add the mixture to the pan and cook, stirring constantly, until the sauce thickens slightly. Drizzle with the sesame oil and serve.

grey mullet with pork

THIS UNUSUAL **COMBINATION** MAKES A **SPECTACULAR** MAIN DISH WITH VERY LITTLE EFFORT.

method

SERVES 4

1 Make four diagonal cuts on either side of the fish and rub with a little salt. Place the fish on a large, shallow, heatproof serving dish.

2 Cut the pork into thin strips. Place in a bowl. Drain the soaked mushrooms, remove and discard the stems and slice the caps thinly.

3 Add the mushrooms to the pork, with the cornstarch and half the soy sauce. Stir in 1 teaspoon of the oil and a generous grinding of black pepper. Arrange the pork mixture along the length of the fish. Scatter the ginger shreds over the top.

4 Cover the fish loosely with aluminum foil. Have ready a large saucepan or roasting pan with about 2 inches boiling water, big enough to fit the heatproof dish inside it on a metal trivet. Place the dish in the pan or roasting pan, cover and steam over a high heat for 15 minutes.

5 Test the fish by pressing the flesh gently. If it comes away from the bone with a slight resistance, the fish is cooked. Carefully pour away any excess liquid from the dish.

6 Heat the remaining oil in a small pan. When it is hot, fry the shredded scallion for a few seconds, then pour it over the fish, taking great care as it will splatter. Drizzle with the remaining soy sauce, garnish with sliced scallions and serve immediately with rice.

cook's tip

If the fish is too big to fit into the steamer whole, simply cut it in half for cooking, then reassemble it to serve.

ingredients

1 **grey mullet**, about 2 pounds, gutted and cleaned
2 ounces lean **pork**
3 dried **Chinese mushrooms**, soaked in boiling water until soft
½ teaspoon **cornstarch**
2 tablespoons **light soy sauce**
1 tablespoon **vegetable oil**
1 tablespoon finely shredded fresh **ginger root**
1 tablespoon shredded **scallion**
salt and freshly ground **black pepper**
sliced **scallion**, to garnish
rice, to serve

asparagus with crabmeat sauce

THE **SUBTLE** FLAVOR OF FRESH ASPARAGUS IS ENHANCED BY THE EQUALLY **DELICATE** TASTE OF **CRAB** IN THIS **CLASSIC DISH**.

method

SERVES 4

1 Bring a large pan of lightly salted water to a boil. Poach the asparagus for about 5 minutes, until just crisp-tender. Drain well and keep hot in a shallow serving dish.

2 Heat the oil in a frying pan or wok. Cook the ginger and garlic for 1 minute to release their flavor, then lift them out with a slotted spoon and discard them.

3 Add the crabmeat, sherry and milk to the flavored oil and cook, stirring frequently, for 2 minutes.

4 In a small bowl, mix the cornstarch to a paste with the water and add to the pan. Cook, stirring constantly, until the sauce is thick and creamy. Season to taste with salt and pepper, spoon over the asparagus, garnish with shreds of scallion and serve.

ingredients

1 pound **asparagus**, trimmed
1 tablespoon **vegetable oil**
4 thin slices of fresh **ginger root**
2 **garlic** cloves, finely chopped
2/3 cup fresh or thawed frozen white **crabmeat**
1 teaspoon **dry sherry**
2/3 cup **milk**
1 tablespoon **cornstarch**
3 tablespoons cold **water**
salt and freshly ground **white pepper**
1 **scallion**, thinly shredded, to garnish

THIS TASTY, **COLORFUL** SALAD IS A **REFRESHING** WAY OF SERVING **SUCCULENT** SQUID.

ingredients

1 pound **squid**
1 1/4 cups **fish stock**
6 ounces **green beans**, trimmed and halved
3 tablespoons **cilantro leaves**
2 teaspoons **sugar**
2 tablespoons **rice vinegar**
1 teaspoon **sesame oil**
1 tablespoon **light soy sauce**
1 tablespoon **vegetable oil**
2 **garlic** cloves, finely chopped
2 teaspoons finely chopped fresh **ginger root**
1 fresh **chile**, seeded and chopped
salt, to taste

spicy squid salad

method

SERVES 4

1 Prepare the squid. Holding the body in one hand, gently pull off the head and tentacles. Discard the head. Trim and reserve the tentacles. Remove the transparent "quill" from inside the body of the squid and peel off the purplish skin on the outside.

2 Cut the body of the squid open lengthwise and wash thoroughly. Score criss-cross patterns on the inside, taking care not to cut through the squid, then cut into 3 x 2-inch pieces.

3 Bring the fish stock to a boil in a wok or saucepan. Add all the squid pieces, then lower the heat and cook for about 2 minutes, until they are tender and have curled. Drain.

4 In a separate pan of lightly salted boiling water, cook the beans until crisp-tender. Drain, refresh under cold water, then drain again. Mix the squid and beans in a serving bowl.

5 In a bowl or cup, mix the cilantro leaves, sugar, rice vinegar, sesame oil and soy sauce. Pour the mixture over the squid and beans.

6 Heat the vegetable oil in a wok or small pan until very hot. Stir-fry the garlic, ginger and chile for a few seconds, then pour the dressing over the squid mixture. Toss gently and set aside for at least 5 minutes. Add salt to taste and serve warm or cold.

cook's tip

If you hold your knife at an angle when scoring the squid, there is less of a risk of cutting right through it.

three sea flavors stir-fry

THIS **DELECTABLE** SEAFOOD COMBINATION IS **ENHANCED** BY THE USE OF **FRESH GINGER ROOT** AND SCALLIONS.

ingredients

4 large **scallops**, with the corals
8 ounces firm **white fish** fillet, such as **monkfish** or **cod**
4 ounces **jumbo shrimp**
1 1/4 cups **fish stock**
1 tablespoon **vegetable oil**
2 **garlic** cloves, coarsely chopped
2-inch piece of fresh **ginger root**, thinly sliced
8 **scallions**, cut into 1 1/2-inch pieces
2 tablespoons **dry white wine**
1 teaspoon **cornstarch**
1 tablespoon cold **water**
salt and freshly ground **white pepper**
noodles or **rice**, to serve

cook's tip

Do not overcook the seafood or it will become rubbery.

method

SERVES 4

1 Separate the corals and slice each scallop in half horizontally. Cut the fish fillet into bite-size chunks. Peel and devein the shrimp.

2 Bring the fish stock to a boil in a saucepan. Add the seafood, lower the heat and poach gently for 1–2 minutes, until the fish, scallops and corals are just firm and the shrimp have turned pink. Drain the seafood, reserving about 1/4 cup of the stock.

3 Heat the oil in a frying pan or wok over high heat until very hot. Stir-fry the garlic, ginger and scallions for a few seconds.

4 Add the seafood and wine. Stir-fry for 1 minute, then add the reserved stock and simmer for 2 minutes.

5 Mix the cornstarch to a paste with the water. Add the mixture to the pan or wok and cook, stirring gently just until the sauce thickens.

6 Season the stir-fry with salt and pepper to taste. Serve immediately, with noodles or rice.

福

monkfish & scallop skewers

USING **LEMONGRASS** STALKS AS SKEWERS IMBUES THE SEAFOOD WITH A **SUBTLE CITRUS** FLAVOR.

method

SERVES 4

1 Remove any membrane from the monkfish fillet, then cut it into 16 large chunks.

2 Remove the outer leaves from the lemongrass to leave thin rigid stalks. Chop the tender parts of the lemongrass leaves finely and place in a bowl. Stir in the lemon juice, oil, chopped cilantro, salt and pepper.

3 Thread the fish and scallop chunks alternately on the 8 lemongrass stalks. Arrange the skewers of fish and shellfish in a shallow dish and pour over the marinade.

4 Cover and set aside in a cool place for at least 1 hour, turning occasionally. Transfer the skewers to a heatproof dish or bamboo steamer, cover and steam over boiling water for 10 minutes, until just cooked. Garnish with cilantro and serve with rice and the cooking juices poured over.

ingredients

1 pound **monkfish** fillet
8 **lemongrass stalks**
2 tablespoons fresh **lemon juice**
1 tablespoon **olive oil**
1 tablespoon finely chopped **cilantro**
½ teaspoon **salt**
large pinch of freshly ground **black pepper**
12 large **scallops**, halved crosswise
cilantro leaves, to garnish
rice, to serve

variation

Jumbo shrimp and salmon make excellent alternative ingredients for the skewers, with or without the monkfish.

THE SLIGHTLY CHEWY SQUID **CONTRASTS BEAUTIFULLY** WITH THE **CRISP CRUNCH** OF THE BROCCOLI TO GIVE THIS DISH THE **PERFECT COMBINATION** OF TEXTURES THAT IS SO **HIGHLY PRIZED** BY THE CHINESE.

ingredients

- 1¼ cups **fish stock**
- 12 ounces prepared **squid**, cut into large pieces
- 8 ounces **broccoli**
- 1 tablespoon **vegetable oil**
- 2 **garlic** cloves, finely chopped
- 1 tablespoon **dry sherry**
- 2 teaspoons **cornstarch**
- ½ teaspoon **sugar**
- 3 tablespoons **water**
- 1 tablespoon **oyster sauce**
- ½ teaspoon **sesame oil**
- **noodles**, to serve

squid with broccoli

method

SERVES 4

1 Bring the fish stock to a boil in a wok or saucepan. Cook the squid pieces for 2 minutes, until they are tender and have curled. Drain and set aside.

2 Trim the broccoli and cut into small florets. Cook in a saucepan of boiling water for 2 minutes until crisp-tender. Drain thoroughly.

3 Heat the vegetable oil in a wok or frying pan. Stir-fry the garlic for a few seconds, then add the squid, broccoli and sherry. Stir-fry for about 2 minutes.

4 Mix the cornstarch and sugar to a paste with the water. Stir the mixture into the wok or pan with the oyster sauce. Cook, stirring, until the sauce thickens slightly. Just before serving, stir in the sesame oil. Serve with noodles.

gong boa shrimp

A PLEASANTLY SPICY **SWEET-&-SOUR** DISH THAT TAKES ONLY **MINUTES** TO MAKE.

ingredients

12 ounces **jumbo shrimp**
1/2 **cucumber**, about 3 ounces
1 1/4 cups **fish stock**
1 tablespoon **vegetable oil**
1/2 teaspoon crushed dried **chiles**
1/2 **green bell pepper**, seeded and cut into 1-inch strips
1 small **carrot**, thinly sliced
2 tablespoons **ketchup**
3 tablespoons **rice vinegar**
1 tablespoon **sugar**
2/3 cup **vegetable stock**
1/2 cup drained canned **pineapple** chunks
2 teaspoon **cornstarch**
1 tablespoon **water**
salt

cook's tip

If you don't have any fish stock, make a quick stock by boiling the shrimp shells with an onion and a carrot in 2 cups of water for 10 minutes. Strain and use as indicated in the recipe.

method

SERVES 4

1 Peel and devein the shrimp. Rub them gently with 1/2 teaspoon salt, set aside for a few minutes and then wash and dry thoroughly.

2 Using a narrow peeler or channel knife, pare strips of skin from the cucumber to give a striped effect. Cut the cucumber in half lengthwise and scoop out the seeds with a teaspoon. Cut the flesh into 1/4-inch crescents.

3 Bring the fish stock to a boil in a saucepan. Add the shrimp, lower the heat and poach the shrimp for about 2 minutes, until they turn pink, then drain and set aside.

4 Heat the oil in a frying pan or wok over high heat. Fry the chiles for a few seconds, then add the pepper strips and carrot slices and stir-fry for 1 minute.

5 Mix together the ketchup, vinegar, sugar and vegetable stock, with 1/4 teaspoon salt. Pour the mixture into the pan and cook for 3 more minutes.

6 Add the shrimp, cucumber and pineapple and cook for 2 more minutes. Mix the cornstarch to a paste with the water. Add the mixture to the pan and cook, stirring constantly, until the sauce thickens. Serve immediately.

variation

You can omit the dried chiles if you like, or increase the quantity for a much spicier dish.

有限公司
特快成立
酒吧聘請
卡拉OK
韓國餐

poultry

chicken with lemon sauce

SUCCULENT CHICKEN WITH A **REFRESHING** LEMONY SAUCE AND **JUST** A **HINT** OF LIME IS A **SURE WINNER**.

method

SERVES 4

1 Arrange the chicken breasts in a single layer in a shallow bowl. Mix the sesame oil with the sherry and add 1/2 teaspoon salt and 1/4 teaspoon pepper. Pour over the chicken, cover and marinate for 15 minutes.

2 Mix together the egg white and cornstarch. Add the mixture to the chicken and turn the chicken with tongs until thoroughly coated. Heat the vegetable oil in a frying pan or wok and fry the chicken for about 15 minutes, until golden brown on both sides.

3 Meanwhile, make the sauce. Combine all the ingredients in a small pan. Add 1/4 teaspoon salt. Bring to a boil over low heat, stirring constantly, until the sauce is smooth and has thickened slightly.

4 Cut the chicken into pieces and arrange on a warm serving plate. Pour the sauce over, garnish with the cilantro, scallions and lemon wedges and serve.

ingredients

4 small skinless boneless **chicken** breasts
1 teaspoon **sesame oil**
1 tablespoon **dry sherry**
salt and freshly ground **white pepper**
1 **egg white**, lightly beaten
2 tablespoons **cornstarch**
1 tablespoon **vegetable oil**
chopped **cilantro leaves** and **scallions** and **lemon wedges**, to garnish

For the sauce
3 tablespoons fresh **lemon juice**
2 tablespoons **lime cordial**
3 tablespoons **sugar**
2 teaspoons **cornstarch**
6 tablespoons **water**

ingredients

12 ounces skinless, boneless **chicken** breasts
4 teaspoons **vegetable oil**
1 1/4 cups **chicken stock**
3/4 cup drained, canned **straw mushrooms**
1/2 cup sliced, drained, canned **bamboo shoots**
1/3 cup drained, canned **water chestnuts**, sliced
1 small **carrot**, sliced
1/2 cup **snow peas**
1 tablespoon **dry sherry**
1 tablespoon **oyster sauce**
1 teaspoon **sugar**
1 teaspoon **cornstarch**
1 tablespoon **cold water**
salt and freshly ground **white pepper**

chicken with mixed vegetables

A **RIOT** OF **COLOR**, THIS FLAVORFUL DISH HAS PLENTY OF **CONTRASTS** IN **TEXTURE** AND **TASTE**.

method

SERVES 4

1 Put the chicken in a shallow bowl. Add 1 teaspoon of the oil, 1/4 teaspoon salt and a pinch of pepper. Cover and set aside for 10 minutes in a cool place.

2 Bring the stock to a boil in a saucepan. Add the chicken and cook for 12 minutes, or until tender. Drain and slice, reserving 5 tablespoons of the stock.

3 Heat the remaining oil in a frying pan or wok, add all the vegetables and stir-fry for 2 minutes. Stir in the sherry, oyster sauce, sugar and reserved stock. Add the chicken to the pan and cook for 2 more minutes.

4 Mix the cornstarch to a paste with the water. Add the mixture to the pan and cook, stirring, until the sauce thickens slightly. Season to taste with salt and pepper and serve immediately.

salt-baked chicken

THIS IS A **FABULOUS** WAY OF COOKING CHICKEN. THE DELICIOUS, **SUCCULENT** JUICES ARE **SEALED** INSIDE THE **SALT CRUST**, YET THE FLAVOR ISN'T SALTY.

ingredients

3–3½-pound free-range **chicken**
¼ teaspoon fine **sea salt**
5 pounds coarse **rock salt**
1 tablespoon **vegetable oil**
1-inch piece fresh **ginger root**, finely chopped
4 **scallions**, cut into fine rings
boiled rice, garnished with shredded **scallions**, to serve

cook's tip

To reduce the fat content, remove and discard the skin from the chicken before eating.

method

SERVES 4

1 Rinse the chicken. Pat it dry, both inside and out, with paper towels, then rub the inside with the sea salt.

2 Place four damp paper towels on the bottom of a heavy frying pan or wok just large enough to hold the chicken.

3 Sprinkle a layer of rock salt over the paper towels, about ½-inch thick. Place the chicken on top of the salt.

4 Pour the remaining salt over the chicken until it is completely covered. Dampen six more paper towels and place them around the rim of the pan or wok. Cover with a tight-fitting lid. Put the pan or wok over high heat for 10 minutes, or until it gives off a slightly smoky smell.

5 Immediately reduce the heat to medium and continue to cook the chicken for 30 minutes without lifting the lid. After 30 minutes, turn off the heat and set aside for another 10 minutes before carefully lifting the chicken out of the salt. Brush off any salt still clinging to the chicken and allow the bird to cool for 20 minutes before cutting it into serving-size pieces.

6 Heat the oil in a small saucepan until very hot. Add the ginger and scallions and fry for a few seconds, then pour into a heatproof bowl and use as a dipping sauce for the chicken. Serve the chicken with boiled rice, garnished with shredded scallions.

BEER

ingredients

12 ounces skinless, boneless **chicken** breasts
1/4 teaspoon **salt**
pinch of freshly ground **white pepper**
1 tablespoon **dry sherry**
1 1/4 cups **chicken stock**
1 tablespoon **vegetable oil**
1 **garlic** clove, finely chopped
1 small **carrot**, cut into cubes
1/2 **cucumber**, about 3 ounces, cut into 1/2-inch cubes
1/2 cup drained canned **bamboo shoots**, cut into 1/2-inch cubes
1 teaspoon **cornstarch**
1 tablespoon light **soy sauce**
1 teaspoon **sugar**
1/4 cup dry-roasted **cashews**
1/2 teaspoon **sesame oil**
noodles, to serve

chicken with cashews

AN **ALL-TIME** FAVORITE, THIS **CLASSIC DISH** IS DELIGHTFULLY **QUICK** AND **EASY** TO PREPARE.

method

SERVES 4

1 Cut the chicken into 3/4-inch cubes. Place the cubes in a bowl, stir in the salt, pepper and sherry, cover and let marinate for 15 minutes.

2 Bring the stock to a boil in a large saucepan. Add the chicken and cook, stirring, for 3 minutes. Drain, reserving 6 tablespoons of the stock, and set aside.

3 Heat the vegetable oil in a frying pan until very hot, add the garlic and stir-fry for a few seconds. Add the carrot, cucumber and bamboo shoots and continue to stir-fry over medium heat for 2 minutes.

4 Stir in the chicken and reserved stock. Mix the cornstarch with the soy sauce and sugar and add the mixture to the pan. Cook, stirring, until the sauce thickens slightly. Finally, add the cashews and sesame oil. Toss to mix thoroughly, then serve with noodles.

cook's tip

Peanuts or almonds can be used in this recipe instead of cashews if desired.

bang bang chicken

THE SAUCE GETS ITS **AUTHENTIC FLAVOR** FROM **SESAME PASTE**, ALTHOUGH PEANUT BUTTER CAN BE USED INSTEAD.

method

SERVES 4

1 Place the chicken breasts in a saucepan. Just cover with water, add the onion and garlic and bring to a boil. Skim the surface and stir in salt and pepper to taste. Cover and cook for 25 minutes, until the chicken is just tender. Drain, reserving the stock.

2 Make the sauce by mixing the sesame paste with 3 tablespoons of the stock. Add the soy sauce, vinegar, scallions, garlic, ginger and peppercorns. Stir in sugar to taste.

3 Make the chili oil by gently heating the oil and chili powder together until foaming. Simmer for 2 minutes, cool, then strain off the red-colored oil. Discard the sediment.

4 Spread out the cucumber sticks on a platter. Cut the chicken into pieces about the same size as the cucumber and arrange on top. Pour the sauce over, drizzle on the chili oil and serve. Guests will toss their own servings before eating.

cook's tip

Crunchy peanut butter can be used instead of sesame paste, if desired. Mix 3 tablespoons with 2 tablespoons sesame oil and proceed as in step 2.

ingredients

3 skinless, boneless **chicken** breasts, about 1 pound
1 small **onion**, halved
1 **garlic** clove, crushed
salt and freshly ground **black pepper**
1 large **cucumber**, peeled, seeded and cut into sticks, to serve

For the sauce
3 tablespoons **sesame paste**
1 tablespoon **light soy sauce**
1 tablespoon **wine vinegar**
2 **scallions**, finely chopped
2 **garlic** cloves, crushed
½-inch piece of fresh **ginger root**, grated
1 tablespoon **Szechuan peppercorns**, dry-fried and crushed
1 teaspoon **light brown sugar**

For the chili oil
¼ cup **peanut oil**
1 teaspoon **chili powder**

anita wong's duck

THE CHINESE ARE **PASSIONATELY** FOND OF DUCK AND REGARD IT AS AN **ESSENTIAL** ON **CELEBRATORY** OCCASIONS. DUCK DENOTES **MARITAL HARMONY**.

method

SERVES 4–6

1 Use the giblets to make a duck stock. Blot the surface with paper towels to remove excess fat, then strain. Reserve 1¾ cups.

2 Heat the oil in a deep frying pan. Fry the garlic without browning, then add the duck. Turn frequently until the outside is slightly brown. Lift the duck onto a plate.

3 Add the ginger to the pan, then stir in the bean paste. Cook for 1 minute, then add both soy sauces, the sugar and the five-spice powder. Return the duck to the pan and fry until the outside is coated. Add the star anise and stock or water, and season to taste. Cover and cook over low heat for 2–2½ hours or until tender, stirring occasionally. Skim or blot the surface to remove the excess fat, then set aside the duck in the sauce to cool.

4 Cut the duck into serving portions and pour the sauce over. Garnish with scallion curls and serve cold.

ingredients

1 **duck** with giblets, about 5–5¼ pounds
¼ cup **vegetable oil**
2 **garlic** cloves, chopped
1-inch piece fresh **ginger root**, thinly sliced
3 tablespoons **bean paste**
2 tablespoons **light soy sauce**
1 tablespoon **dark soy sauce**
1 tablespoon **sugar**
½ teaspoon **five-spice powder**
3 points **star anise**
1¾ cups **duck stock** or **water** (see step 1)
salt
scallion curls, to garnish

cook's tip

Store any leftover sauce in a jar in the refrigerator for a few days. Use as a marinade for steak or chicken drumsticks, or stir into gravy for extra flavor.

ingredients

- 1 tablespoon **dry sherry**
- 1 tablespoon **dark soy sauce**
- 2 small skinless **duck** breasts
- 1 tablespoon **vegetable oil**
- 2 **garlic** cloves, finely chopped
- 1 small **onion**, sliced
- 1 **red bell pepper**, seeded and cut into 1-inch squares
- ½ cup drained, canned **pineapple** chunks
- 6 tablespoons **pineapple** juice
- 1 tablespoon **rice vinegar**
- 1 teaspoon **cornstarch**
- 1 tablespoon cold **water**
- 1 teaspoon **sesame oil**
- salt and freshly ground **white pepper**
- 1 **scallion**, shredded, to garnish

duck with pineapple

DUCK AND PINEAPPLE IS A FAVORITE **COMBINATION**, BUT THE FRUIT MUST NOT BE ALLOWED TO DOMINATE. HERE THE PROPORTIONS ARE **PERFECT** AND THE DISH HAS A WONDERFULLY **SUBTLE** SWEET-AND-SOUR FLAVOR.

method

SERVES 4

1 Mix together the sherry and soy sauce. Stir in ½ teaspoon salt and ¼ teaspoon pepper. Put the duck breasts in a bowl and add the marinade. Cover and set aside in a cool place for 1 hour.

2 Drain the duck breasts and place them on a rack in a broiler pan. Broil under medium to high heat for 10 minutes on each side. Allow to cool for 10 minutes, then cut into bite-size pieces.

3 Heat the vegetable oil in a frying pan or wok and stir-fry the garlic and onion for 1 minute. Add the red pepper, pineapple chunks, duck, pineapple juice and vinegar and stir-fry for 2 minutes.

4 Mix the cornstarch to a paste with the water. Add the mixture to the pan with ¼ teaspoon salt. Cook, stirring, until the sauce thickens. Stir in the sesame oil and serve immediately, garnished with scallion shreds.

duck with pancakes

ingredients

1 tablespoon **honey**
1/4 teaspoon Chinese **five-spice powder**
1 **garlic** clove, finely chopped
1 tablespoon **hoisin sauce**
1/2 teaspoon **salt**
a large pinch of freshly ground **white pepper**
2 small skinless **duck** breasts
1/2 **cucumber**
10 **scallions**
3 **Chinese cabbage leaves**
12 **Chinese pancakes** (see cook's tip)

For the sauce
1 teaspoon **vegetable oil**
2 **garlic** cloves, chopped
2 **scallions**, chopped
1/2-inch piece of fresh **ginger root**, bruised
1/4 cup **hoisin sauce**
1 tablespoon **dry sherry**
1 tablespoon **water**
1/2 teaspoon **sesame oil**

cook's tip

Chinese pancakes can be bought frozen from Chinese markets. Let them thaw before steaming.

CONSIDERABLY LOWER IN FAT THAN TRADITIONAL **PEKING DUCK**, AND JUST AS DELICIOUS. GUESTS SPREAD THEIR **PANCAKES** WITH SAUCE, ADD DUCK AND VEGETABLES, THEN **ROLL THEM UP**.

method

SERVES 4

1 Mix the honey, five-spice powder, garlic, hoisin sauce and salt and pepper in a shallow dish large enough to hold the duck breasts side by side. Add the duck breasts, turning them in the marinade. Cover and set aside in a cool place to marinate for 2 hours.

2 Cut the cucumber in half lengthwise. Using a teaspoon, scrape out and discard the seeds. Cut the flesh into thin sticks 2 inches long.

3 Cut off and discard the green tops from the scallions. Finely shred the white parts and place on a serving plate with the cucumber sticks.

4 Make the sauce. Heat the oil in a small saucepan and gently fry the garlic for a few seconds without browning. Add the scallions, ginger, hoisin sauce, sherry and water. Cook gently for 5 minutes, stirring often, then strain and mix with the sesame oil.

5 Remove the duck breasts from the marinade and drain them well. Place the duck breasts on a rack of a broiler pan. Broil under medium to high heat for 8–10 minutes on each side. Let cool for 5 minutes before cutting into thin slices. Arrange on a serving platter, cover and keep warm.

6 Line a steamer with the cabbage leaves and place the pancakes on top. Have ready a large pan with 2 inches boiling water. Cover the steamer and place on a trivet in the pan. Steam over high heat for 2 minutes, or until the pancakes are hot. Serve immediately with the duck, cucumber, scallions and sauce.

pork & beef

sticky spareribs

A DELICIOUS DISH THAT HAS TO BE **EATEN** WITH **FINGERS** TO BE ENJOYED FULLY.

method

SERVES 4

1 Combine the sugar, five-spice powder, hoisin sauce, yellow bean sauce, garlic, cornstarch and salt in a bowl, then mix together well.

2 Place the spareribs in an ovenproof dish and pour the marinade over them. Mix thoroughly, cover and set aside in a cool place for 1 hour.

3 Preheat the oven to 350°F. Cover the dish tightly with aluminum foil and bake the spareribs for 40 minutes. Baste the ribs from time to time with the cooking juices.

4 Remove the aluminum foil, baste the ribs and continue to cook for 20 minutes, until glossy and brown. Garnish with chives and scallions and serve with a salad or rice.

cook's tip

These ribs barbecue well. Bake as described in step 3, then transfer them to the charcoal grill to finish cooking. The sauce coating makes the ribs liable to burn, so watch them closely.

ingredients

2 tablespoons **sugar**
½ teaspoon Chinese **five-spice powder**
3 tablespoons **hoisin sauce**
2 tablespoons **yellow bean sauce**
3 **garlic** cloves, finely chopped
1 tablespoon **cornstarch**
½ teaspoon **salt**
16 **spareribs**
chives and sliced **scallion**, to garnish
salad or **rice**, to serve

ingredients

1 tablespoon **vegetable oil**
1 tablespoon **hoisin sauce**
1 tablespoon **yellow bean sauce**
1/4 teaspoon Chinese
five-spice powder
1/2 teaspoon **cornstarch**
1 tablespoon **sugar**
1/4 teaspoon **salt**
1/4 teaspoon freshly ground
white pepper
1 pound **pork tenderloin**,
trimmed
2 teaspoons **honey**
shredded **scallion**, to garnish
rice, to serve

char-siu pork

MARINATED PORK, ROASTED AND GLAZED **WITH HONEY**, IS SIMPLY IRRESISTIBLE ON ITS OWN AND CAN ALSO BE USED AS THE BASIS FOR **SALADS** OR **STIR-FRIES**.

method

SERVES 4

1 Mix the oil, sauces, five-spice powder, cornstarch, sugar and salt and pepper in a shallow dish. Add the pork and coat it with the mixture. Cover and chill for 4 hours or overnight.

2 Preheat the oven to 375°F. Drain the pork and place it on a wire rack over a deep roasting pan. Roast for 40 minutes, turning the pork over occasionally.

3 Check that the pork is cooked by inserting a skewer or fork into the meat; the juices should run clear. If they are still tinged with pink, roast the pork for 5–10 minutes more.

4 Remove the pork from the oven and brush it with the honey. Let cool for 10 minutes before cutting into thin slices. Garnish with scallion shreds and serve hot or cold with rice.

sweet-&-sour pork

AN **IRRESISTIBLY EASY** VERSION OF THIS POPULAR, **CLASSIC** CHINESE DISH.

ingredients

1 tablespoon **dry sherry**
12 ounces lean **pork** steaks
1 tablespoon **vegetable oil**
1 **garlic** clove, finely chopped
½ **onion**, diced
1 **green bell pepper**, seeded and cut into 1-inch squares
1 small **carrot**, sliced
½ cup drained, canned **pineapple** chunks
2 tablespoons **malt** or **cider vinegar**
3 tablespoons **ketchup**
⅔ cup **pineapple juice**
2 teaspoons **sugar**
2 teaspoons **cornstarch**
1 tablespoon **water**
salt and freshly ground **black pepper**
rice, to serve

cook's tip

This is a great way of giving leftover pork a new lease on life. Cut into bite-size pieces and proceed from step 3.

method

SERVES 4

1 Mix the sherry, ½ teaspoon salt and a large pinch of pepper in a shallow dish. Add the pork, turn to coat, then cover and set aside to marinate in a cool place for 15 minutes.

2 Drain the pork steaks and place them on a rack over a broiling pan. Broil under high heat for 5 minutes on each side, or until cooked, then remove and let cool. Cut the cooked pork into bite-size pieces.

3 Heat the oil in a frying pan or wok until very hot. Stir-fry the garlic and onion for a few seconds, then add the green pepper and carrot and stir-fry for 1 minute.

4 Stir in the pineapple chunks, vinegar, ketchup, pineapple juice and sugar. Bring to a boil, lower the heat and simmer for 3 minutes.

5 Add the cooked pork to the vegetable mixture and cook for about 2 minutes.

6 Mix the cornstarch to a paste with the water. Add the mixture to the pan or wok and cook, stirring, until slightly thickened. Serve with rice.

beef in oyster sauce

THE **OYSTER SAUCE** GIVES THE BEEF **EXTRA RICHNESS** AND **DEPTH** OF FLAVOR. TO COMPLETE THE DISH, ALL YOU NEED IS PLAIN BOILED **RICE** OR **NOODLES**.

ingredients

12 ounces sirloin **steak**, trimmed
1 tablespoon **vegetable oil**
1 1/4 cups **beef stock**
2 **garlic** cloves, finely chopped
1 small **carrot**, thinly sliced
3 **celery** stalks, sliced
1 tablespoon **dry sherry**
1 teaspoon **sugar**
3 tablespoons **oyster sauce**
1 teaspoon **cornstarch**
1 tablespoon **water**
4 **scallions**, cut into 1-inch lengths
freshly ground **white pepper**
rice or **noodles**, to serve

method

SERVES 4

1 Slice the beef thinly. Place the slices in a bowl, add 1 teaspoon of the vegetable oil and stir to coat.

2 Bring the stock to a boil in a large saucepan. Add the beef and cook, stirring, for 2 minutes. Drain, reserving 3 tablespoons of the stock, and set aside.

3 Heat the remaining oil in a frying pan or wok. Stir-fry the garlic for a few seconds, then add the carrot and celery and stir-fry for 2 minutes.

4 Stir in the sherry, sugar, oyster sauce and a large pinch of pepper. Add the beef to the pan with the reserved stock. Simmer for 2 minutes.

5 Mix the cornstarch to a paste with the water. Add the mixture to the pan and cook, stirring, until thickened.

6 Stir in the scallions, mixing well, then serve at once, with boiled rice or noodles.

variation

To increase the number of servings without adding any extra beef, add more vegetables, such as peppers, snow peas, water chestnuts, baby corn and mushrooms.

beef with peppers & black bean sauce

A **SPICY**, **RICH** DISH WITH THE **DISTINCTIVE** FLAVOR OF **BLACK BEAN** SAUCE.

method

SERVES 4

1 Place the prepared beef in a large bowl. Add 1 teaspoon of the vegetable oil and stir well to coat.

2 Bring the stock to a boil in a saucepan. Add the beef and cook for 2 minutes, stirring constantly to prevent the slices from sticking together. Drain the beef and set aside.

3 Heat the remaining oil in a frying pan or wok. Stir-fry the garlic, ginger and chile with the black bean sauce for a few seconds. Add the pepper squares and a little water. Cook for about 2 minutes more, then stir in the sherry. Add the beef slices to the pan and spoon the sauce over.

4 Mix the cornstarch and sugar to a paste with the water. Pour the mixture into the pan. Cook, stirring, until the sauce has thickened. Season to taste with salt. Serve immediately, with rice noodles.

ingredients

12 ounces sirloin **steak**, trimmed and thinly sliced
1 tablespoon **vegetable oil**
1 1/4 cups **beef stock**
2 **garlic** cloves, finely chopped
1 teaspoon grated fresh **ginger root**
1 fresh **red chile**, seeded and finely chopped
1 tablespoon **black bean sauce**
1 **green bell pepper**, seeded and cut into 1-inch squares
1 tablespoon **dry sherry**
1 teaspoon **cornstarch**
1 teaspoon **sugar**
3 tablespoons **water**
salt
rice noodles, to serve

cook's tip

For extra color, use half each of a green and red bell pepper or a mixture that includes yellow and orange bell peppers.

ingredients

12 ounces sirloin **steak**, trimmed
1 tablespoon **vegetable oil**
1¼ cups **beef stock**
1 **garlic** clove, finely chopped
1 small **onion**, sliced into rings
5 **tomatoes**, quartered
1 tablespoon **tomato paste**
1 teaspoon **sugar**
1 tablespoon **dry sherry**
1 tablespoon **water**
salt and freshly ground
white pepper
noodles, to serve

Cook's Tip

Use plum tomatoes or vine tomatoes from the garden, if you can. The store-bought ones are a little more expensive than standard tomatoes, but have a far better flavor.

beef with tomatoes

COLORFUL AND **FRESH**-TASTING, THIS IS THE PERFECT WAY OF SERVING **SUN-RIPENED** TOMATOES FROM THE GARDEN.

method

SERVES 4

1 Slice the beef thinly. Place the slices in a bowl, add 1 teaspoon of the vegetable oil and stir to coat.

2 Bring the stock to a boil in a saucepan. Add the beef and cook for 2 minutes, stirring constantly. Drain the beef and set it aside.

3 Heat the remaining oil in a frying pan or wok until very hot. Stir-fry the garlic and onion for a few seconds.

4 Add the beef and tomatoes and cook for 1 more minute. Mix the tomato paste, sugar, sherry and water in a cup or small bowl. Stir the mixture into the pan, add salt and pepper to taste and mix thoroughly. Cook for 1 minute, then serve with noodles.

vegetables

stir-fried bean sprouts

THIS **FRESH**, **CRUNCHY** VEGETABLE, WHICH IS ALMOST SYNONYMOUS WITH CHINESE COOKING, TASTES SO **MUCH BETTER** WHEN **STIR-FRIED** AT HOME.

method

SERVES 4

1 Heat the vegetable oil in a frying pan or wok. Add the chopped garlic and grated ginger and stir-fry for a few minutes.

2 Add the bamboo shoot and carrot matchsticks to the pan or wok and stir-fry for a few minutes.

3 Add the bean sprouts to the pan or wok with the salt and a pinch of pepper. Drizzle over the sherry and toss the bean sprouts over the heat for 3 minutes until hot.

4 Sprinkle the soy sauce and sesame oil over, toss to mix thoroughly, then serve immediately.

cook's tip

Bean sprouts keep best when stored in the refrigerator or other cool place in a bowl of cold water, but you must remember to change the water daily.

ingredients

1 tablespoon **vegetable oil**
1 **garlic** clove, finely chopped
1 teaspoon grated fresh **ginger root**
½ cup drained, canned **bamboo shoots**, cut into fine matchsticks
1 small **carrot**, cut into fine matchsticks
8 cups **bean sprouts**
½ teaspoon **salt**
freshly ground **white pepper**
1 tablespoon **dry sherry**
1 tablespoon **light soy sauce**
½ teaspoon **sesame oil**

ingredients

1 pound **green beans**
1 tablespoon **vegetable oil**
3 **garlic** cloves, finely chopped
5 **scallions**, cut into 1-inch lengths
1 ounce dried **shrimp**, soaked in warm water and drained
1 tablespoon **light soy sauce**
salt

sautéed green beans

THE **SMOKY** FLAVOR OF THE DRIED SHRIMP ADDS AN **EXTRA DIMENSION** TO **GREEN BEANS** COOKED THIS WAY.

method

SERVES 4

1 Trim the green beans. Cut each green bean in half.

2 Bring a saucepan of lightly salted water to a boil and cook the beans for 3–4 minutes, until crisp-tender. Drain, refresh under cold water and drain again.

3 Heat the oil in a frying pan or wok until very hot. Stir-fry the garlic and scallions for 30 seconds, then add the shrimp. Mix lightly.

4 Add the green beans and soy sauce. Toss the mixture over the heat until the beans are hot. Serve immediately.

cook's tip

Don't be tempted to use too many dried shrimp. The flavor is very strong and could overwhelm the more delicate taste of the beans.

braised eggplant & zucchini

EGGPLANT, ZUCCHINI AND FRESH **RED CHILES** FORM THE BASIS OF A VEGETARIAN DISH THAT IS **SIMPLE**, SPICY AND **QUITE SENSATIONAL**.

ingredients

1 **eggplant**, about 12 ounces
2 small **zucchini**
1 tablespoon **vegetable oil**
2 **garlic** cloves, finely chopped
2 fresh **red chiles**, seeded and finely chopped
1 small **onion**, diced
1 tablespoon **black bean sauce**
1 tablespoon **dark soy sauce**
3 tablespoons **cold water**
salt
chile flowers (optional), to garnish (see cook's tip)

cook's tip

Chile flowers make a pretty garnish. Using a small pair of scissors, slit a fresh red chile from the tip to within ½-inch of the stem end. Repeat this at regular intervals around the chile so that you have slender "petals" attached at the stem. Rinse the chile to remove the seeds, then place it in a bowl of ice water for at least 4 hours, until the "petals" curl.

method

SERVES 4

1 Trim the eggplant and slice it in half lengthwise, then across into ½-inch thick slices. Layer the slices in a colander, sprinkling each layer with salt. Let the eggplant drain in the sink for about 20 minutes.

2 Roll-cut the zucchini by slicing off one end diagonally, then rolling the zucchini through 180 degrees and taking off another diagonal slice, which will form a triangular wedge. Make more wedges of zucchini in the same way.

3 Rinse the eggplant slices well, drain and dry thoroughly on paper towels.

4 Heat the oil in a wok or frying pan. Stir-fry the garlic, chiles and onion with the black bean sauce for a few seconds.

5 Add the eggplant slices and stir-fry for 2 minutes, sprinkling a little water over to prevent them from burning.

6 Stir in the zucchini, soy sauce and measured water. Cook, stirring occasionally, for 5 minutes. Serve hot, garnished with chile flowers.

broccoli with soy sauce

A **WONDERFULLY** SIMPLE DISH THAT YOU WILL WANT TO MAKE **AGAIN** AND **AGAIN**. THE BROCCOLI COOKS IN MINUTES, SO DON'T START COOKING UNTIL YOU ARE ALMOST **READY** TO EAT.

method

SERVES 4

1 Trim and discard the thick stalk of the broccoli and then cut the head into large florets.

2 Bring a saucepan of lightly salted water to a boil. Add the broccoli and cook for 3–4 minutes, until crisp-tender. Drain thoroughly and arrange in a heated serving dish.

3 Heat the oil in a small saucepan. Fry the garlic for 2 minutes to release the flavor, then remove it with a slotted spoon. Pour the oil carefully over the broccoli, taking care because it will splatter. Drizzle the soy sauce over the broccoli, scatter the fried garlic slices over and serve.

ingredients

1 pound **broccoli**
1 tablespoon **vegetable oil**
2 **garlic** cloves, crushed
2 tablespoons **light soy sauce**
salt
fried **garlic** slices, to garnish

variation

Most leafy vegetables taste delicious prepared this way. Try blanched lettuce and you may be surprised at how crisp and clean the taste is.

ingredients

1½ pounds **Chinese cabbage**
1 tablespoon **vegetable oil**
2 **garlic** cloves, finely chopped
1-inch piece of fresh
  ginger root, finely chopped
½ teaspoon **salt**
1 tablespoon **oyster sauce**
4 **scallions**, cut into
  1-inch lengths

stir-fried chinese cabbage

THIS SIMPLE WAY OF COOKING **CHINESE CABBAGE** PRESERVES ITS **DELICATE FLAVOR**.

method

SERVES 4

1 Stack the cabbage leaves together and cut them into 1-inch slices.

2 Heat the oil in a wok or large deep saucepan. Stir-fry the garlic and ginger for 1 minute.

3 Add the cabbage to the wok or saucepan and stir-fry for 2 minutes. Add the salt and drizzle with the oyster sauce. Toss the cabbage over the heat for 2 minutes more.

4 Stir in the scallions. Toss the mixture well, transfer it to a heated serving plate and serve.

cook's tip

For guests who are vegetarian, substitute 1 tablespoon light soy sauce and 1 teaspoon sugar for the oyster sauce.

monk-style mixed vegetables

CHINESE MONKS EAT NEITHER **MEAT** NOR **FISH**, SO "MONK-STYLE" DISHES ARE IDEAL FOR **VEGETARIANS**.

ingredients

2 ounces dried **tofu sticks**
4 ounces fresh **lotus root**, or
2 ounces dried
1/4 ounces dried **wood ears**
8 dried **Chinese mushrooms**
1 tablespoon **vegetable oil**
3/4 cup drained, canned **straw mushrooms**
1 cup **baby corn,** cut in half
2 tablespoons **light soy sauce**
1 tablespoon **dry sherry**
2 teaspoons **sugar**
2/3 cup **vegetable stock**
3oz **snow peas**, trimmed and cut in half
1 teaspoon **cornstarch**
1 tablespoon **water**
salt

cook's tip

The flavor of this tasty mix improves on keeping, so any leftovers will taste even better next day.

method

SERVES 4

1 Put the tofu sticks in a bowl. Cover with hot water and let soak for 1 hour. If using fresh lotus root, peel and slice it; if using dried lotus root, place in a bowl of boiling water and let soak for 1 hour.

2 Prepare the wood ears and dried Chinese mushrooms by soaking them in separate bowls of boiling water for 15 minutes. Drain the wood ears, trim off and discard the hard bits from each and cut the rest into bite-size pieces. Drain the soaked mushrooms, trim off and discard the stems and chop the caps roughly.

3 Drain the tofu sticks. Cut them into 2-inch long pieces, discarding any hard pieces. If using dried lotus root, drain well.

4 Heat the oil in a frying pan or wok. Stir-fry the wood ears, Chinese mushrooms and lotus root for about 30 seconds.

5 Add the pieces of tofu straw mushrooms, baby corn, soy sauce, sherry, sugar and stock. Bring to a boil, then cover the pan or wok, lower the heat and simmer for about 20 minutes.

6 Stir in the snow peas with salt to taste, and cook, uncovered, for 2 more minutes. Mix the cornstarch to a paste with the water. Add the mixture to the pan or wok. Cook, stirring, until the sauce thickens. Serve immediately.

braised tofu with mushrooms

THE **MARINADE** AND **MUSHROOMS** FLAVOR THE TOFU **BEAUTIFULLY** IN THIS **PERFECT** VEGETARIAN MAIN COURSE.

ingredients

12 ounces **tofu**
½ teaspoon **sesame oil**
2 teaspoons **light soy sauce**
1 tablespoon **vegetable oil**
2 **garlic** cloves, finely chopped
½ teaspoon grated fresh **ginger root**
1 cup fresh **shiitake mushrooms**, stems removed
1½ cups fresh **oyster mushrooms**
1 cup drained, canned **straw mushrooms**
1 cup **button mushrooms**, cut in half
1 tablespoon **dry sherry**
1 tablespoon **dark soy sauce**
6 tablespoons **vegetable stock**
1 teaspoon **cornstarch**
1 tablespoon **water**
salt and freshly ground **white pepper**
2 **scallions**, shredded, to garnish

method

SERVES 4

1 Put the tofu in a dish and sprinkle with the sesame oil, light soy sauce and a large pinch of pepper. Let marinate for 10 minutes, then drain and cut into 1 x ½-inch pieces.

2 Heat the vegetable oil in a frying pan or wok. When it is very hot, fry the garlic and ginger for a few seconds. Add all the mushrooms and stir-fry for 2 minutes.

3 Stir in the sherry, soy sauce and stock, with salt, if needed, and pepper. Simmer for 4 minutes.

4 Mix the cornstarch to a paste with the water. Stir the mixture into the pan or wok and cook, stirring, until thickened.

5 Carefully add the pieces of tofu, toss gently to coat thoroughly and simmer for 2 minutes.

6 Scatter the shredded scallions over the top of the mixture, transfer to a serving dish and serve immediately.

cook's tip

If fresh shiitake mushrooms are not available, use dried Chinese mushrooms soaked in boiling water. Use the soaking liquid instead of vegetable stock for a more intense flavor.

rice & noodles

festive rice

THIS **ATTRACTIVE** RICE DISH IS TRADITIONALLY **SHAPED** INTO A CONE AND SURROUNDED BY A **VARIETY OF ACCOMPANIMENTS** BEFORE BEING SERVED.

method

SERVES 8

1 Put the rice in a strainer and rinse thoroughly under cold running water. Drain well.

2 Heat the oil in a frying pan that has a lid. Fry the garlic, onions and turmeric over a low heat for a few minutes, until the onions are softened but not browned. Add the rice and stir well so that each grain is thoroughly coated.

3 Pour in the water and coconut milk and add the lemongrass. Bring to a boil, stirring well. Cover the pan and let cook gently for 15–20 minutes, or until all the liquid has been absorbed.

4 Remove the pan from heat and lift the lid. Cover with a clean dish towel, replace the lid and let stand in a warm place for 15 minutes. Remove the lemongrass, mound the rice mixture into a cone on a serving platter and garnish with the accompaniments. Serve immediately.

cook's tip

Look for fresh turmeric at Asian markets or food stores. It is a rhizome and looks rather like fresh ginger root.

ingredients

2⅓ cups **jasmine** or **basmati rice**
¼ cup **oil**
2 **garlic** cloves, crushed
2 **onions**, finely sliced
2-inch piece of fresh **turmeric**, peeled and crushed or ¼ teaspoon **ground turmeric**
3 cups **water**
14-ounce can **coconut milk**
1–2 **lemongrass stalks**, bruised

For the accompaniments
omelet strips
2 fresh **red chiles**, shredded
cucumber chunks
tomato wedges
deep-fried **onions**
shrimp crackers

ingredients

1 $1/3$ cups **black glutinous rice** or **brown rice**
3$3/4$ cups **vegetable stock**
1 tablespoon **vegetable oil**
8 ounces **Chinese cabbage**, cut into $1/2$-inch strips
4 **scallions**, thinly sliced
salt and freshly ground **white pepper**
$1/2$ teaspoon **sesame oil**

chinese cabbage & black rice stir-fry

THE **SLIGHTLY NUTTY**, CHEWY BLACK **GLUTINOUS RICE** CONTRASTS BEAUTIFULLY WITH THE CHINESE CABBAGE.

method

SERVES 4

1 Rinse the rice until the water runs clear, then drain and place in a saucepan. Add the stock and bring to a boil. Lower the heat, cover the pan and cook gently for 30 minutes. Remove from heat and let stand for 15 minutes without lifting the pan lid.

2 Heat the vegetable oil in a frying pan or wok. Stir-fry the cabbage for 2 minutes, sprinkling with a little water to prevent them from burning.

3 Drain the rice, stir it into the cabbage and cook for 4 minutes, using two spatulas or spoons to toss the mixture over the heat.

4 Add the scallions, with salt and pepper to taste and the sesame oil. Cook for 1 more minute. Serve immediately.

fried rice with mushrooms

A **TASTY RICE** DISH THAT IS ALMOST A MEAL IN ITSELF. **SESAME** OIL ADDS A **HINT** OF **NUTTY FLAVOR**.

ingredients

- 1¼ cups **long-grain rice**
- 1 tablespoon **vegetable oil**
- 1 **egg**, lightly beaten
- 2 **garlic** cloves, crushed
- 1¼ cups **button mushrooms**, sliced
- 1 tablespoon **light soy sauce**
- ¼ teaspoon **salt**
- ½ teaspoon **sesame oil**
- **cucumber** matchsticks, to garnish

cook's tip

When you cook rice this way, you may find there is a crust at the bottom of the pan. Simply soak the crust in water for a couple of minutes to break it up, then drain it and fry it with the rest of the rice.

method

SERVES 4

1. Rinse the rice until the water runs clear, then drain. Place it in a saucepan. Measure the depth of the rice against your index finger, then bring the finger up to just above the surface of the rice and add cold water to the same depth as the rice.

2. Bring the water to a boil. Stir, boil for a few minutes, then cover the pan. Lower the heat to a simmer and cook the rice gently for 5–8 minutes, until all the water has been absorbed. Remove the pan from heat and, without lifting the lid, set aside for another 10 minutes before stirring or forking up the rice.

3. Heat 1 teaspoon of the vegetable oil in a frying pan or wok. Add the egg and cook, stirring with a chopstick or wooden spoon, until scrambled. Remove and set aside.

4. Heat the remaining vegetable oil in the clean pan or wok. Stir-fry the garlic for a few seconds, then add the mushrooms and stir-fry for 2 minutes, adding a little water, if needed, to prevent burning.

5. Stir in the cooked rice and cook, stirring occasionally, for 4 minutes, or until the rice is hot.

6. Add the scrambled egg, soy sauce, salt and sesame oil. Cook for 1 minute to heat through. Serve immediately, garnished with cucumber matchsticks.

sticky rice parcels

THIS **SUPERB** DISH IS **PACKED** WITH **FLAVOR**. THE PARCELS LOOK PRETTY AND ARE A **PLEASURE** TO **EAT**.

method

SERVES 4

1 Rinse the glutinous rice until the water runs clear, then set aside to soak in water for 2 hours. Drain and stir in 1 teaspoon of the oil and ½ teaspoon salt. Line a large steamer with a piece of clean muslin or cheesecloth. Transfer the rice into this. Cover and steam over boiling water for 45 minutes, stirring the rice from time to time and adding water if needed.

2 Mix the soy sauce, five-spice powder and sherry. Put the chicken pieces in a bowl, add the marinade, stir to coat, then cover and let marinate for 20 minutes.

3 Drain the Chinese mushrooms, cut out and discard the stems, then chop the caps roughly. Drain the dried shrimp. Heat the remaining oil in a frying pan or wok. Stir-fry the chicken for 2 minutes, then add the mushrooms, shrimp, bamboo shoots and stock. Lower the heat and to simmer for 10 minutes.

4 Mix the cornstarch to a paste with the water. Add the mixture to the pan and cook, stirring, until the sauce has thickened. Season with salt and white pepper to taste. Lift the cooked rice out of the steamer and set it aside to cool slightly.

5 With lightly dampened hands, divide the rice into four equal portions. Put half of one portion in the center of a lotus leaf. Spread it into a round and place a quarter of the chicken mixture on top. Cover with the remaining half portion of rice. Fold the leaf around the filling to make a neat rectangular parcel. Make three more parcels in the same way.

6 Prepare a steamer. Put the rice parcels, seam-side down, into the steamer. Cover and steam over high heat for about 30 minutes. Serve the parcels on individual heated plates, inviting the diners to unwrap their own parcels.

ingredients

2⅔ cups **glutinous rice**
4 teaspoons **vegetable oil**
1 tablespoon dark **soy sauce**
¼ teaspoons Chinese **five- spice powder**
1 tablespoon **dry sherry**
4 skinless boneless **chicken** thighs, each cut into 4 pieces
8 dried **Chinese mushrooms,** soaked in hot water until soft
1 ounce dried **shrimp**, soaked in hot water until soft
½ cup sliced, drained, canned **bamboo shoots**
1¼ cups **chicken stock**
2 teaspoons **cornstarch**
1 tablespoon cold **water**
4 **lotus leaves**, soaked in warm water until soft
salt and freshly ground **white pepper**

ingredients

2 ounces cooked **ham**
2 ounces cooked **shrimp**, peeled and deveined
3 **eggs**
1 teaspoon **salt**
2 **scallions**, finely chopped
1 cup **green peas**, thawed if frozen
¼ cup **vegetable oil**
1 tablespoon **light soy sauce**
1 tablespoon **Chinese rice wine** or **dry sherry**
4 cups cooked **rice**

chinese fried rice

CHINESE **FRIED RICE** IS AN **ELABORATE** VERSION OF FRIED RICE—ALMOST A **MEAL** IN **ITSELF**.

method

SERVES 4

1 Dice the ham finely. Pat the shrimp dry on paper towels.

2 In a bowl, beat the eggs lightly with a pinch of the salt and a few pieces of the scallions.

3 Heat about half the oil in a wok or frying pan, stir-fry the peas, shrimp and ham for 1 minute, then add the soy sauce and wine or sherry. Transfer to a bowl and keep hot.

4 Heat the remaining oil in the wok or pan and scramble the eggs lightly. Add the rice and stir to make sure that each grain of rice is separate. Add the remaining salt, the remaining scallions and the shrimp mixture. Toss over the heat to mix. Serve hot or cold.

variations

This is one of those good-tempered recipes that are ideal for using up leftovers. Use cooked chicken or turkey instead of the ham, doubling the quantity if you omit the shrimp.

special fried rice

THIS DELICIOUS RECIPE COMBINES **CHICKEN**, **SHRIMP** AND **VEGETABLES** WITH FRIED RICE. LETTUCE AND A **SPRINKLING** OF NUTS ARE ADDED FOR **EXTRA CRUNCH**.

ingredients

scant 1 cup **long-grain white rice**
3 tablespoons **peanut oil**
1½ cups **water**
1 **garlic** clove, crushed
4 **scallions**, finely chopped
1 cup diced cooked **chicken**
1 cup cooked peeled **shrimp**, rinsed if canned
1 **egg**, beaten with a pinch of **salt**
1 cup shredded **lettuce**
2 tablespoons **light soy sauce**
pinch of **sugar**
salt and freshly ground **black pepper**
roasted **cashews** and fresh **herbs**, to garnish

method

SERVES 4

1 Rinse the rice in two to three changes of warm water to wash away some of the starch. Drain well.

2 Put the rice in a saucepan and add 1 tablespoon of the oil. Pour in the measured water. Bring to a boil, stir once, then cover and simmer for 12–15 minutes, until nearly all the water has been absorbed. Turn off the heat and set aside, covered, to stand for 10 minutes. Fluff up with a fork and let cool.

3 Heat the remaining oil in a frying pan or wok, add the garlic and scallions and stir-fry for 30 seconds.

4 Add the chicken and shrimp and stir-fry for 1–2 minutes, then add the cooked rice and stir-fry for 2 more minutes. Pour in the egg and stir-fry until just set. Stir in the lettuce, soy sauce and sugar and season to taste with salt and pepper.

5 Transfer to a warm serving bowl, garnish with the cashews and herbs and serve immediately, with more soy sauce, if desired.

chinese jeweled rice

ANOTHER **FRIED RICE MEDLEY**, THIS TIME WITH CRABMEAT AND WATER CHESTNUTS PROVIDING **CONTRASTING TEXTURES** AND **FLAVORS**.

ingredients

1¾ cups **long-grain rice**
3 tablespoons **vegetable oil**
1 **onion**, roughly chopped
4 dried **black Chinese mushrooms**, soaked for 10 minutes in warm water
4 ounces cooked **ham**, diced
6 ounces drained canned **white crabmeat**
½ cup drained canned **water chestnuts**, cubed
1 cup **peas**, thawed if frozen
2 tablespoons **oyster sauce**
1 teaspoon **sugar**
salt

method

SERVES 4

1 Rinse the rice, then cook for 10–12 minutes in a saucepan of lightly salted boiling water. Drain, refresh under cold water and drain again. Heat half the oil in a wok or frying pan. When very hot, stir-fry the rice for 3 minutes. Transfer to a bowl and set aside.

2 Heat the remaining oil in the wok and cook the onion until softened but not colored. Drain the mushrooms, cut off and discard the stems, then chop the caps.

3 Add the chopped mushrooms to the wok, with all the remaining ingredients except the rice. Stir-fry for 2 minutes, then add the rice and stir-fry for 3 more minutes. Serve immediately.

cook's tip

When adding the oil to the hot wok, drizzle it in a "necklace" just below the rim. As it runs down, it will coat the inner surface as it heats.

toasted noodles with vegetables

CRISP NOODLE **CAKES** TOPPED WITH VEGETABLES MAKE AN **UNUSUAL** AND **TASTY** DISH.

method

SERVES 4

1 Bring a saucepan of water to a boil. Add the egg vermicelli and cook according to the instructions on the package until just tender. Drain, refresh under cold water, drain again, then dry thoroughly on paper towels.

2 Heat ½ teaspoon of the oil in a frying pan or wok. When it starts to smoke, spread half the noodles over the bottom. Fry for 2–3 minutes, until lightly toasted. Turn the noodles over (they stick together like a cake), fry the other side, then slide onto a heated serving plate. Repeat with the remaining noodles to make 2 cakes. Keep hot.

3 Heat the remaining oil in the clean pan or wok, then fry the garlic for a few seconds. Halve the corn lengthwise, add to the pan with the mushrooms, then stir-fry for 3 minutes, adding water to prevent burning. Add the celery, carrot, snow peas and bamboo shoots. Stir-fry for 2 minutes, until the vegetables are tender-crisp.

4 Mix the cornstarch to a paste with the water. Add the mixture to the pan or wok with the soy sauce, sugar and vegetable stock. Cook, stirring, until the sauce thickens. Season to taste with salt and pepper. Divide the vegetable mixture between the noodle cakes, garnish with the scallion curls and serve. Each noodle cake serves 2 people.

ingredients

1½ cups dried **egg vermicelli**
1 tablespoon **vegetable oil**
2 **garlic** cloves, finely chopped
1 cup **baby corn**
1 cup fresh **shiitake mushrooms**, halved
3 **celery** stalks, sliced
1 **carrot**, sliced diagonally
1 cup **snow peas**
¾ cup sliced, drained, canned **bamboo shoots**
1 tablespoon **cornstarch**
1 tablespoon **water**
1 tablespoon **dark soy sauce**
1 teaspoon **sugar**
1¼ cups **vegetable stock**
salt and freshly ground **white pepper**
scallion curls, to garnish

ingredients

1 1/2 cups dried **egg noodles**
1 tablespoon **vegetable oil**
1 **garlic** clove, finely chopped
1 small **onion**, halved and sliced
4 cups **bean sprouts**
1 small **red bell pepper**, seeded and cut into strips
1 small **green bell pepper**, seeded and cut into strips
1/2 teaspoon **salt**
1/4 teaspoon freshly ground **white pepper**
2 tablespoons **light soy sauce**

stir-fried noodles with bean sprouts

A **CLASSIC** CHINESE **NOODLE** DISH THAT IS A MARVELOUS **SIDE DISH**.

method

SERVES 4

1 Bring a saucepan of water to a boil. Cook the noodles for 4 minutes, until just tender, or according to the instructions on the package. Drain, refresh under cold water and drain again.

2 Heat the oil in a frying pan or wok. When the oil is very hot, add the garlic, stir briefly, then add the onion slices. Cook, stirring constantly, for 1 minute, then add the bean sprouts and peppers. Stir-fry for 2–3 minutes.

3 Stir in the cooked noodles and toss over the heat, using two spatulas or wooden spoons, for 2–3 minutes, or until the ingredients are well mixed and have heated through.

4 Add the salt, pepper and soy sauce and stir thoroughly before serving the noodle mixture in heated bowls.

ingredients

2 **duck** breasts
1 tablespoon **vegetable oil**
5 ounces **sugar snap peas**
2 **carrots**, cut into 3-inch sticks
8 ounces medium **egg noodles**
6 **scallions**, sliced
salt
2 tablespoons **cilantro leaves**, to garnish

For the marinade
1 tablespoon **sesame oil**
1 teaspoon **ground coriander**
1 teaspoon **Chinese five-spice powder**

For the dressing
1 tablespoon **garlic vinegar**
1 teaspoon **light brown sugar**
1 teaspoon **light soy sauce**
1 tablespoon toasted **sesame seeds** (see cook's tip)
3 tablespoons **sunflower oil**
2 tablespoons **sesame oil**
freshly ground **black pepper**

sesame duck & noodle salad

THIS SALAD IS A COMPLETE MEAL IN ITSELF AND MAKES A LOVELY **SUMMER LUNCH**. THE **MARINADE** IS A SUPERB BLEND OF DELICIOUS **SPICES.**

method

SERVES 4

1 Slice the duck breasts thinly across the grain and place them in a shallow dish. Mix together all the ingredients for the marinade, pour it over the duck and mix well to coat thoroughly. Cover and set aside in a cool place for 30 minutes.

2 Heat the oil in a frying pan or wok, add the slices of duck breast and stir-fry for 3–4 minutes, until cooked. Set aside.

3 Bring a saucepan of lightly salted water to a boil. Place the sugar snap peas and carrots in a steamer that will fit on top of the pan. When the water boils, add the noodles. Place the steamer on top and steam the vegetables, while cooking the noodles for the time suggested on the package. Set the steamed vegetables aside. Drain the noodles, refresh them under cold running water and drain again. Place them in a large serving bowl.

4 Make the dressing. Mix the vinegar, sugar, soy sauce and sesame seeds in a bowl. Add a generous grinding of black pepper, then beat in the oils.

5 Pour the dressing over the noodles and mix well. Add the sugar snap peas, carrots, scallions and duck slices and toss to mix. Scatter the cilantro leaves over and serve.

cook's tip

To toast the sesame seeds, place them in a dry, heavy pan and heat gently, stirring frequently, until they are lightly browned.

singapore rice vermicelli

SIMPLE AND **SPEEDILY** PREPARED, THIS LIGHTLY **CURRIED** RICE NOODLE DISH IS A **FULL MEAL** IN A BOWL.

method

SERVES 4

1 Soak the rice vermicelli in a bowl of boiling water for 4 minutes, or according to the instructions on the package, then drain thoroughly and set aside.

2 Heat 1 teaspoon of the oil in a frying pan or wok. Add the egg and scramble until set. Remove with a slotted spoon and set aside.

3 Heat the remaining oil in the clean pan. Stir-fry the garlic and chile for a few seconds, then stir in the curry powder. Cook for 1 minute, stirring, then stir in the peppers, carrot sticks, salt and stock.

4 Bring to a boil. Add the shrimp, ham, scrambled egg, rice vermicelli and soy sauce. Mix well. Cook, stirring, until all the liquid has been absorbed and the mixture is hot. Serve immediately.

ingredients

2 cups dried **rice vermicelli**
1 tablespoon **vegetable oil**
1 **egg**, lightly beaten
2 **garlic** cloves, finely chopped
1 large fresh **red** or **green chile**, seeded and finely chopped
1 tablespoon medium **curry powder**
1 **red bell pepper**, seeded and thinly sliced
1 **green bell pepper**, seeded and thinly sliced
1 **carrot**, cut into matchsticks
½ teaspoon **salt**
¼ cup **vegetable stock**
4 ounces cooked peeled **shrimp**, thawed if frozen
3 ounces lean **ham**, cut into ½-inch cubes
1 tablespoon **light soy sauce**

seafood soup noodles

AUDIBLE SOUNDS OF **ENJOYMENT** ARE A COMPLIMENT TO THE CHINESE COOK, SO **SLURPING** THIS **SOUP** IS NOT ONLY **PERMISSIBLE**, IT IS POSITIVELY **DESIRABLE**.

ingredients

- 6 ounces **jumbo shrimp**, peeled and deveined
- 8-ounce **monkfish** fillet, cut into chunks
- 8-ounce **salmon** fillet, cut into chunks
- 1 teaspoon **vegetable oil**
- 1 tablespoon **dry white wine**
- 2 cups dried **egg vermicelli**
- 5 cups **fish stock**
- 1 **carrot**, thinly sliced
- 8 ounces **asparagus**, cut into 2-inch lengths
- 2 tablespoons **dark soy sauce**
- 1 teaspoon **sesame oil**
- **salt** and freshly ground **black pepper**
- 2 **scallions**, cut into thin rings, to garnish

variation

Try this simple recipe using rice vermicelli for a slightly different texture and taste.

method

SERVES 4

1. Mix the shrimp and fish in a bowl. Add the vegetable oil and wine with 1/4 teaspoon salt and a little pepper. Mix lightly, cover and marinate in a cool place for 15 minutes.

2. Bring a large saucepan of water to a boil and cook the noodles for 4 minutes, until just tender, or according to the instructions on the package. Drain the noodles thoroughly and divide among four serving bowls. Keep hot.

3. Bring the fish stock to a boil in a separate pan. Add the shrimp and monkfish, cook for 1 minute, then add the salmon and cook for 2 more minutes.

4. Using a slotted spoon, lift the fish and shrimp out of the stock, add to the noodles in the bowls and keep hot.

5. Strain the stock through a sieve lined with cheesecloth into a clean pan. Bring to a boil and cook the carrot and asparagus for 2 minutes, then add the soy sauce and sesame oil, with salt to taste. Stir well.

6. Pour the stock and vegetables over the noodles and seafood, garnish with the scallions and serve.

desserts

golden steamed sponge cake

CAKES ARE **NOT TRADITIONALLY** SERVED FOR DESSERT IN CHINA, BUT THIS **LIGHT CAKE** IS VERY **POPULAR** WITH DIM SUM AT TEAHOUSES.

method

SERVES 8

1 Sift the flour, baking powder and baking soda into a bowl. Line a 7-inch diameter bamboo steamer or cake pan with nonstick baking parchment.

2 In a mixing bowl, beat the eggs with the sugar until thick and frothy. Beat in the oil and syrup, then let the mixture stand for about 30 minutes.

3 Add the dry ingredients to the egg mixture with the vanilla extract, beating rapidly to form a thick batter.

4 Pour the batter into the lined steamer or pan. Cover and steam over boiling water for 30 minutes, or until the sponge springs back when it is gently pressed with a finger. Allow to cool for a few minutes before serving.

ingredients

1 1/2 cups **all-purpose flour**
1 teaspoon **baking powder**
1/4 teaspoon **baking soda**
3 large **eggs**
2/3 cup **light brown sugar**
3 tablespoons **walnut oil**
2 tablespoons **golden syrup** or **light corn syrup**
1 teaspoon **vanilla extract**

ingredients

6 tablespoons **sugar**
1 1/4 cups **white dessert wine**
thinly pared zest and juice of
 1 **lemon**
3-inch piece of fresh
 ginger root, bruised
5 **star anise**
10 **cloves**
2 1/2 cups **water**
6 slightly unripe **pears**
3 tablespoons drained,
 preserved ginger
 in syrup, sliced
fromage frais, to serve

pears with ginger & star anise

STAR ANISE AND GINGER GIVE A **REFRESHING TWIST** TO THESE POACHED PEARS. SERVE THEM **CHILLED**.

method

SERVES 4

1 Place the sugar, dessert wine, lemon zest and juice, ginger, star anise, cloves and water in a saucepan just large enough to hold the pears snugly in an upright position. Bring to a boil.

2 Meanwhile, peel the pears, leaving the stems intact. Add them to the wine mixture, making sure that they are totally immersed in the liquid.

3 Return the wine mixture to a boil, lower the heat, cover and simmer for 15–20 minutes, or until the pears are tender. Lift out the pears with a slotted spoon and place them in a heatproof dish. Boil the wine syrup rapidly until it is reduced by about half, then pour over the pears. Allow them to cool, then chill.

4 Cut the pears into thick slices and arrange these on four serving plates. Remove the ginger and whole spices from the wine sauce, stir in the preserved ginger and spoon the sauce over the pears. Serve with fromage frais.

heavenly jellies with fruit

DELICATE, **VANILLA-FLAVORED** JELLY, SET WITH **RIBBONS** OF EGG WHITE WITHIN IT, MAKES A **DELIGHTFUL** DESSERT SERVED WITH FRESH **FRUIT**.

method

SERVES 6

1 Put the agar agar into a saucepan. Add the boiling water, return to a boil and lower the heat. Simmer the mixture for 10–15 minutes, stirring occasionally, until the agar agar has dissolved completely.

2 Stir in the sugar. As soon as it has dissolved, strain the syrup through a fine sieve placed over a bowl. Return the mixture to the saucepan.

3 Immediately stir in the vanilla extract, then gently pour in the egg white in a steady stream; the heat will cook the egg. Stir once to distribute the threads of cooked egg white.

4 Pour the mixture into a shallow 11 x 7-inch baking dish and allow to cool. The jelly will set at room temperature, but will set faster and taste better if it is transferred to the refrigerator as soon as it has cooled completely.

5 Cut the strawberries in halves or quarters. If using fresh lychees, peel them and remove the stones. Divide the fruit among six small serving dishes or cups.

6 Turn the jelly out of the dish and cut it into diamond shapes to serve with the strawberries and lychees.

ingredients

1⁄4 ounce **agar agar**
3 3⁄4 cups boiling **water**
1⁄2 cup **sugar**
1 teaspoon **vanilla extract**
1 **egg white**, lightly beaten
1 1⁄2 cups fresh **strawberries**
1 pound fresh **lychees** or 19-ounce can **lychees**, well drained

variation

The jelly can be made with equal amounts of coconut milk and water and served with mangoes for a more tropical taste.

USUALLY **SERVED WARM**, THIS IS A LIGHT AND **REFRESHING** "SOUP," POPULAR WITH **CHILDREN** AND **ADULTS ALIKE**.

ingredients

- 2⁄3 cup **tapioca**
- 6 1⁄4 cups **water**
- 8 ounces **taro**
- 2⁄3 cup **rock sugar**
- 1 1⁄4 cups **coconut milk**

tapioca & taro pudding

method

SERVES 4–6

1 Rinse the tapioca, drain well, then put into a bowl with fresh water to cover. Set aside to soak for 30 minutes.

2 Drain the tapioca and put it in a saucepan with 3 3⁄4 cups water. Bring to a boil, lower the heat and simmer for about 6 minutes, or until the tapioca is transparent. Drain, refresh under cold water, and drain again.

3 Peel the taro and cut it into diamond-shaped slices, about 1⁄2-inch thick. Pour the remaining water into a saucepan and bring it to a boil. Add the taro and cook for 10–15 minutes or until it is just tender.

4 Using a slotted spoon, lift out half of the taro slices and set them aside. Continue to cook the remaining taro until it is very soft. Place the taro and cooking liquid in a food processor and process until completely smooth.

5 Return the taro "soup" to the clean pan; stir in the sugar and simmer, stirring occasionally, until the sugar has dissolved.

6 Stir in the tapioca, reserved taro and coconut milk. Cook for a few minutes. Serve immediately in heated bowls, or cool and chill before serving.

cook's tip

Taro is a starchy tuber that tastes rather like a potato. If it is difficult to obtain, use sweet potato instead.

toffee apples

ALL THE **FLAVOR** AND **TEXTURE** OF THIS CLASSIC CHINESE DESSERT WITHOUT THE **FUSS** AND FAT OF **DEEP-FRYING**.

ingredients

2 tablespoons **butter**
5 tablespoons cold **water**
6 tablespoons **all-purpose flour**
1 **egg**
1 **apple**
1 teaspoon **vegetable oil**
¾ cup **sugar**
1 teaspoon **sesame seeds**

cook's tip

A slightly unripe, firm banana can be used instead of an apple for a variation.

method

SERVES 6

1 Preheat the oven to 400°F. Put the butter and water into a small saucepan and bring to a boil. Remove from heat and add the flour all at once. Stir vigorously until the mixture forms a smooth paste that leaves the sides of the pan clean.

2 Cool the choux paste for 5 minutes, then beat in the egg, mixing thoroughly until the mixture is smooth and glossy.

3 Peel and core the apple and cut it into ½-inch chunks.

4 Stir the apple into the choux paste and place teaspoonfuls on a dampened nonstick baking sheet. Bake for 20–25 minutes, until brown and crisp on the outside but still soft inside.

5 When the pastries are cooked, heat the oil in a saucepan over low heat and add the sugar. Cook, without stirring, until the sugar has melted and turned golden brown, then sprinkle in the sesame seeds. Remove the pan from heat.

6 Have ready a bowl of ice water. Add the pastries, a few at a time, to the caramel and toss to coat them all over. Remove with a slotted spoon and quickly dip in the iced water to set the caramel; drain well. Serve immediately. If the caramel becomes too thick before all the choux pastries have been coated, re-heat it gently until it liquifies before continuing coating the pastries.

index

Share

a)

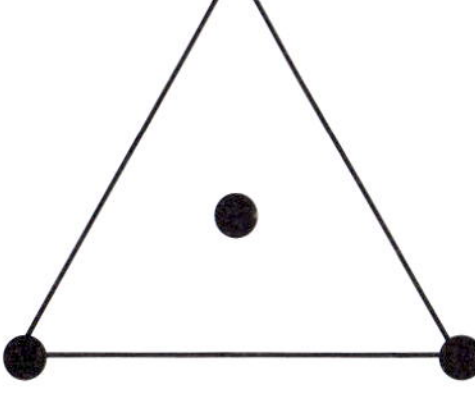

Three children will form a triangle around Amelia.

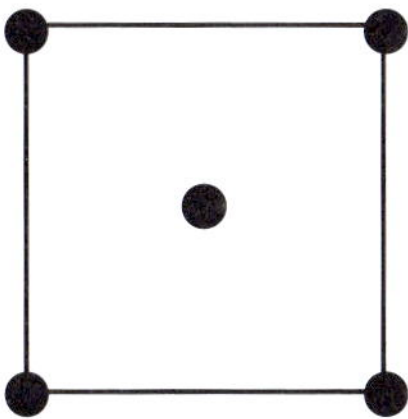

Four children will form a quadrilateral.

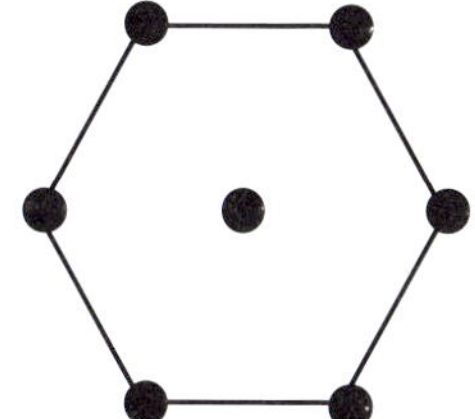

As more children join, the shape has more vertices.

As more children join, they start to form a circle. The distance from the centre is called the **radius**. This circle has a radius of 5 m.

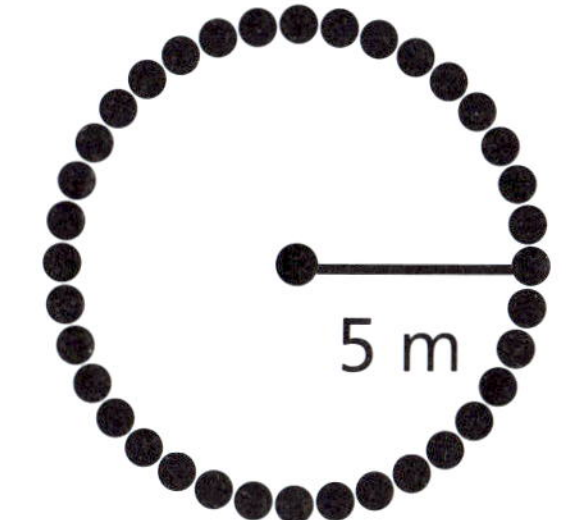

To draw smaller circles, you can use a pair of compasses.

This pair would draw a circle with a radius of 6 cm.

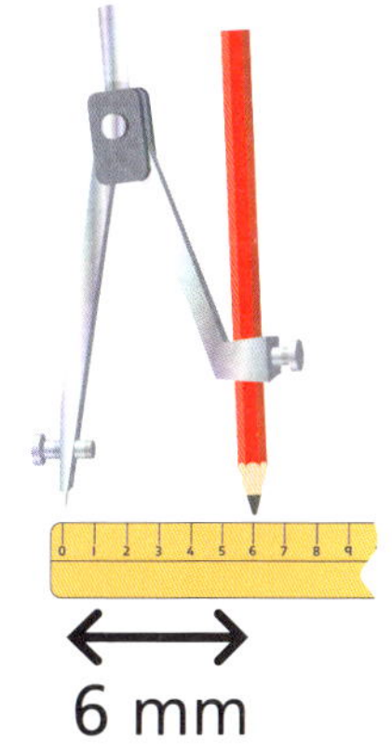

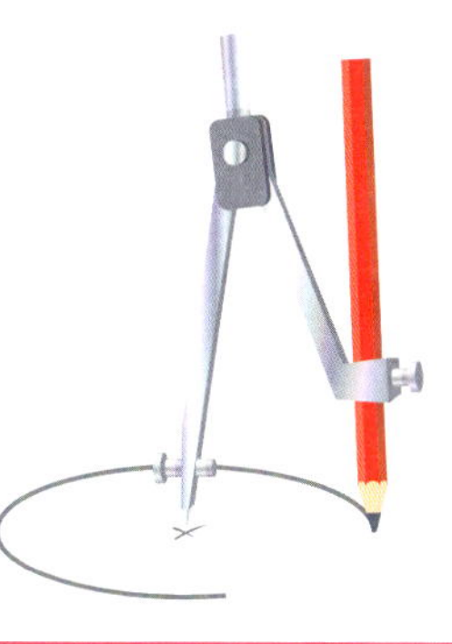

Not actual size

b) The second class will form another circle. The radius will be 6 m, so it will be larger.

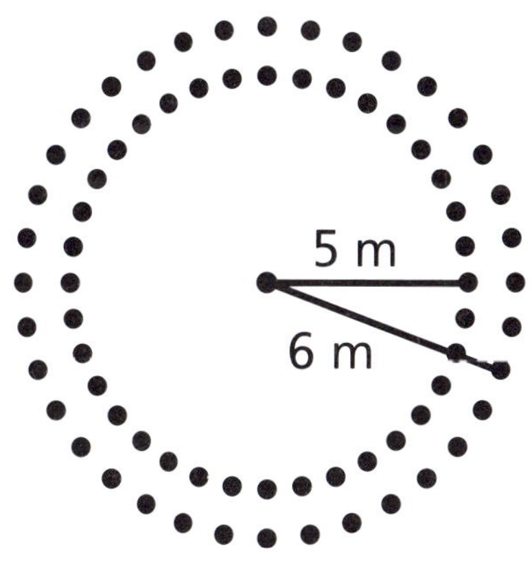

Circles with the same centre are called **concentric** circles.

Think together

1 Measure the radiuses (radii) of the circles below.

a)

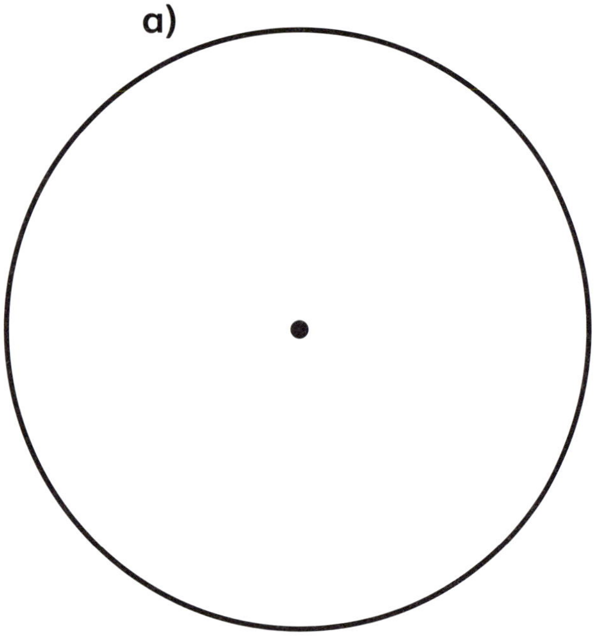

b)

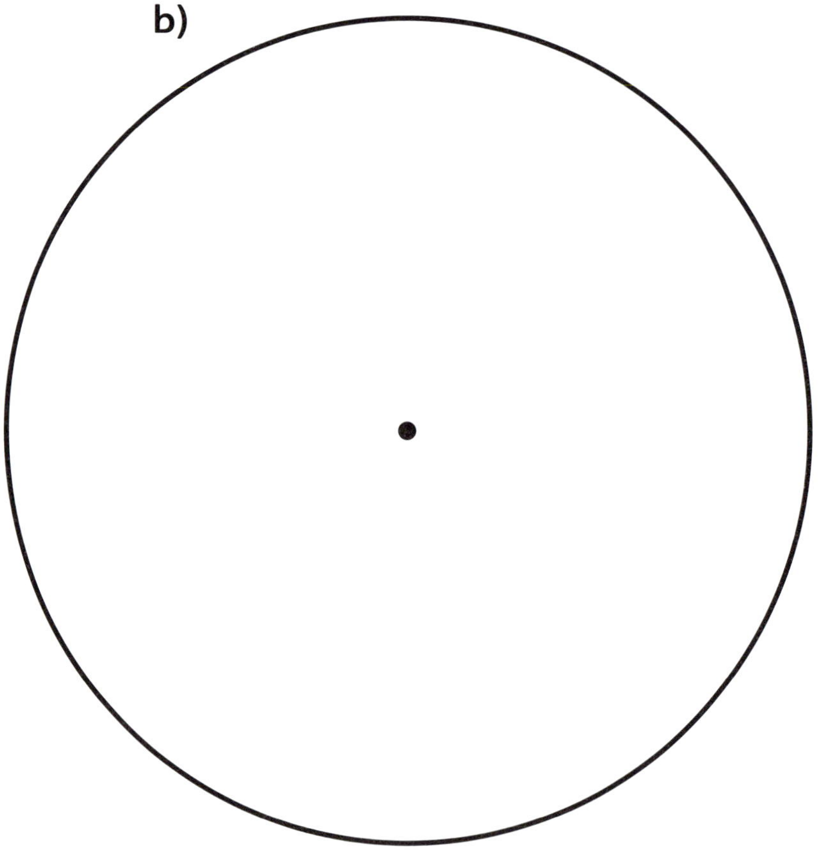

The widest part of a circle is called the **diameter**. The radius is half the diameter.

2 Try copying this design. If you do not have a pair of compasses, you could use string or a ruler to make the design.

Not actual size

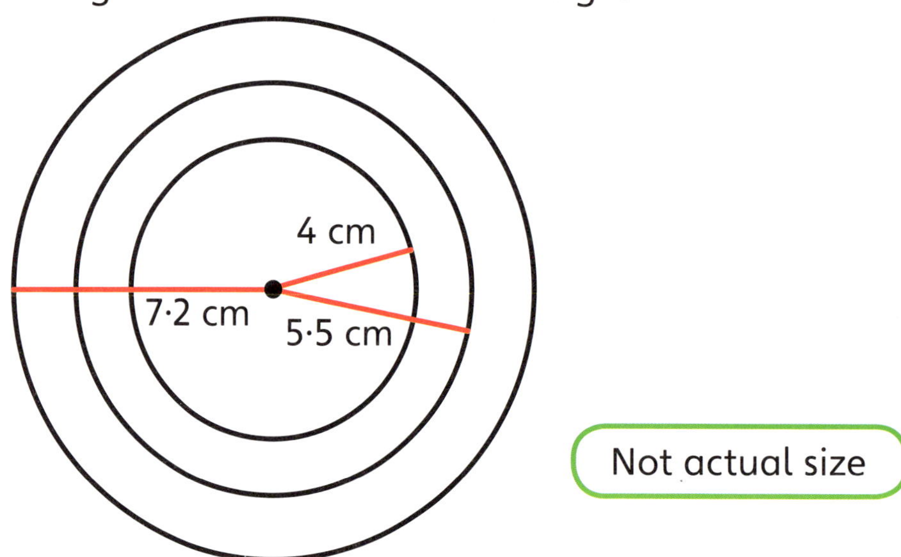

3 Max has drawn some circles, but he forgot to mark the centres. Find the radius of each circle.

i)

iii)

ii)

You can use the diameter to find the radius.

→ Practice book 6C p30

Parts of a circle

Discover

1 **a)** How could Bella find the distance around the edge of her bike's wheel?

b) Which is longest: the diameter, the radius or the distance around the edge of the wheel?

Share

The circumference is the distance all around a circle. It is similar to the perimeter of polygons.

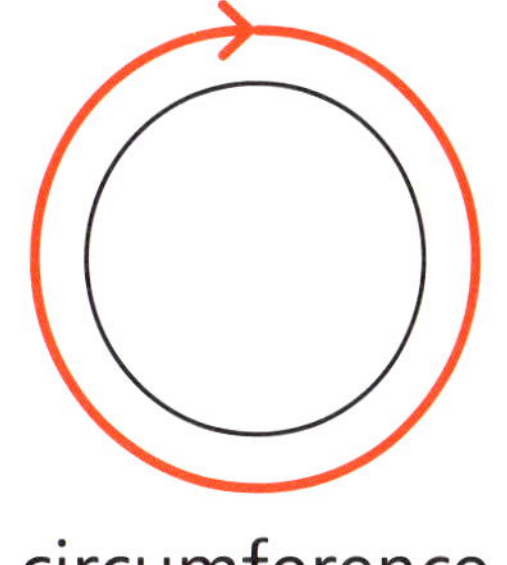

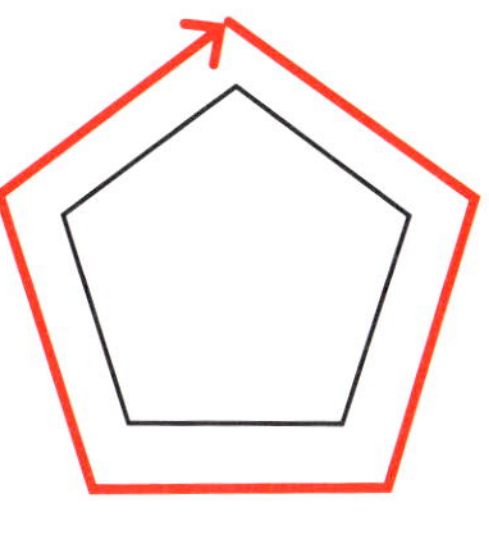

a) There are different methods to measure the circumference of a wheel.

Method 1:

Wrap a piece of rope or string around the circumference, then measure the rope in a straight line.

Method 2:

Choose a point on the wheel, and roll it until the point returns to the starting position. The distance it has rolled is the circumference.

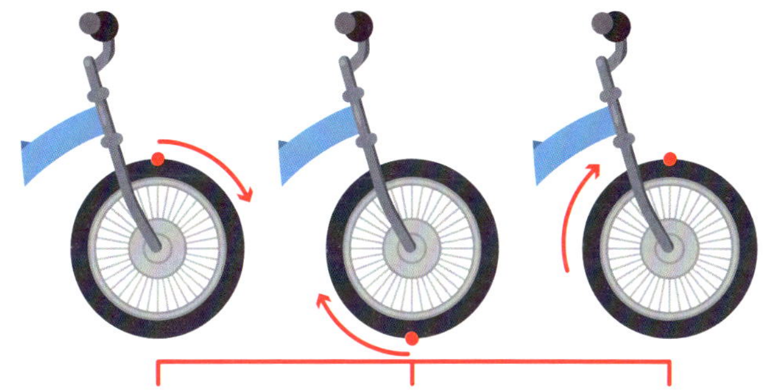

b) The radius is half the diameter, so the diameter is longer.

You can see in a semicircle that the curved part of half a circle is longer than the diameter.

So the circumference of a circle, like the outside of a wheel, is always longer than the diameter.

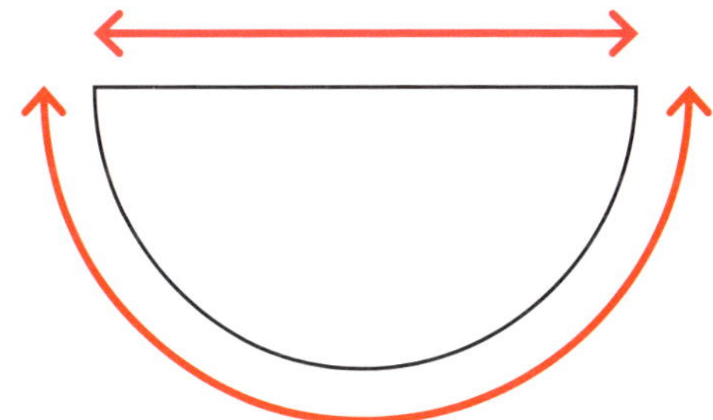

Think together

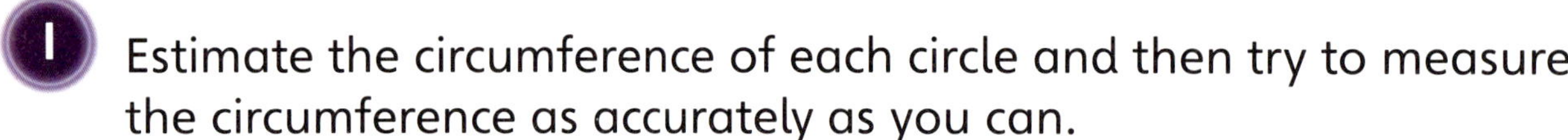

1 Estimate the circumference of each circle and then try to measure the circumference as accurately as you can.

a) 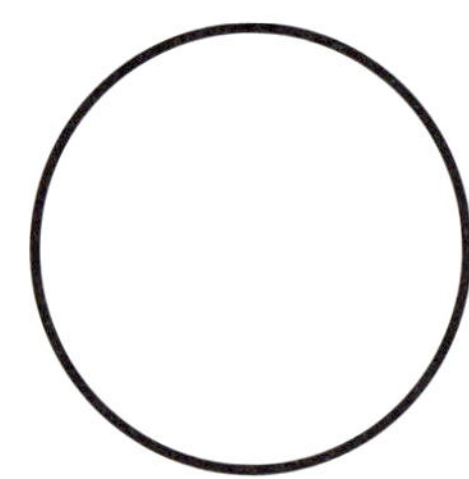

b) 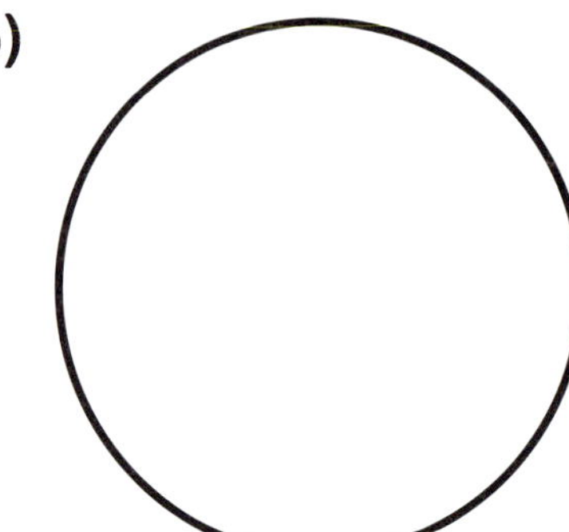

I can use string to measure the circumference of these circles.

2 Bella chooses two points on the circumference of a circle and joins them to the centre to form different triangles.

a) 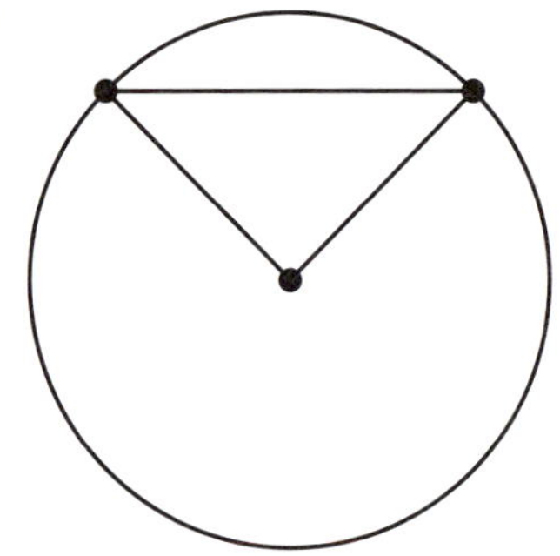

b) 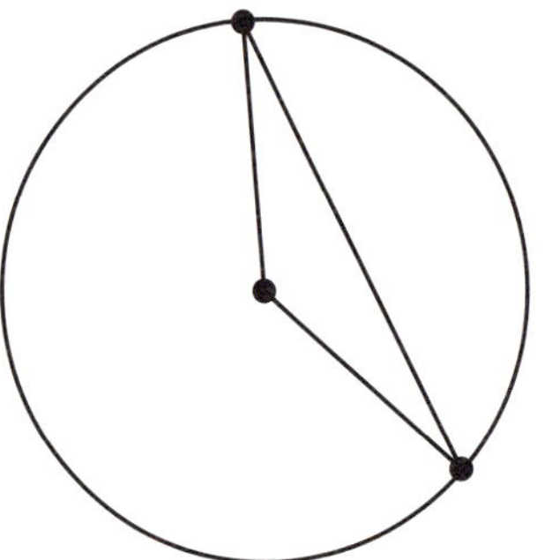

c) 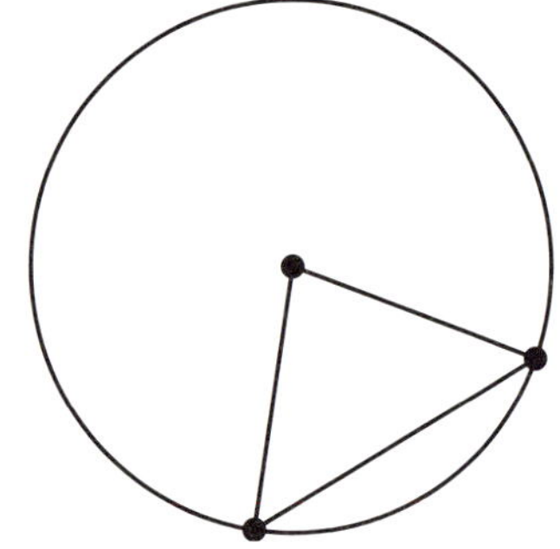

What different types of triangle can Bella form?

3 **a)** These triangles are formed by drawing a diameter through the centre, and joining each end of the diameter to a point on the circumference.

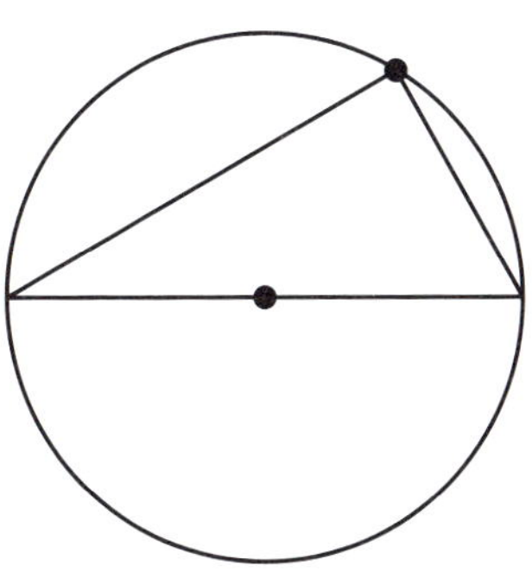

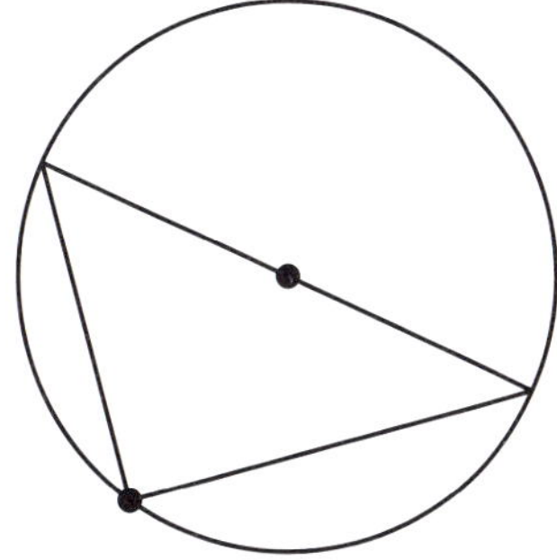

Measure the angles. What do you notice?

b) Isla has an idea about the size of the angle on the circumference. She has shown her reasoning in the diagrams below. Can you see what she has worked out?

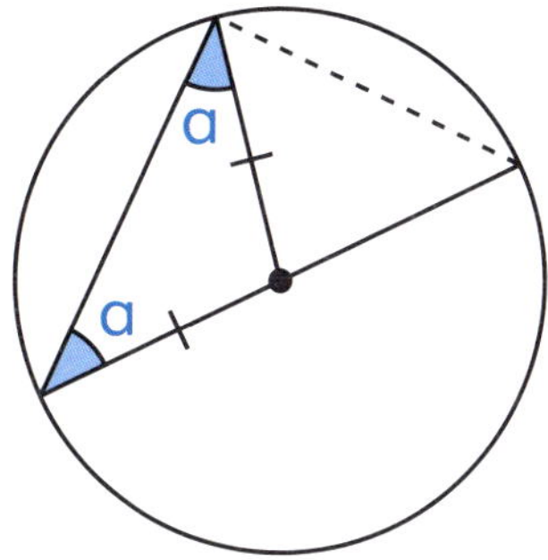

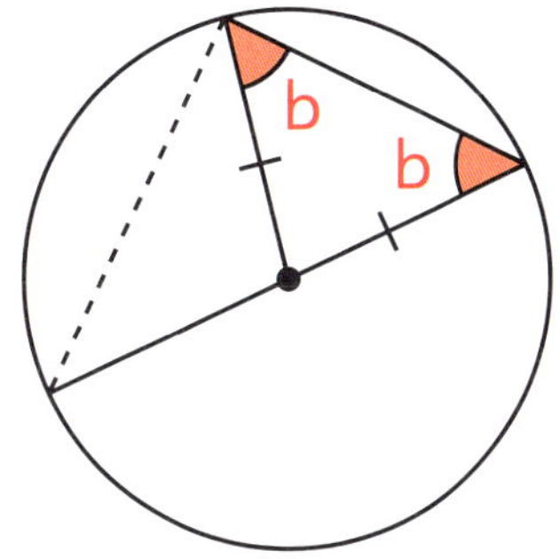

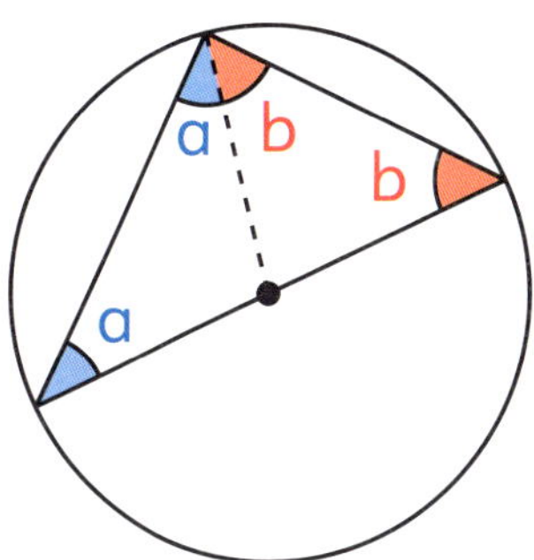

I think I can see isosceles triangles. I wonder why.

So angles a and b join at the circumference. I think I know what they add up to.

There are two a angles and two b angles in the triangle. I wonder what they add up to.

→ Practice book 6C p33

Nets 1

Discover

These are **nets**. They are 2D shapes that fold to make 3D shapes.

1 a) Which shapes will these nets form?

b) Sketch a net for a pentagonal-based pyramid.

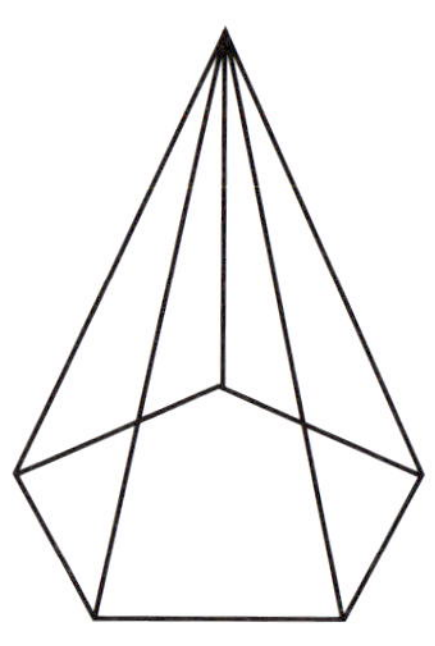

Share

a) Each face of the shape forms one part of the net.

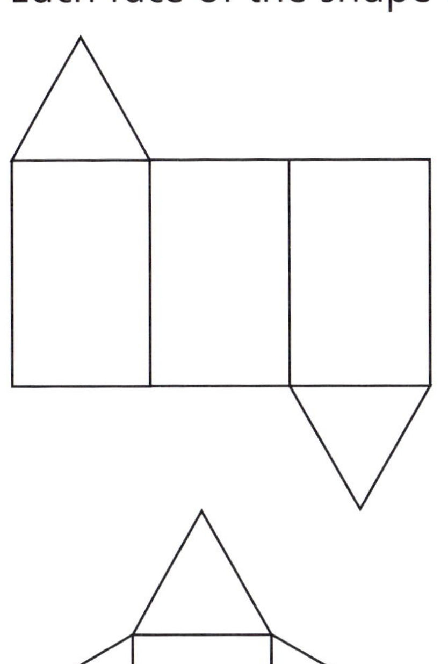

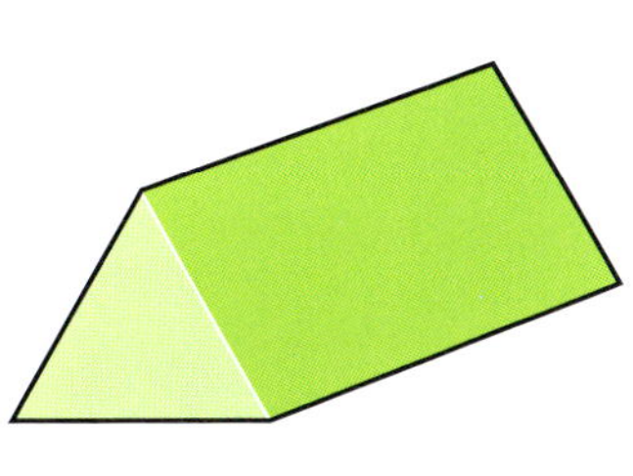

A triangular prism has three rectangular faces and two triangular faces.

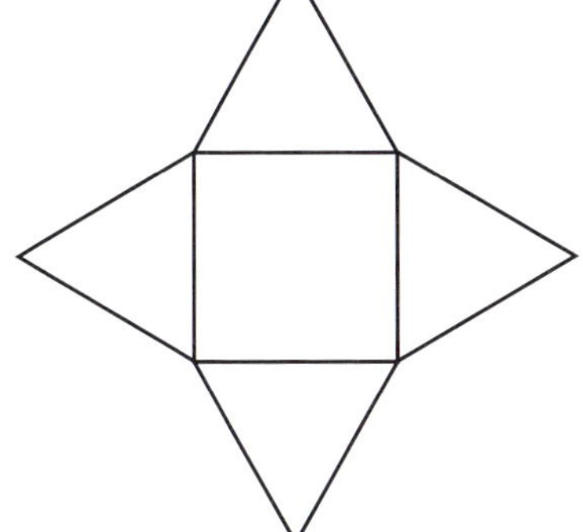

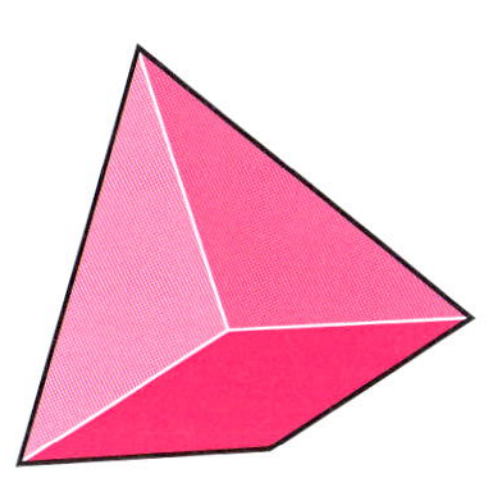

A square-based pyramid has four triangular faces and one square face.

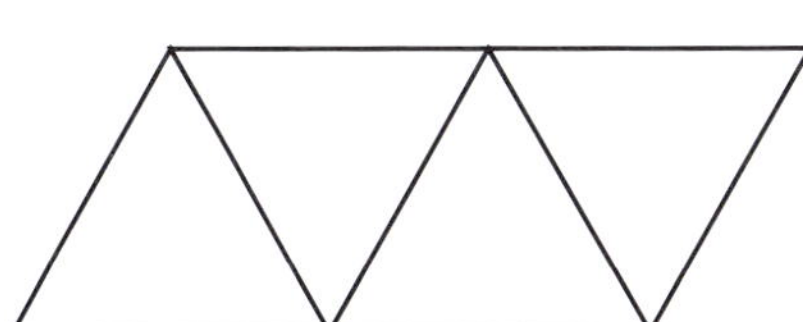

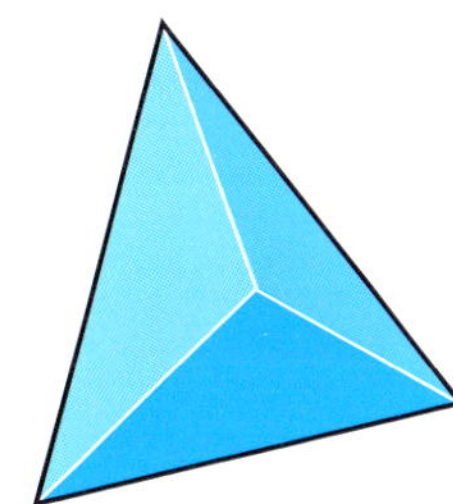

A **tetrahedron** has four triangular faces.

b) There are different possible nets for a pentagonal-based pyramid. One way is to have the base in the centre, and one triangular face for each side of the base.

Think together

1 Which of these nets will form a cuboid?

A

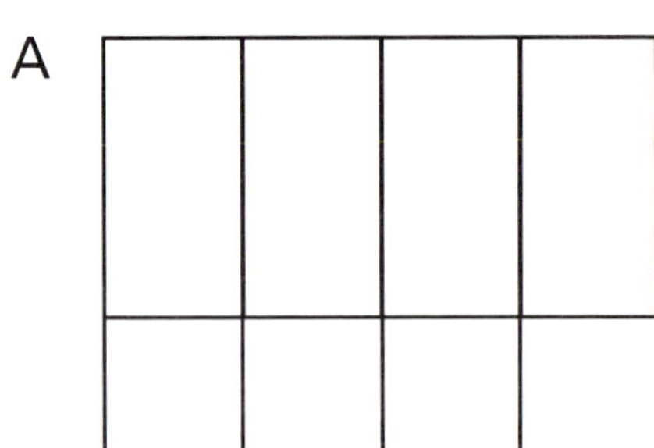

C

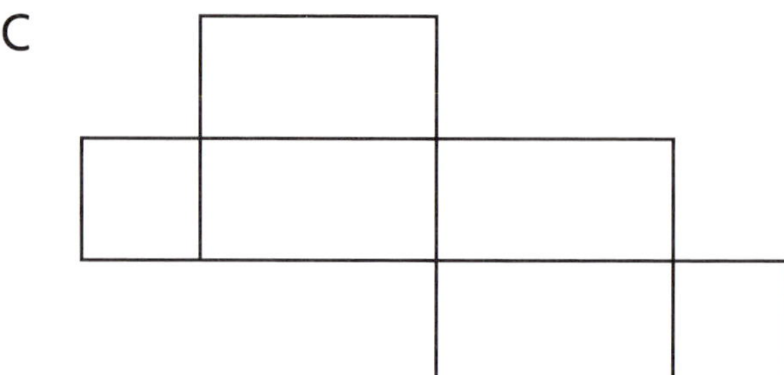

B

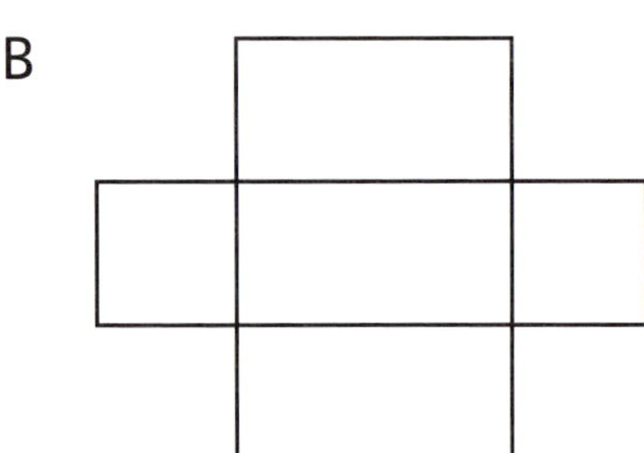

D

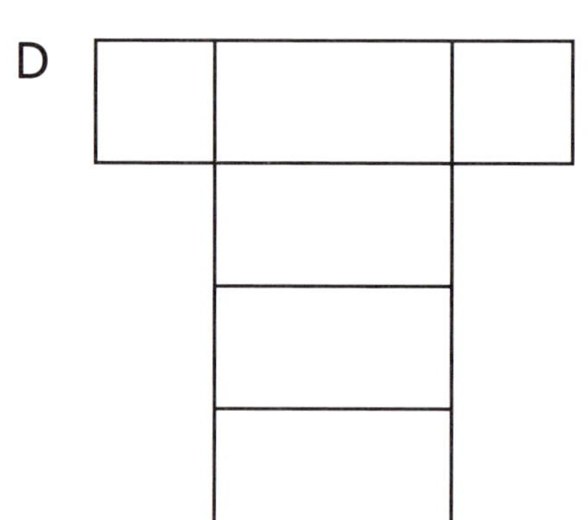

I know how many faces a cuboid has. That could help me spot a mistake.

I will check if any faces will overlap when they fold.

2 Sketch nets for the following 3D shapes.

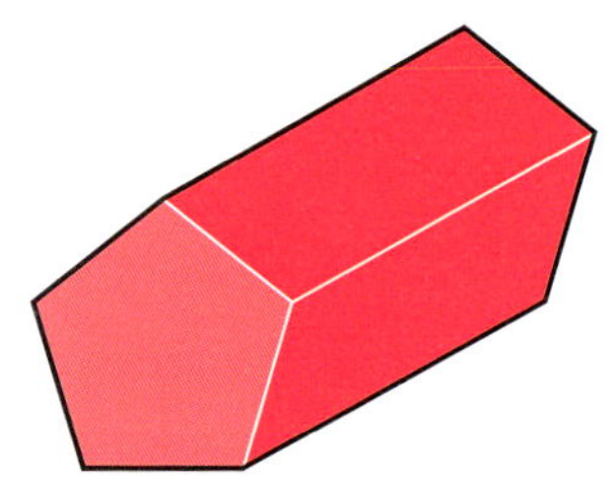

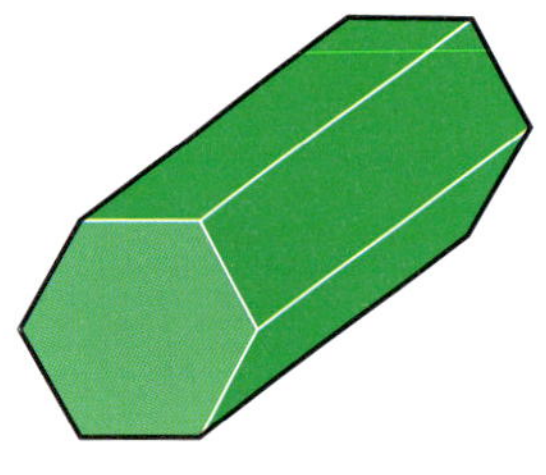

3 Draw a net for the following shape as accurately as you can. The base is a regular shape.

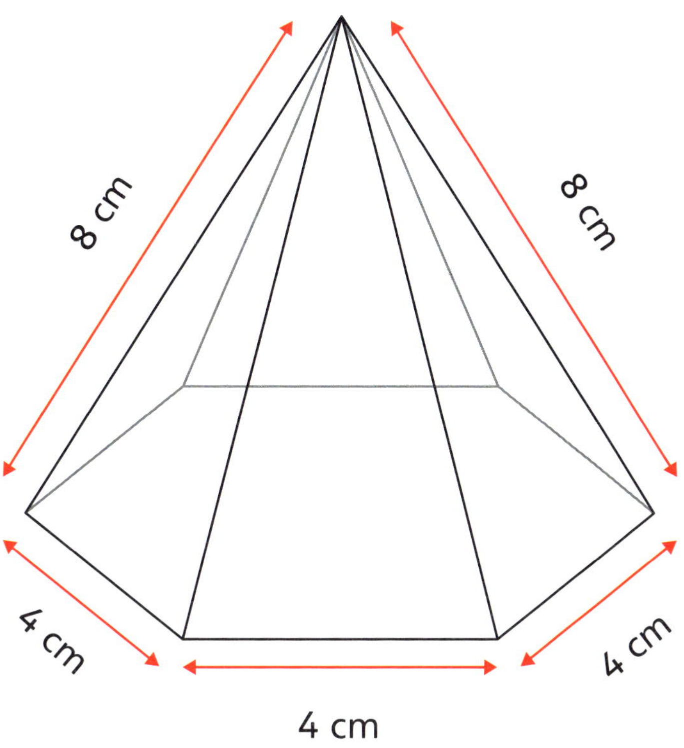

I will use a ruler and a protractor.

I will use grid paper. I wonder if I should use square dotted paper or isometric paper.

→ Practice book 6C p36

Nets 2

Discover

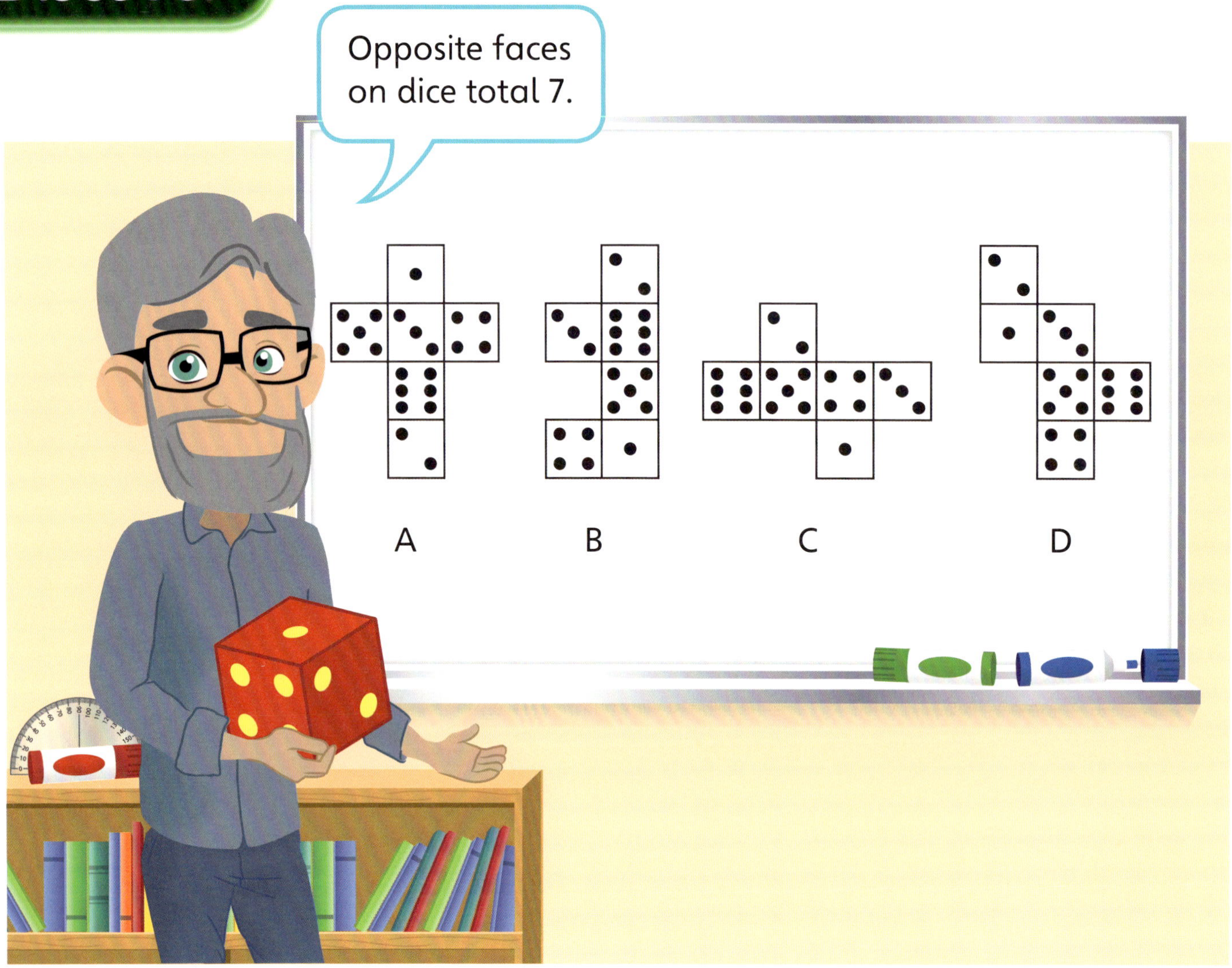

Opposite faces on dice total 7.

A B C D

1 **a)** Which is the correct net of a dice?

b) Try sketching the dots for a dice on a blank net. Are there different ways?

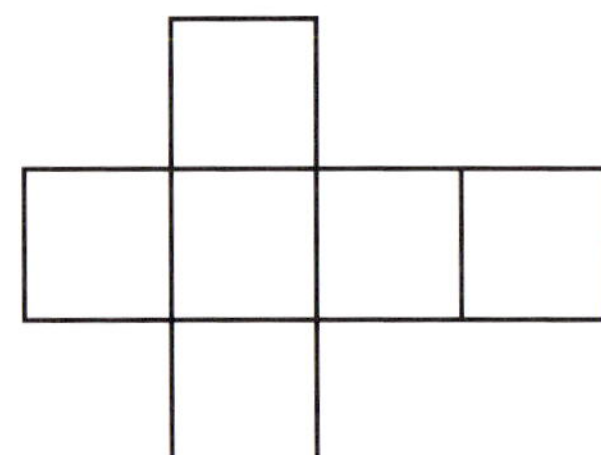

Share

a) Opposite faces of a dice must total 7.

So the following pairs must be opposite each other.

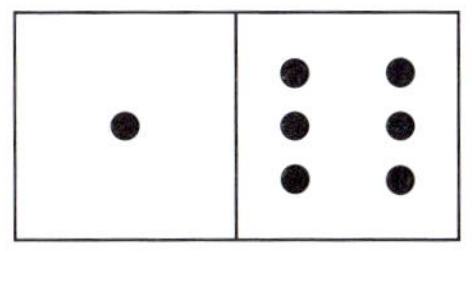 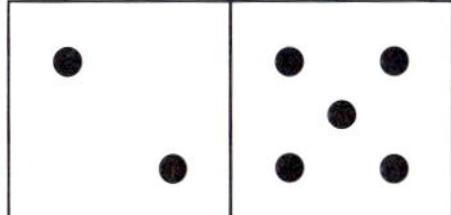 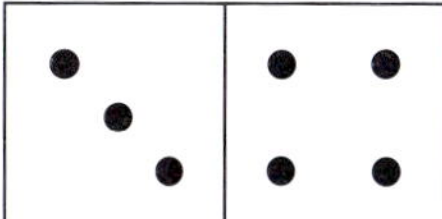

A

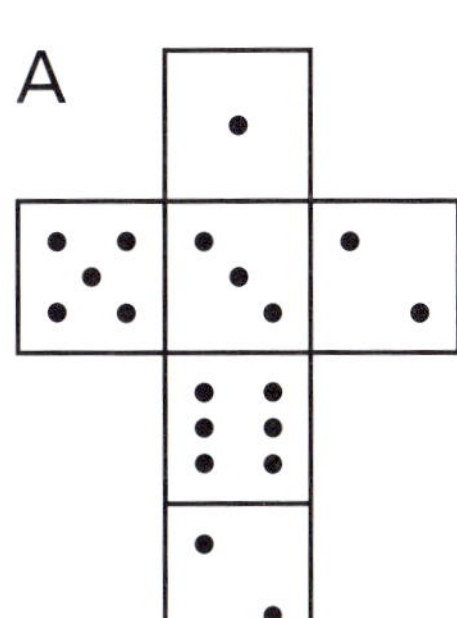

In this net, only 1 and 6 are opposite.

B

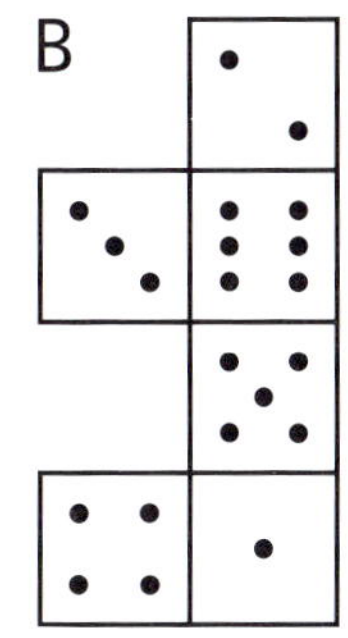

This does not form a cube correctly, as the 3 and the 4 overlap.

C

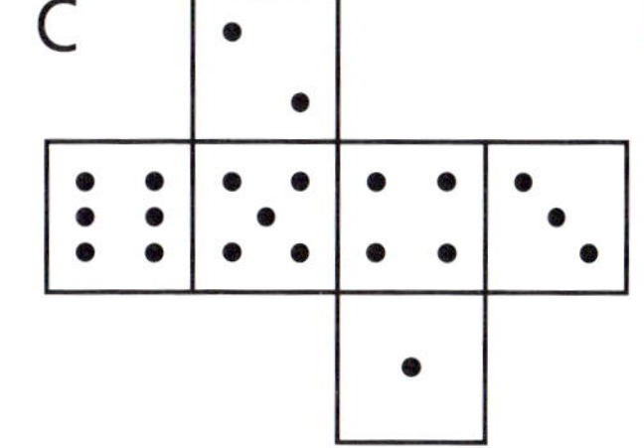

In this net, 3 and 4 are next to each other, and so are 2 and 5.

D

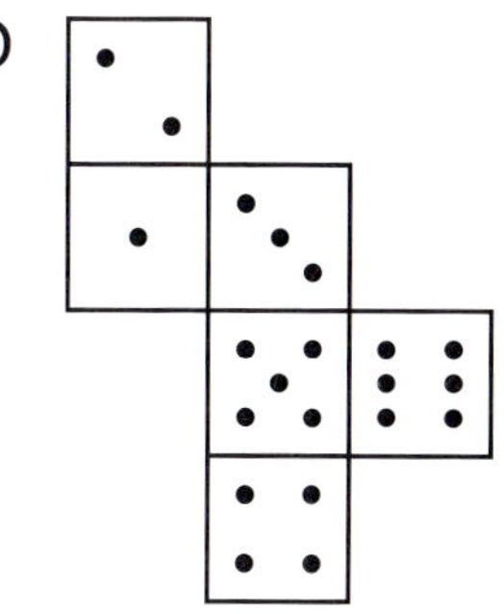

This net folds to make a correct dice.

  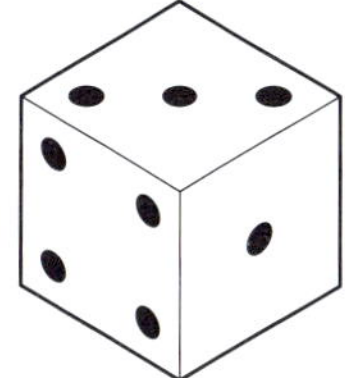 

b) There are multiple solutions. The opposite faces have been colour coded. Pairs totalling 7 must go on the same colour.
Here is one solution.

 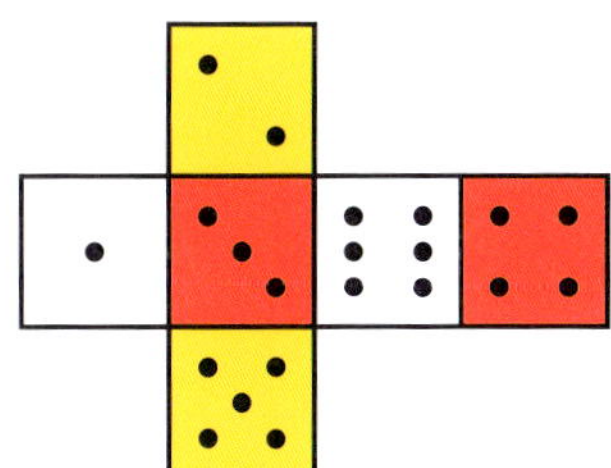

Think together

1 Which of these nets correctly forms a cube?

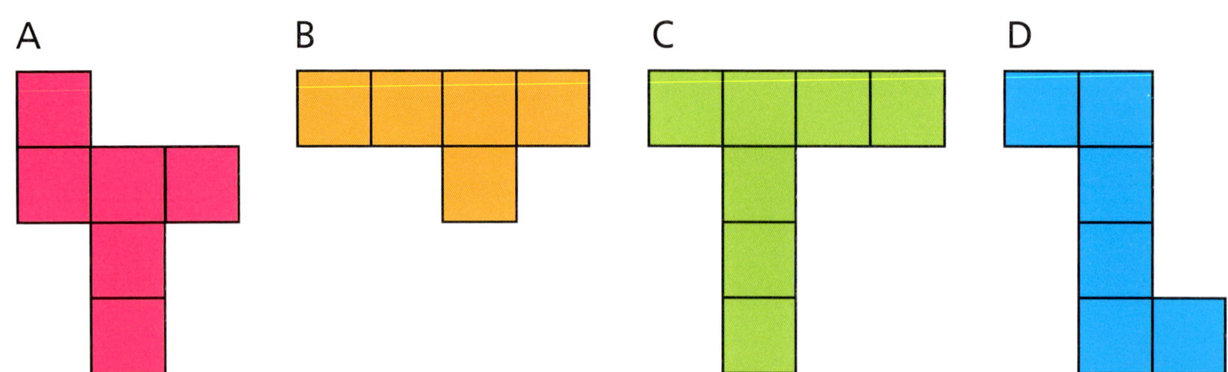

2 Which of the diagrams below could be views of the cube made from this net?

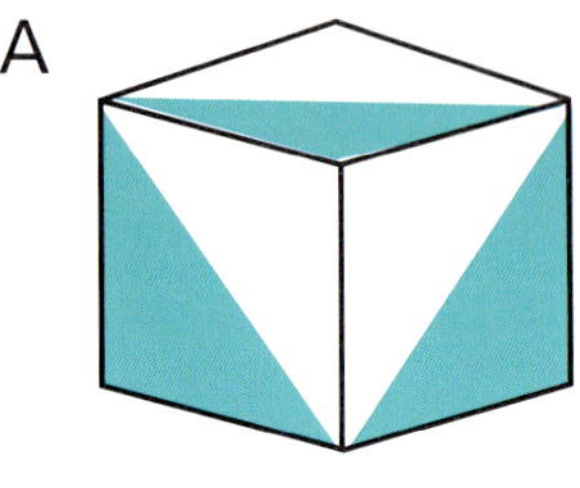

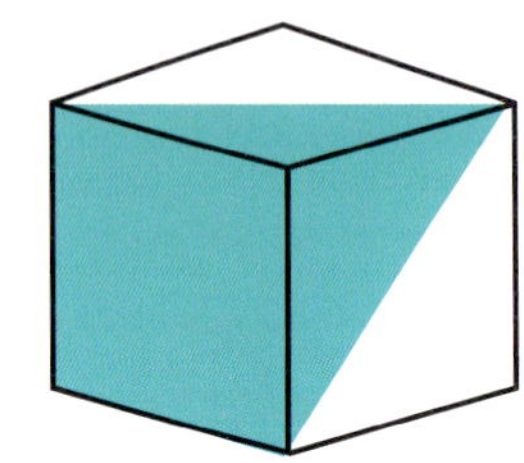

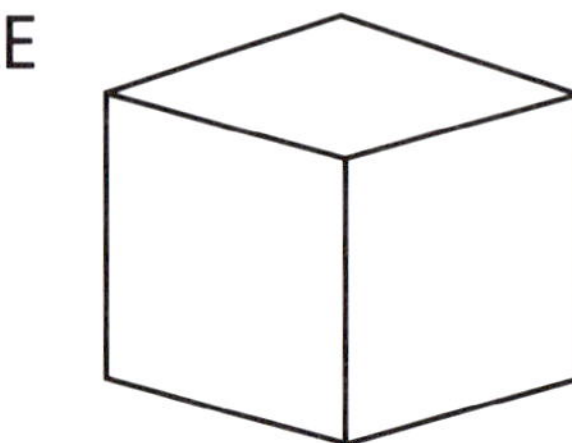

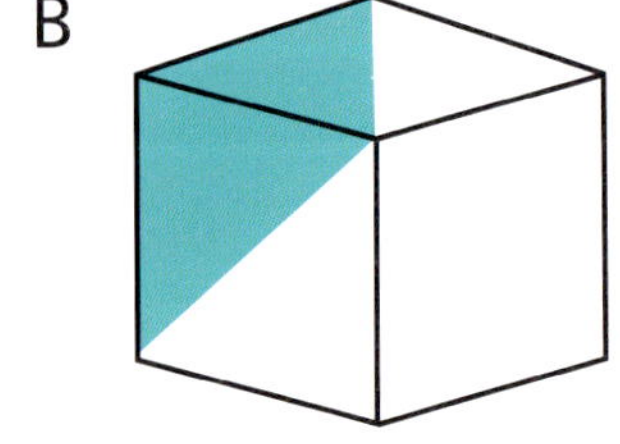

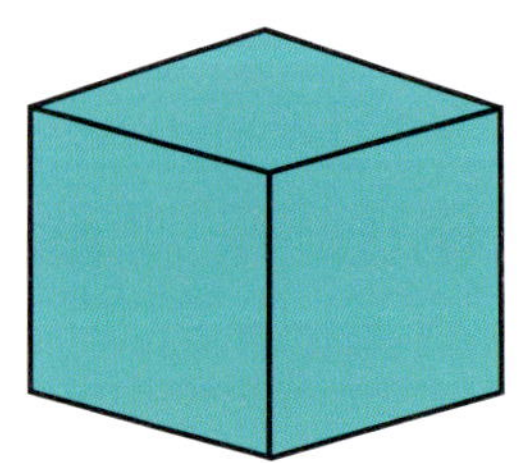

I will make a version of the net on paper and fold it to check.

3 Try to find all the different nets of a cube. How many do you think there are? Is Bella correct?

I think there are more than 10 different nets of a cube.

Bella

I found these two. I do not know if they count as different.

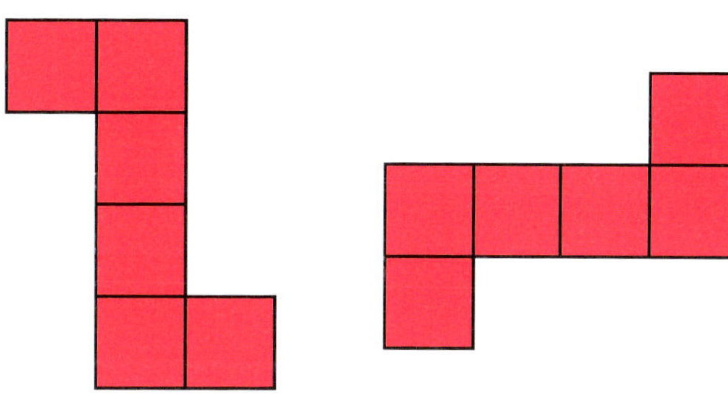

I will use construction materials to help.

→ Practice book 6C p39

End of unit check

1 Measure the angle. What is it?

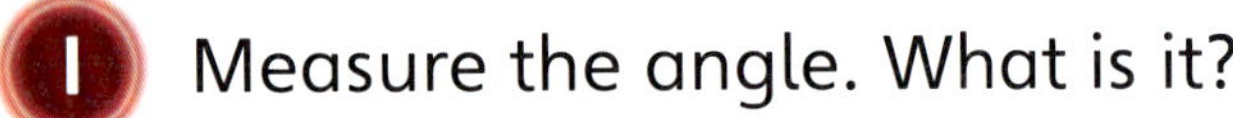

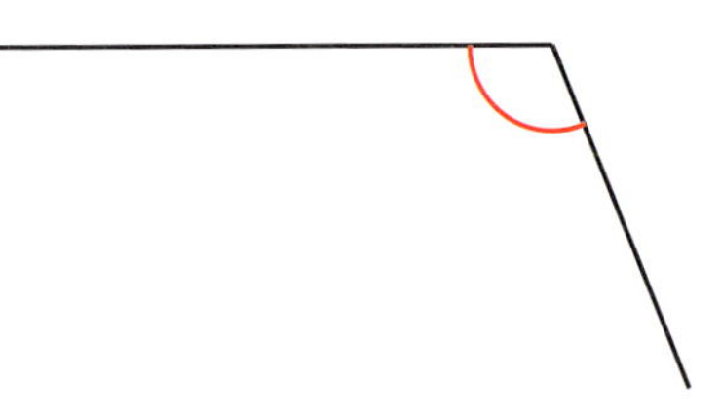

A 118°   B 68°   C 108°   D 112°

2 What is angle x?

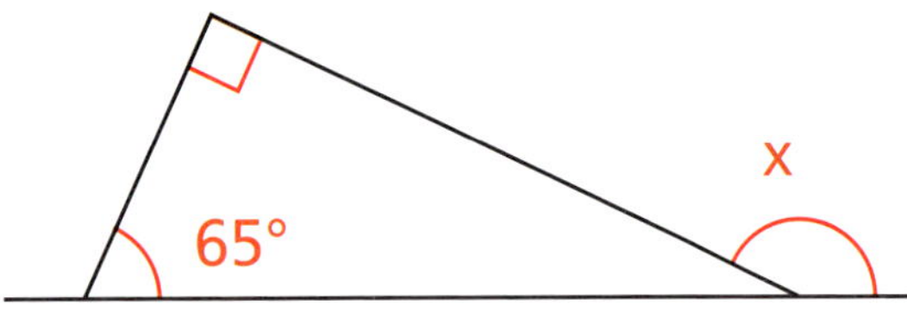

A 175°   B 15°   C 155°   D 165°

3 Which quadrilateral does not have an angle of 45°?

A

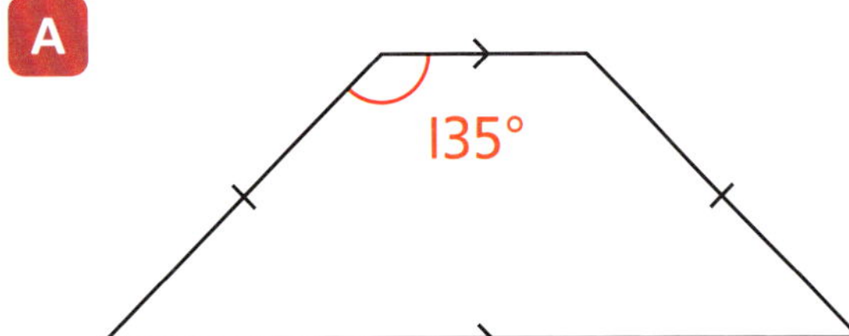

C

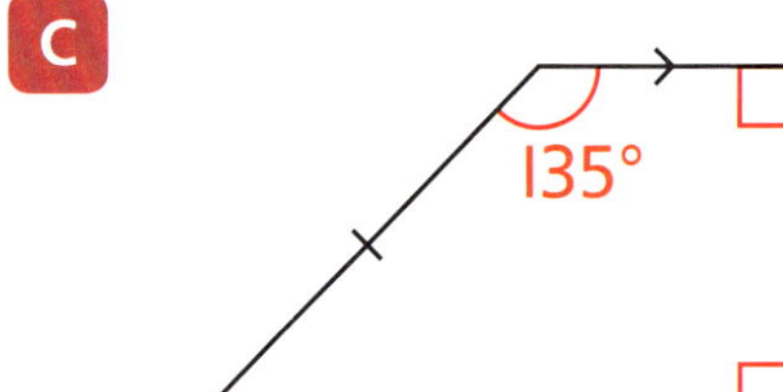

B

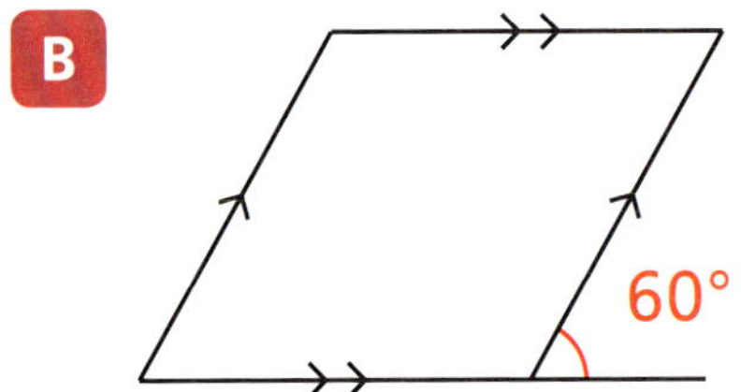

D

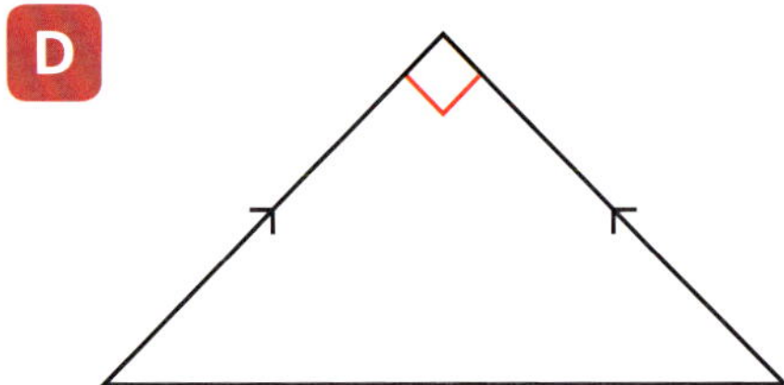

4 Which statement is always true?

A Regular shapes have 90° angles.

B Angles in a polygon sum to 540°.

C Quadrilaterals have 3 right angles.

D Angles in a polygon sum to a multiple of 180°.

5 In which diagram is angle a equal to 28°?

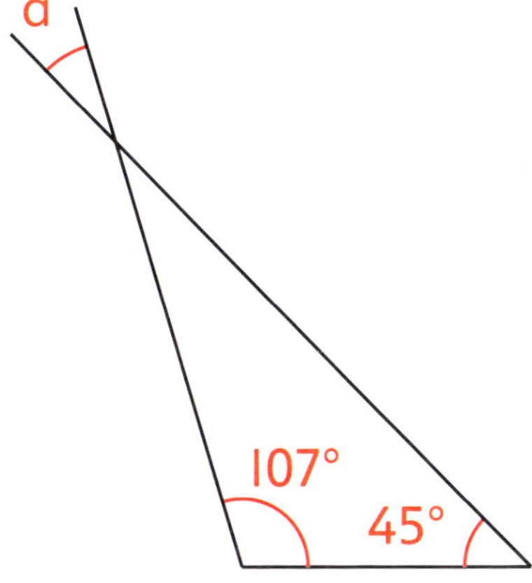

C

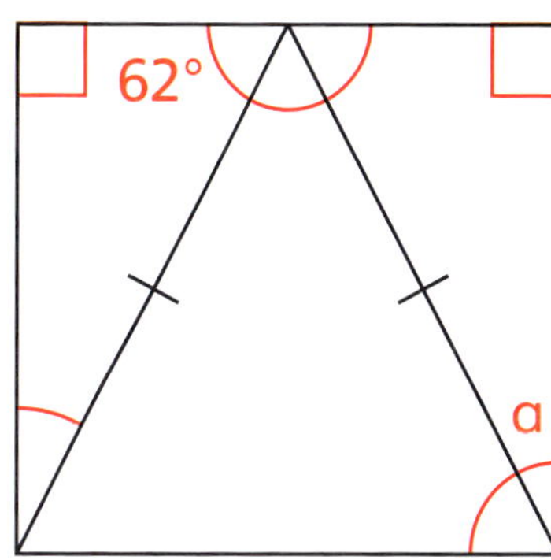

B

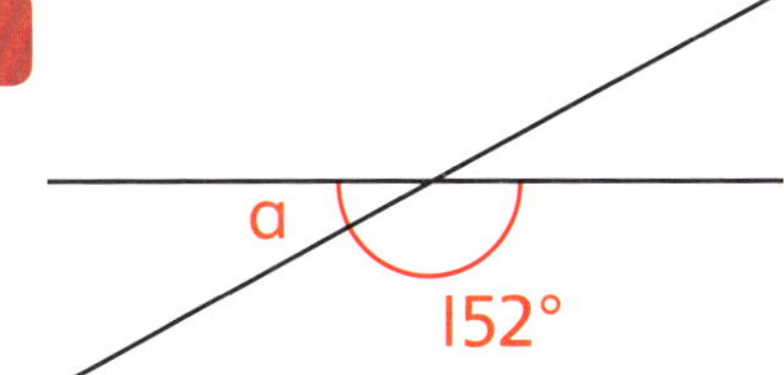

D All – A, B and C.

6 Draw a net of this cuboid.

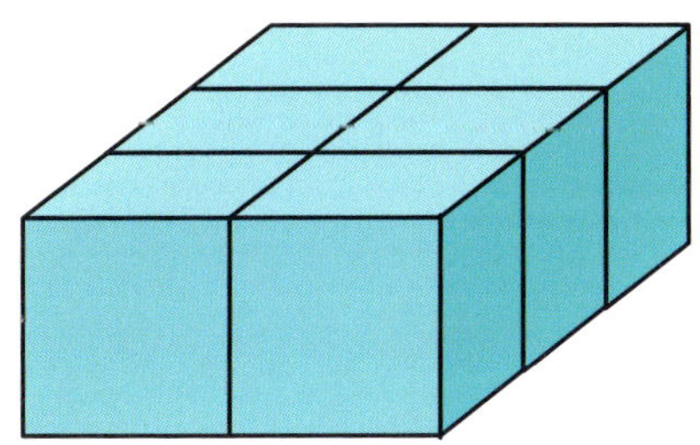

→ Practice book 6C p42

Unit 14
Problem solving

In this unit we will ...

- Solve problems about number, including fractions and ratio
- Use representations to help make sense of problems
- Use the four operations flexibly
- Reason about problems with a context and without a context
- Apply understanding of measurement and geometry to solve problems

In previous units, we used the four operations to solve calculations. Which operations do you need to find the value of the triangle?

$\triangle + \triangle - 120 = 300$

We will need some maths words. Which ones do you remember?

partition estimate round
compare equivalent percentage
ratio proportion convert
common denominator coordinates
translation reflection vertex
scaling isosceles triangle

We will also use bar models and number lines.

What values do the question marks represent in the number line and bar model?

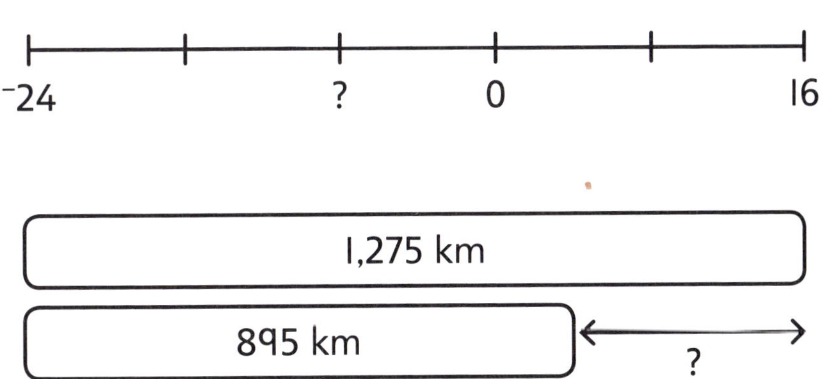

Problem solving – place value

Discover

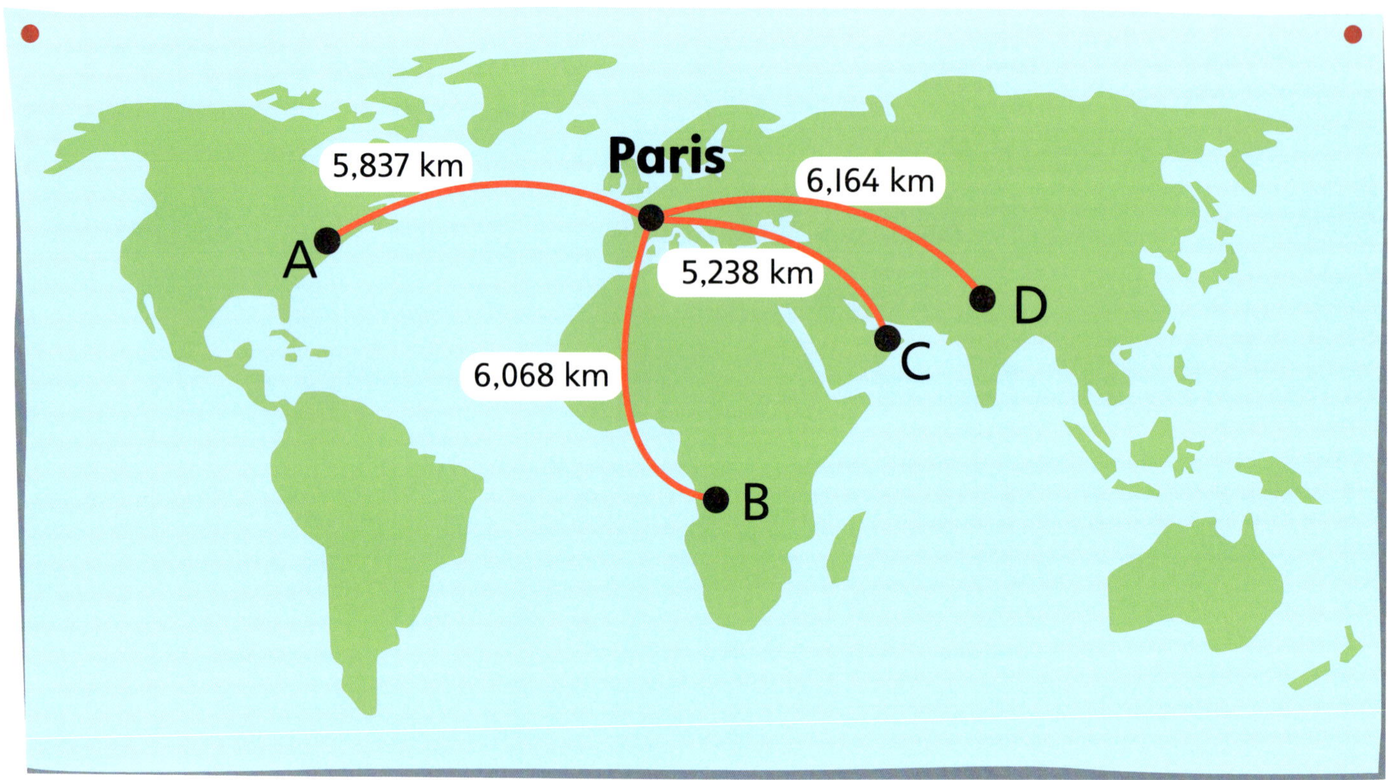

1 **a)** Place each distance shown on the map on this number line.

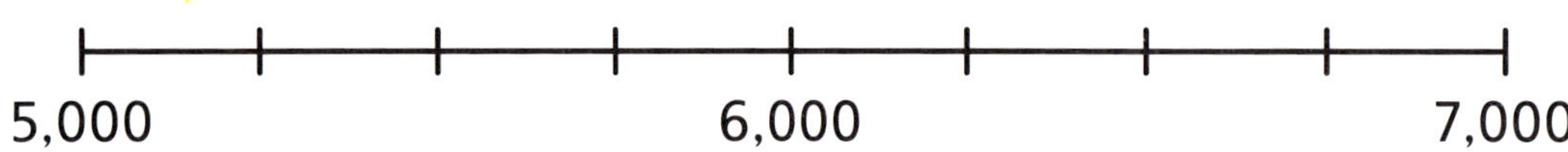

b) The distance from Paris to three of the cities rounds to the same multiple of 1,000 km. What is the multiple, and which are the cities?

Share

a)

I can work out the scale on the number line. There are four intervals for each 1,000. Each interval is 1,000 ÷ 4 = 250.

I can estimate the position of each number. 5,837 is closer to 5,750 than to 6,000.

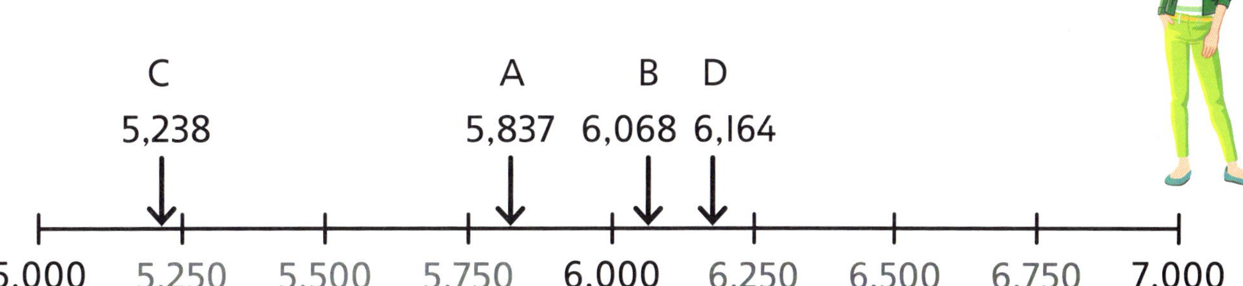

b)

I am going to round each number to the nearest 1,000. I need to check the hundreds digit.

I can round each number by looking at the number line.

City A: 5,837 rounds up to 6,000.

City B: 6,068 rounds down to 6,000.

City C: 5,238 rounds down to 5,000.

City D: 6,164 rounds down to 6,000.

The distance from Paris to cities A, B and D rounds to 6,000 km.

Think together

1 The approximate population of four cities is shown here.

Where will each number be positioned on this number line?

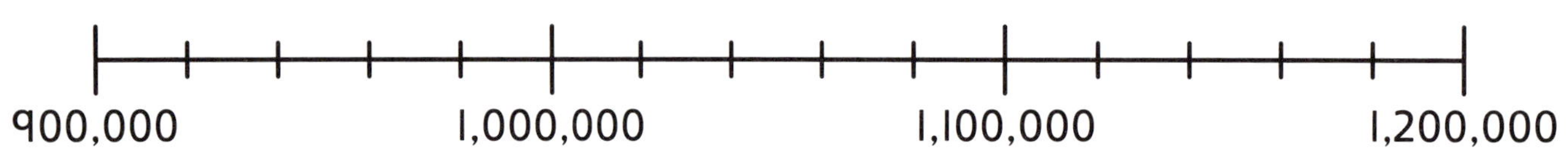

I wonder what intervals the number line is going up in.

Do you think that the next interval after 900,000 is 900,001?

2 The populations of the cities in question 1 are compared. Complete the statements to make them true.

a) 942,000 > ☐

b) 924,500 < ☐ < 1,025,000

You can use the number line from question 1 to help you.

3 Put each number in the correct place in the sorting circles.

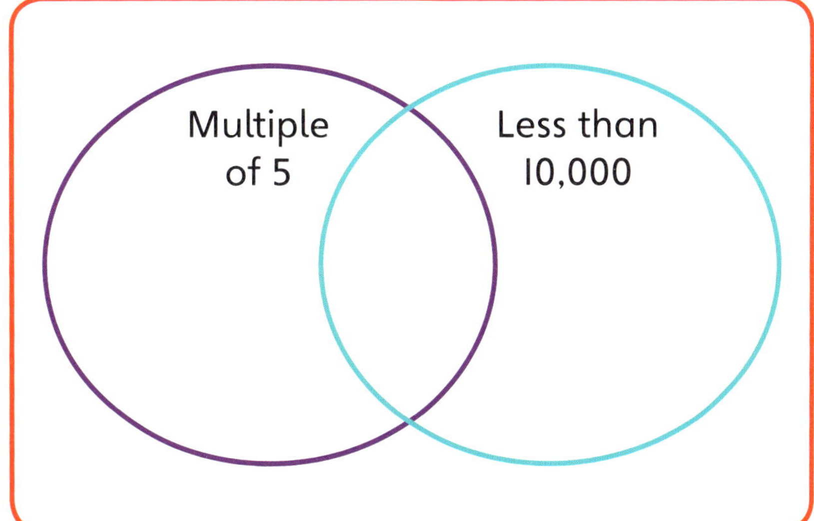

6,551 4,000
12,750 500
10,001 20,615

CHALLENGE

4 Luis makes three different 4-digit numbers using these cards.

He places each number in a different section on the number line.

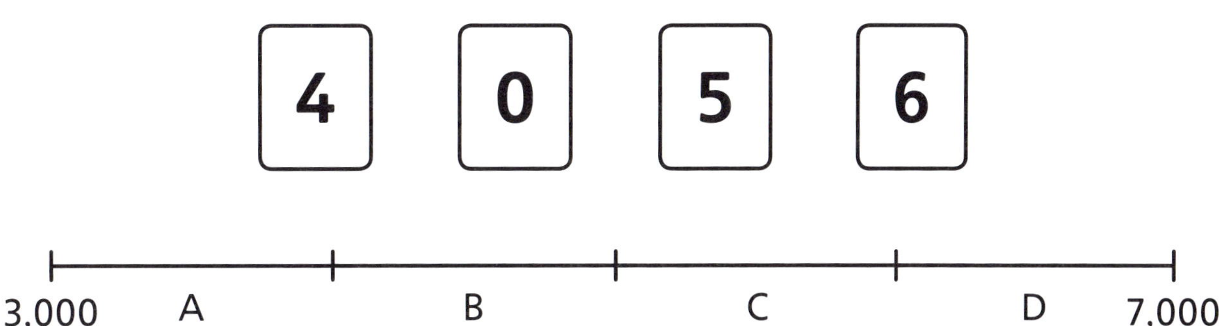

- He places an odd number in section B. It rounds up to the nearest 1,000.
- The number in section D is a multiple of 10 but not a multiple of 50.
- The last number has an even number of hundreds.

I wonder if I can find more than one solution to this problem.

Find three numbers that Luis could have made.

→ Practice book 6C p45

Problem solving – negative numbers

Discover

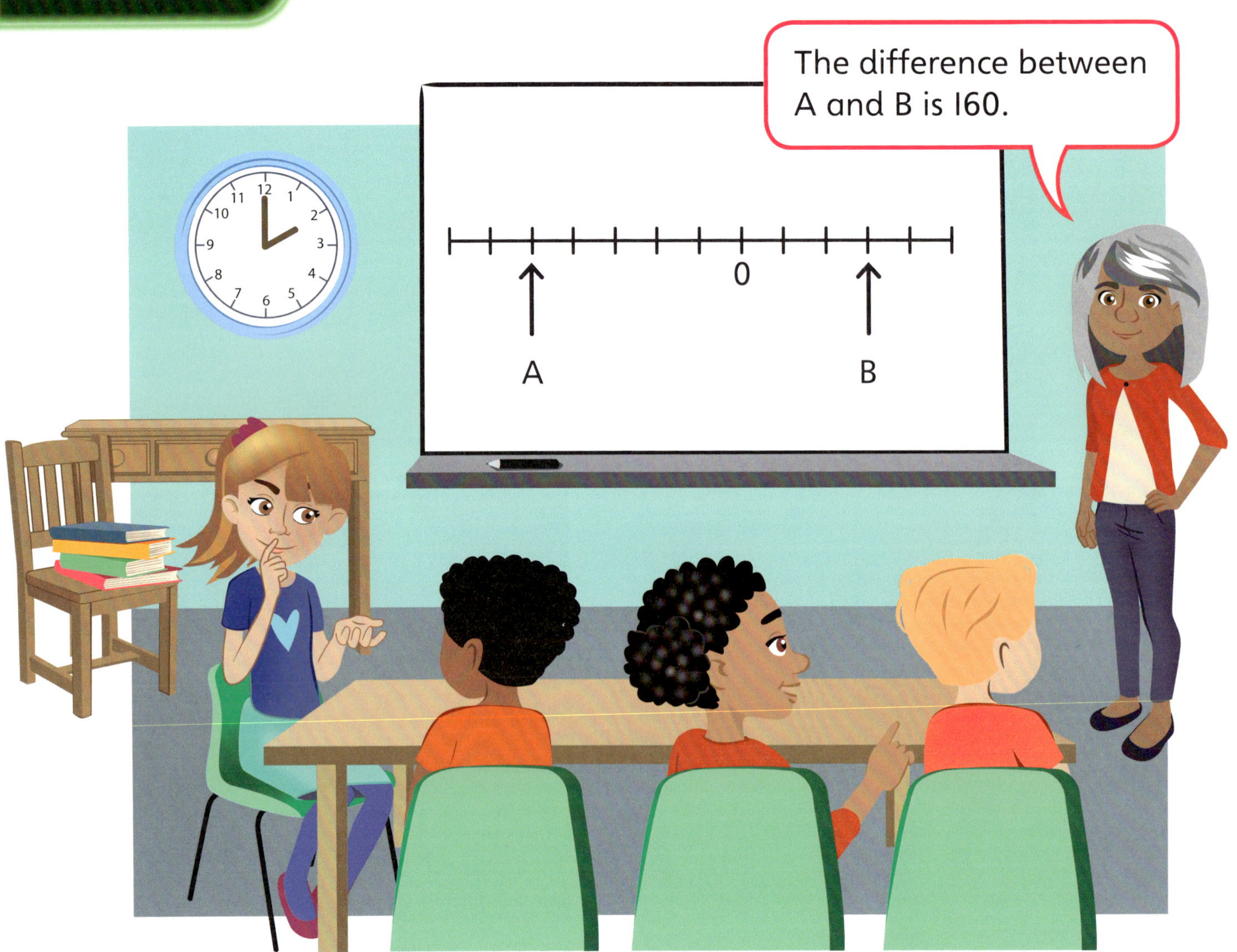

1 **a)** What are the values of A and B?

b) Find the value of the point half-way between A and B.

Share

a) The number line represents positive and negative numbers. A must be negative as it is less than 0, and B must be positive as it is greater than 0.

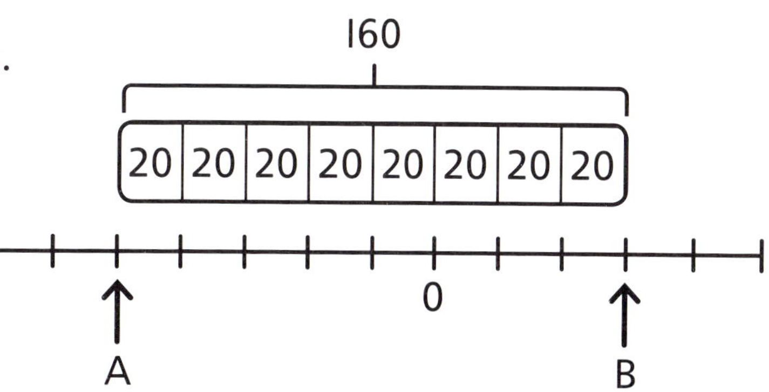

160 must be shared equally between the 8 intervals between A and B.

160 ÷ 8 = 20 so each interval is 20.

Point A is 5 intervals of 20 less than 0. The value of A is −100.

Point B is 3 intervals of 20 more than 0. The value of B is 60.

I tried a different method. I counted in different intervals from A to B until I found a difference of 160. I started with intervals of 10.

b) We need to find the half-way point between −100 and 60.

There are 8 intervals. So it must be 4 intervals of 20 more than −100 and 4 intervals of 20 less than 60.

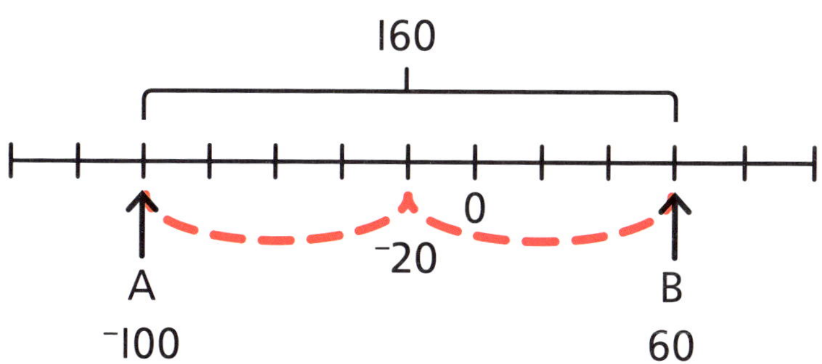

I can either halve the difference of 160 or halve the number of intervals.

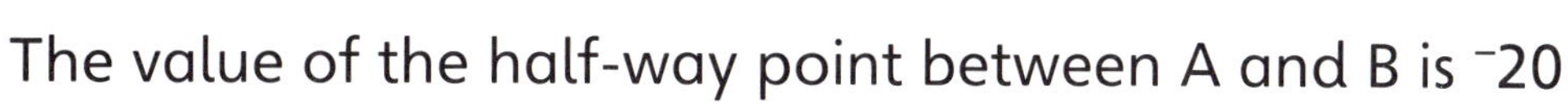

The value of the half-way point between A and B is −20.

Think together

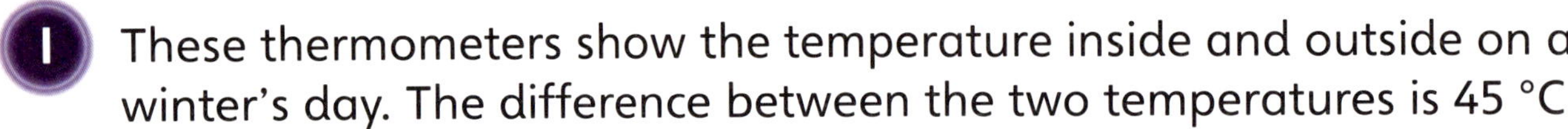

1 These thermometers show the temperature inside and outside on a winter's day. The difference between the two temperatures is 45 °C.

a) What is the inside temperature?

The inside temperature is ☐ °C.

b) What is the outside temperature?

The outside temperature is ☐ °C.

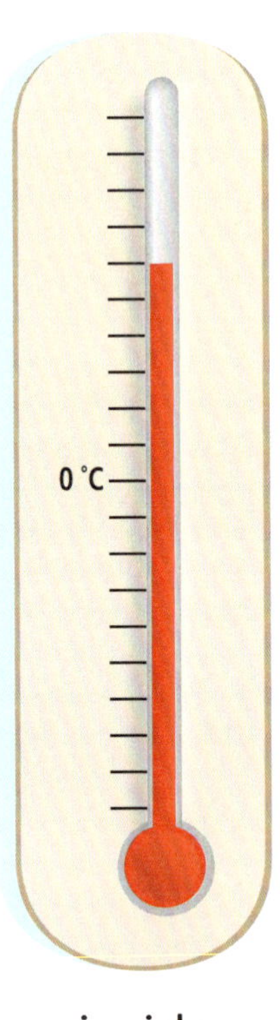

inside

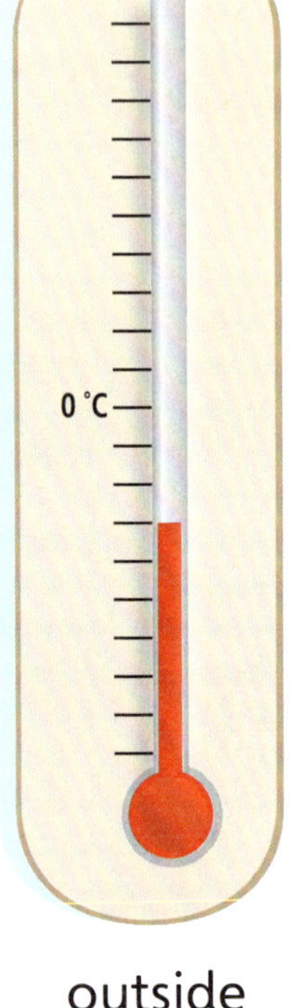

outside

2 This sequence decreases by the same amount each time. What are the missing numbers?

26, 14, ☐, ☐, ⁻22, ☐

3 The graph shows the temperature in °C from 3 am to 3 pm on a winter's day.

a) How many degrees warmer was it at 1 pm than at 5 am?

It was ☐ °C warmer.

b) At 7 pm the temperature was 8 degrees colder than at 3 pm. What was the temperature at 7 pm?

The temperature at 7 pm was ☐ °C.

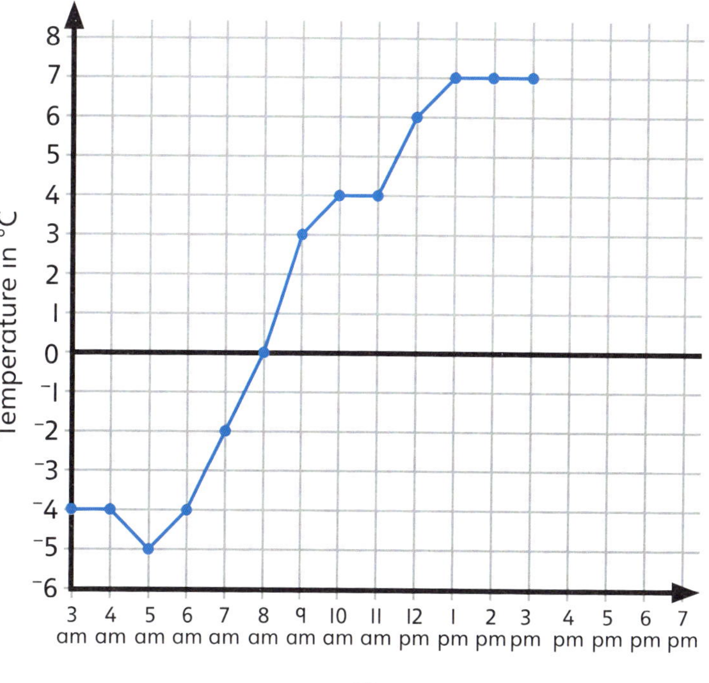

4 The numbers 18 and ⁻30 are shown on this number line.

Calculate the value of the half-way point.

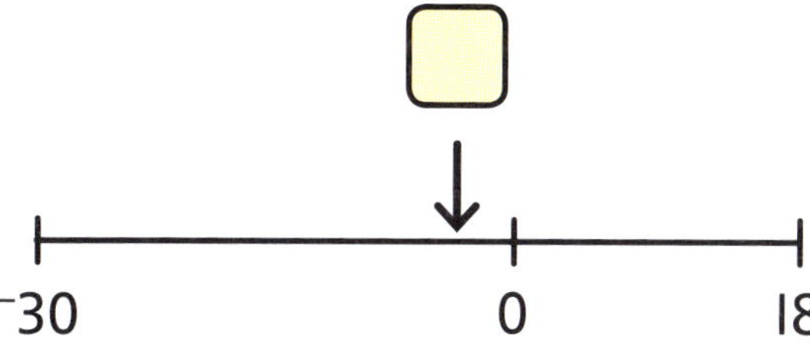

This number line looks different because I cannot see any intervals.

I do not think that matters. We can still work out the difference between the two numbers.

→ Practice book 6C p48

Problem solving – addition and subtraction

Discover

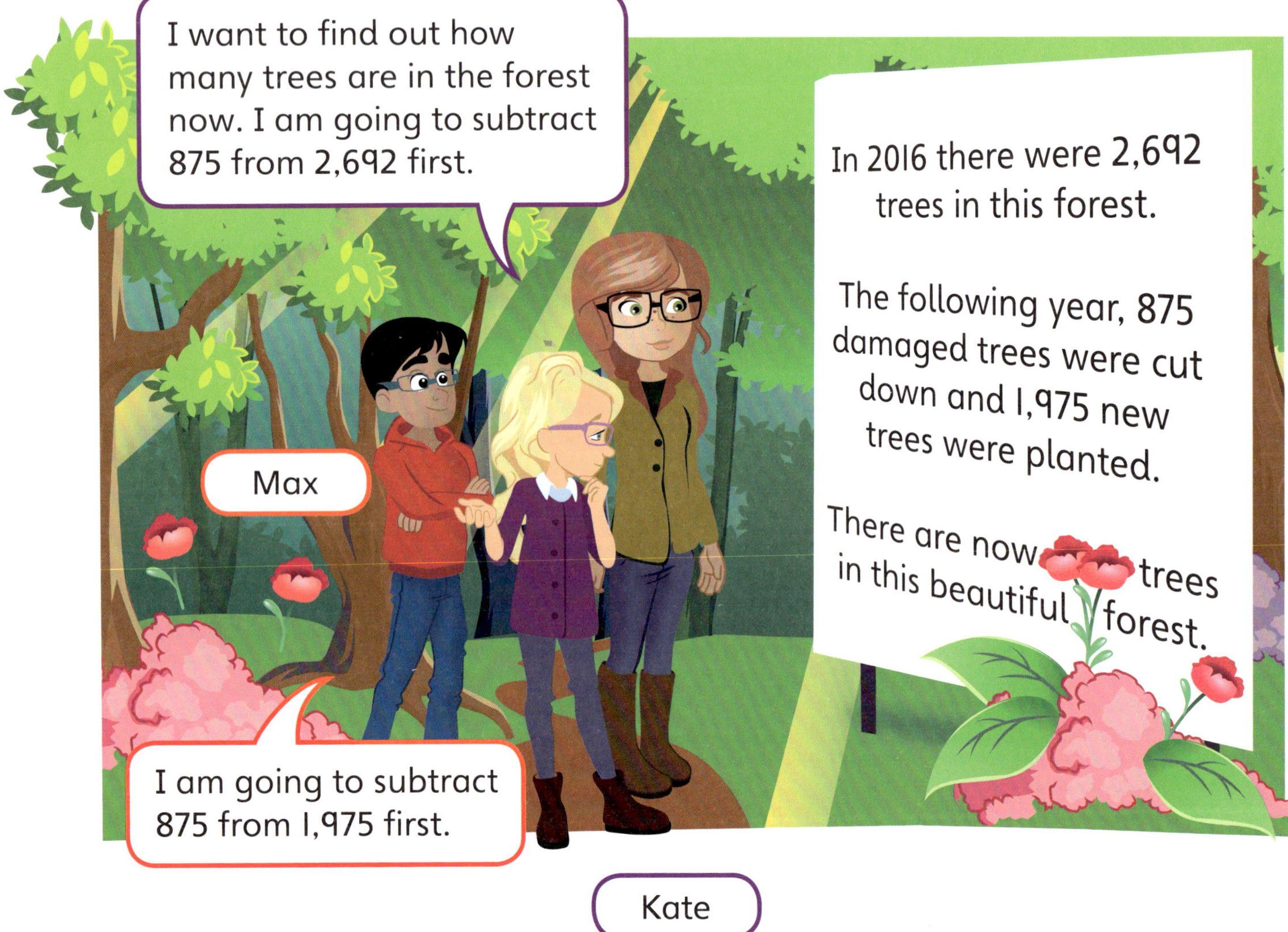

1 a) Use Kate's method to find the number of trees in the forest now.

b) Now use Max's method.

Why do you think Max is going to use this method?

Share

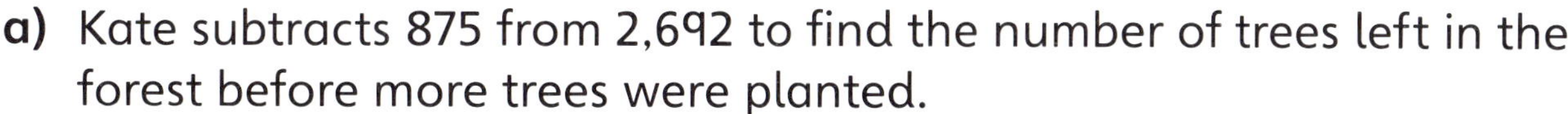

a) Kate subtracts 875 from 2,692 to find the number of trees left in the forest before more trees were planted.

	Th	H	T	O
	$^{1}\not{2}$	$^{1}6$	$^{8}\not{9}$	$^{1}2$
−		8	7	5
	1	8	1	7

Add 1,975 to 1,817 to find the number of trees now.

	Th	H	T	O
	1	8	1	7
+	1	9	7	5
	3	7	9	2
	1		1	

There are 3,792 trees in the forest now.

b) Max subtracts 875 from 1,975 to find the difference between the number of extra trees planted and the number cut down.

1,975 – 875 = 1,100

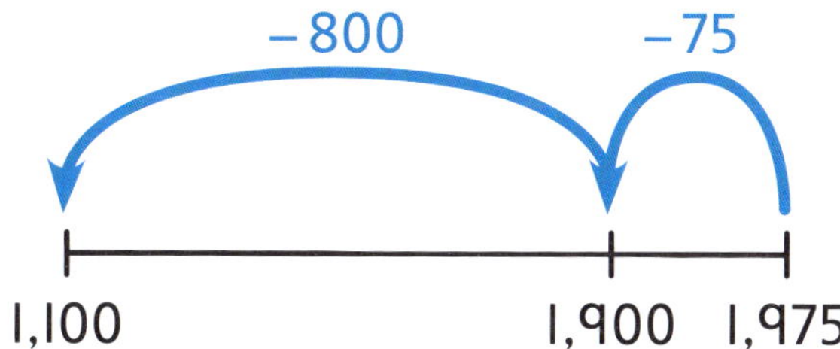

Add the difference of 1,100 to 2,692.

2,692 + 1,100 = 3,792

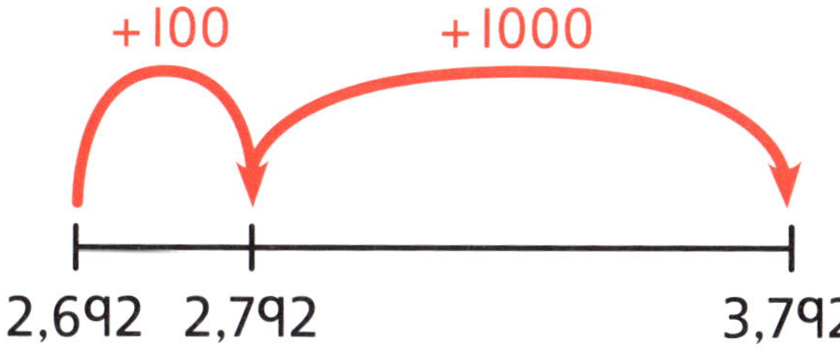

There are 3,792 trees in the forest now.

Think together

1 The bar chart shows the amount of money raised by a fun run and a singing competition over three years.

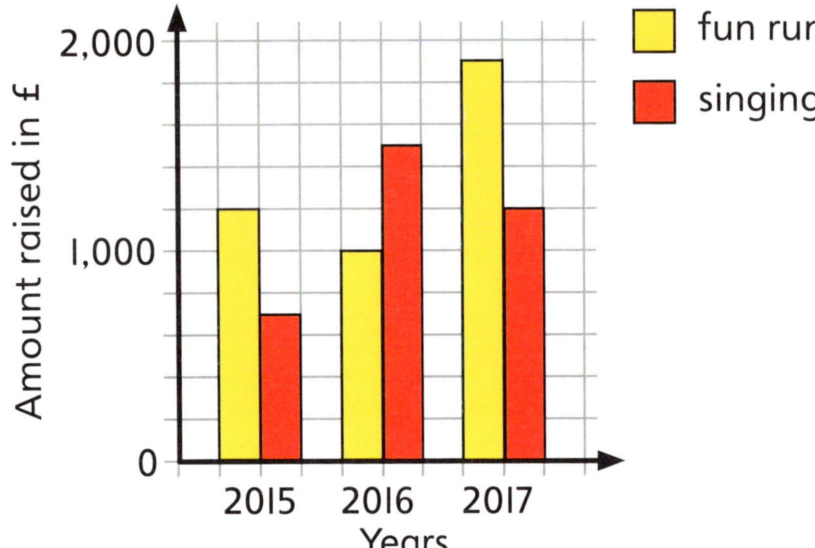

a) How much more money was raised in total in 2017 than in 2015?

£ ☐ more was raised in 2017 than in 2015.

b) What is the difference between the total raised over the three years from fun runs and the total raised from singing competitions?

The difference is £ ☐.

2 Find the value of the triangle and the square.

10,000 + △ – 8,250 = 3,750

999 – ☐ + 500 = 1,200

The value of the triangle is ☐.

The value of the square is ☐.

I wonder if I can use addition or subtraction first to make each calculation easier.

3 Find the missing digits to complete these calculations.

a)

	TTh	Th	H	T	O
		5	3	6	
+			5		9
	1	1		0	3

b)

	T	O	·	Tth	Hth
	6		·	8	
−	2	3	·		6
		6	·	2	9

4 Aki buys a rubber and a pen from the school shop. He pays £1·10.

Jamie buys 1 rubber and 2 pens from the school shop. She pays £1·75.

Calculate the cost of a rubber.

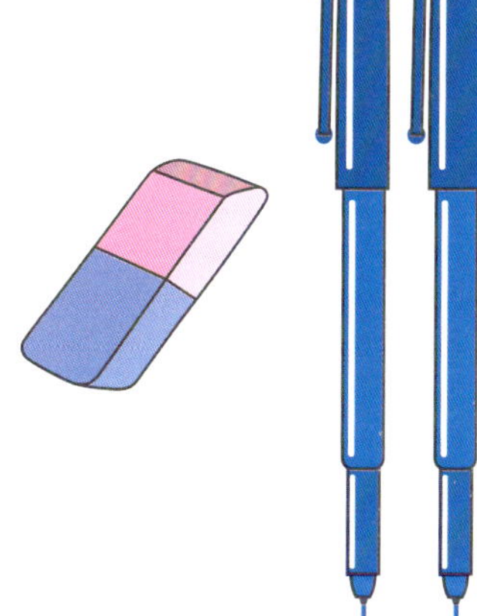

I am going to draw a bar model to help me represent this problem.

Remember to think about the different strategies you can use. Will you add or subtract first?

→ Practice book 6C p51

Problem solving – four operations 1

Discover

1 **a)** A computer game costs £12·50 more than a puzzle book.

Zac buys 1 computer game and 2 puzzle books for £35.

How much does each item cost?

b) A box of pencils is half the price of a computer game.

How many boxes of pencils can Isla buy for £35?

Share

a) A computer game is equal to the cost of a puzzle book + £12·50.

2 puzzle books and 1 computer game costs £35 in total.

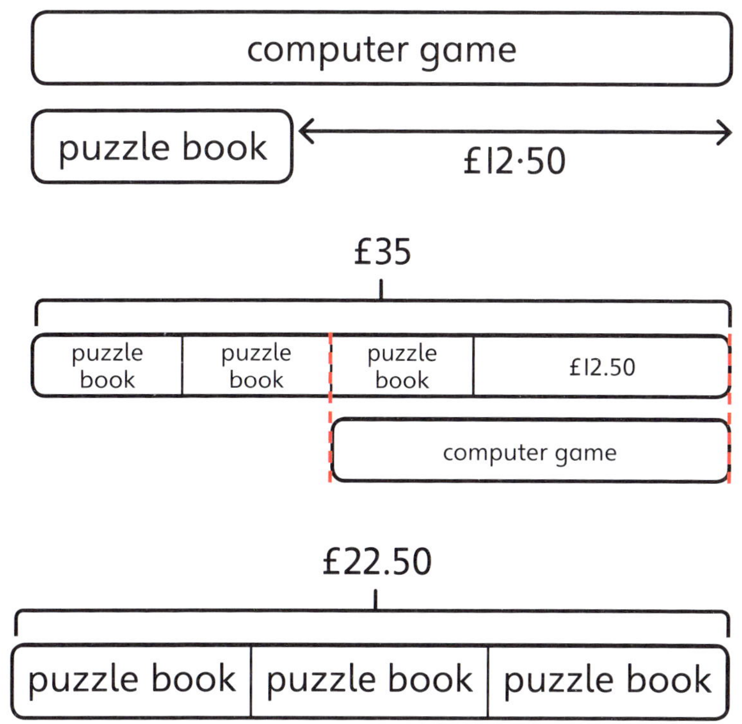

Subtract £12.50 first:

£35 – £12·50 = £22·50

Now divide by 3 to work out the cost of 1 puzzle book.

A puzzle book costs £7·50.
A computer game costs £7·50 + £12·50 = £20.

b) A box of pencils is half the price of a computer game.

Pencils are half of £20 = £10.

35 ÷ 10 = 3·5 but Isla cannot buy half a box.

£35

£10	£10	£10	£5

3 × 10 = 30, so Isla can buy 3 boxes of pencils for £35.
She will have £5 left over.

I can divide 35 by 10 or simply think about the multiple of 10 that is closest to, but less than, 35.

Think together

1 A whistle costs 85p less than a toy car.

Isla buys 3 whistles and 1 toy car for £5·25.

How much does each item cost?

A whistle costs £[ ].

A toy car costs £[ ].

2 Sand is sold in small bags and large bags.

There are 75 small bags and 60 large bags.

The total mass of the small bags is 300 kg. The total mass of the large bags is twice as much.

How much heavier is a large bag than a small bag?

A large bag is [ ] kg heavier than a small bag.

3 A drama group pays £538 to hire a coach to take 40 children to the theatre. The cost of the coach is shared equally between the children, rounded to the nearest £1.

Theatre tickets cost £14·75 each.

a) How much does each child pay in total for the trip?

b) Do the children pay enough money to pay for the coach?

Explain your thinking.

4 The perimeter of the rectangle is a third of the perimeter of the square.

What is the length of the longer side of the rectangle, *x*?

120 cm

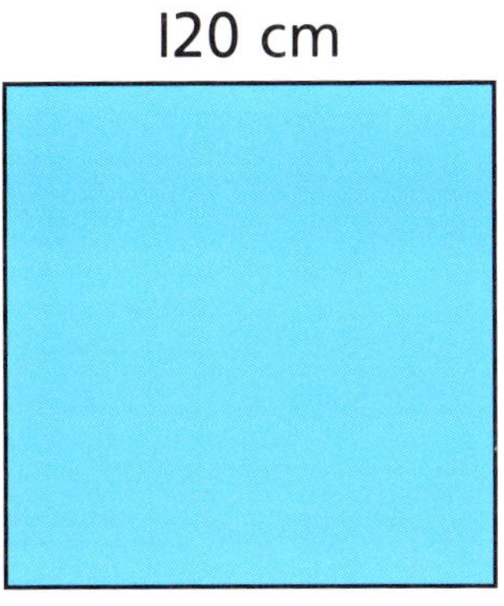

Not drawn to scale

x cm

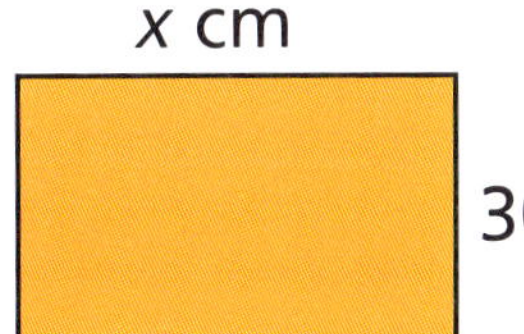

30 cm

I am going to calculate the perimeter of the square first and then find $\frac{1}{3}$.

I wonder if we can do it another way by finding $\frac{1}{3}$ of the length of the square first.

→ Practice book 6C p54

Problem solving – four operations 2

Discover

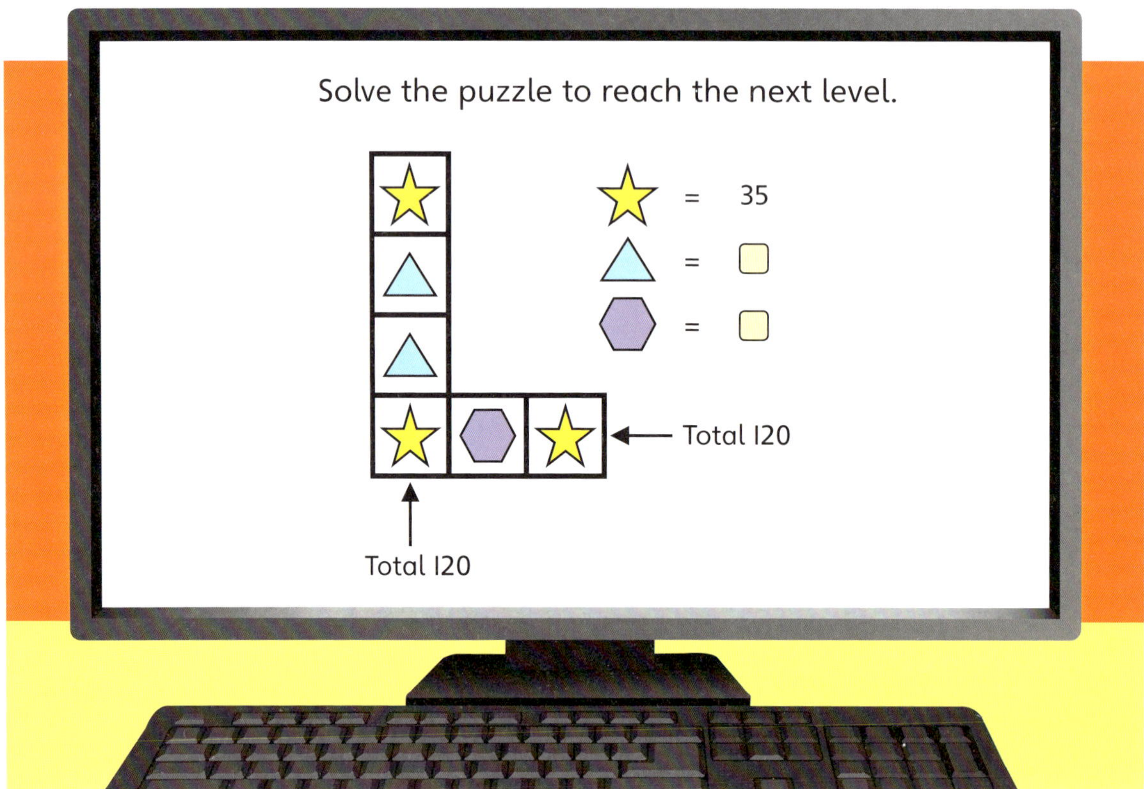

1 **a)** What are the values of the shapes?

b) On the next level of the game, the puzzle looks the same but both the totals are doubled. What are the values of the shapes?

Lexi says, 'That's easy. The value of each shape must be doubled too!'

Do you agree? Explain your answer.

Share

a)

I am going to start by writing down the value of the stars. Then I am going to try other numbers to total 120 each time.

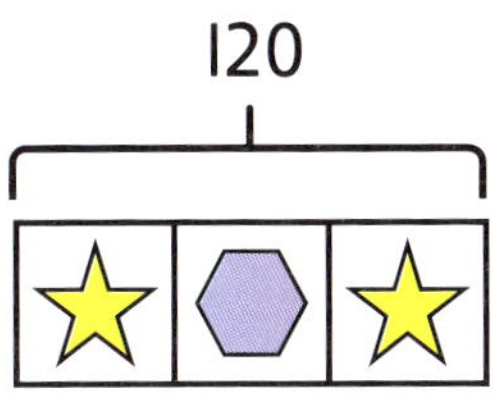

In the row, 2 stars and 1 hexagon total 120.

★ = 35

120 – (35 × 2)

120 – 70 = 50 so ⬡ = 50

It is much easier to use calculations to help. I am going to look at the row first.

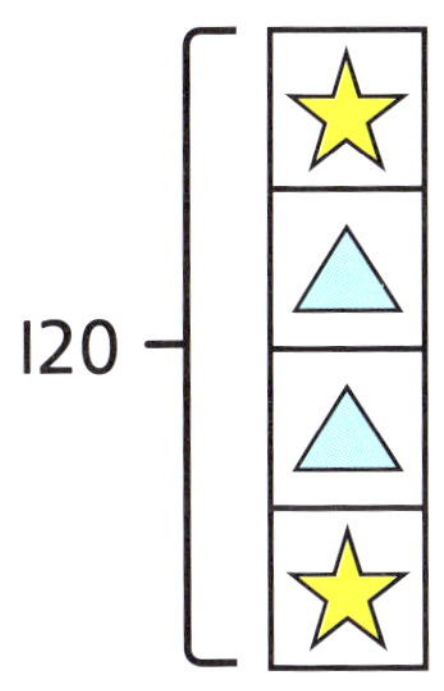

In the column, 2 stars and 2 triangles total 120.

2△ = 120 – 70 = 50

△ is half of 50 so △ = 25

b) Double the value of each shape.

△ = 50 ★ = 70 ⬡ = 100

Work out the row and column totals with these values.

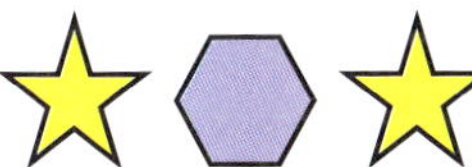

row: 70 + 100 + 70 = 240

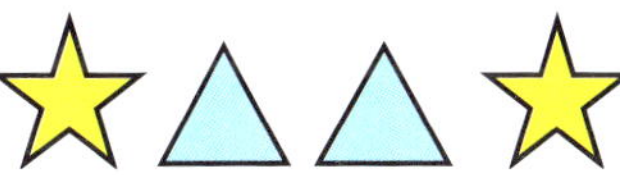

column: 70 + 50 + 50 + 70 = 240

Lexi is correct because doubling the totals is the same as adding the values in the row or column twice.

Think together

1 The shapes are arranged in a pattern.

The base of each triangle is 90 mm.

What is the width of each hexagon?

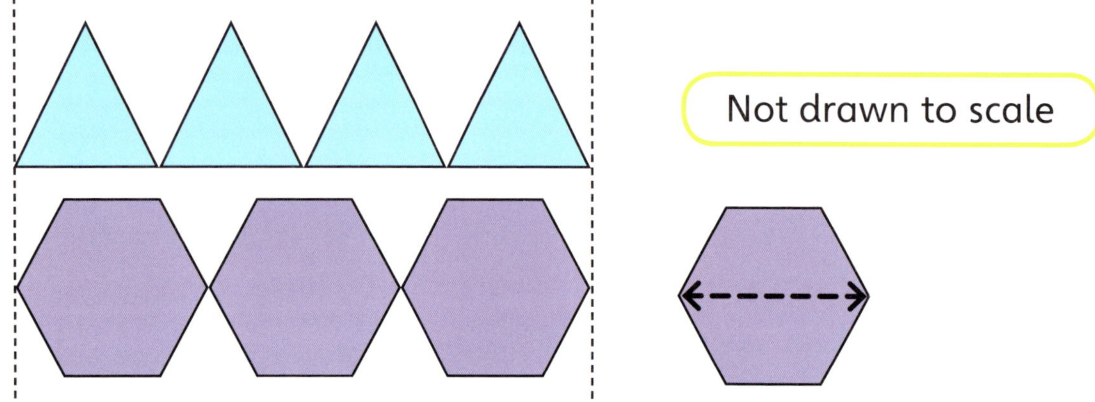

2 The same shapes are arranged in another pattern. What is the height of the dark triangle in the middle of the pattern?

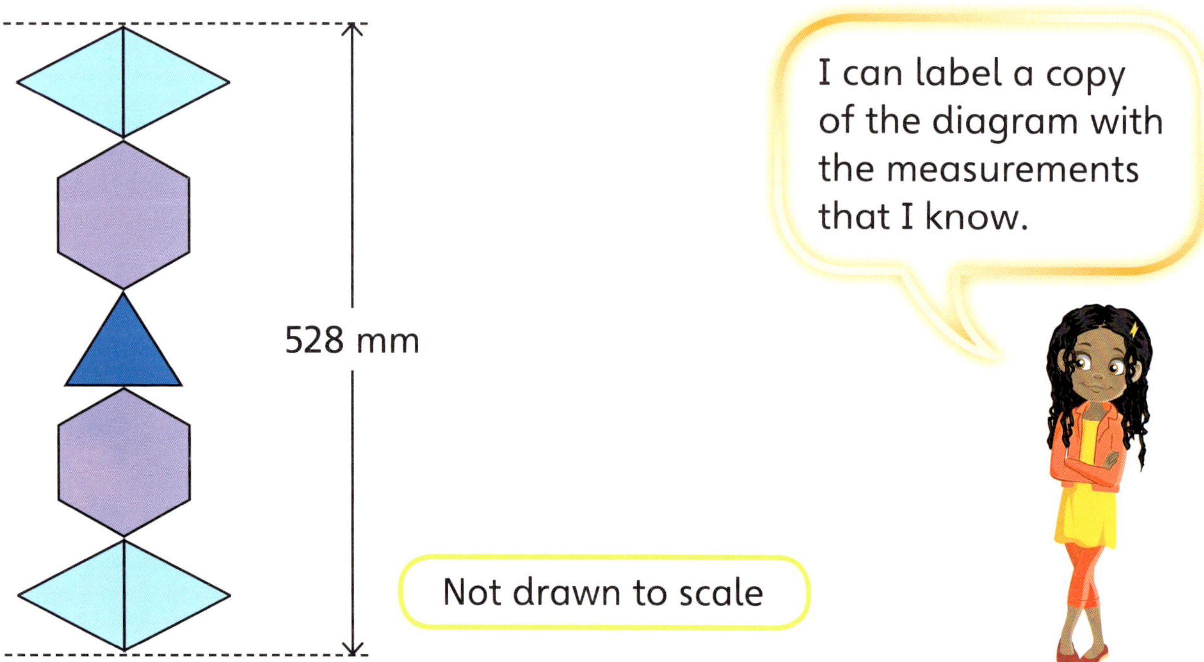

3 Lee does a multiplication calculation.
The ones digit of his answer is 4.

Which of these calculations could it be?

A 583 × 8

B 450 × 4

C 1,235 × 4

D 24,264 × 6

E 3,469 × 6

I wonder if I can solve this without working out the calculations.

4 The diagram shows boxes and tins on a balance scale.

The mass of one box is 448 g.

What is the mass of one tin?

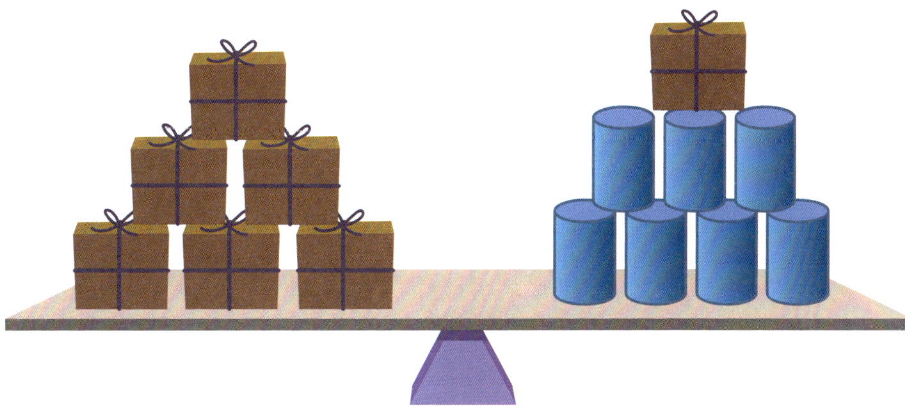

I think that a tin will be lighter because there are more tins than boxes.

I think I will need to use multiplication and division for this problem.

→ Practice book 6C p57

Problem solving – fractions

Discover

1 **a)** Who won the race?

Order the fractions from largest to smallest to prove your answer.

b) Each bucket can hold 4,800 ml of water.

How many millilitres of water did Olivia and Bella collect in total?

Share

I used my reasoning skills to compare the fractions.

a) Compare fractions with the same denominator:

$\frac{5}{8} > \frac{3}{8}$

$\frac{5}{6}$ and $\frac{5}{8}$ share the same numerator:

$\frac{5}{6} > \frac{5}{8}$

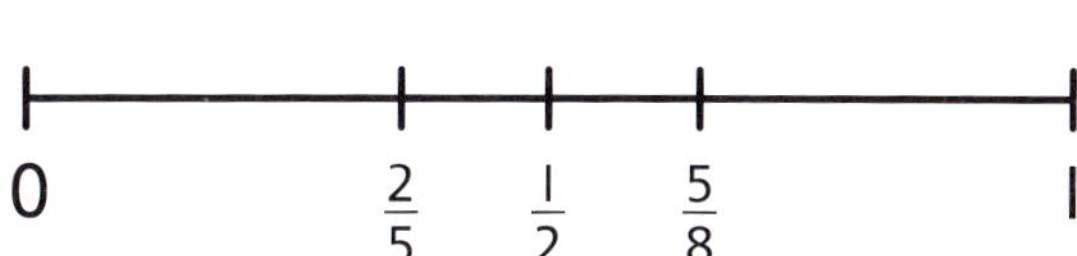

Compare $\frac{2}{5}$ and $\frac{5}{8}$ on a number line.

0 — $\frac{2}{5}$ — $\frac{1}{2}$ — $\frac{5}{8}$ — 1

You can say $\frac{2}{5}$ is less than $\frac{1}{2}$ as the numerator is less than half the denominator.

$\frac{5}{8}$ is greater than $\frac{1}{2}$ as the numerator is greater than half the denominator.

$\frac{5}{8} > \frac{2}{5}$

Find a common denominator to compare $\frac{2}{5}$ and $\frac{3}{8}$: $\frac{16}{40} > \frac{15}{40}$

$\frac{2}{5} > \frac{3}{8}$

$\frac{2}{5} = \frac{16}{40}$ (× 8, × 8)

$\frac{3}{8} = \frac{15}{40}$ (× 5, × 5)

Bella won the race because $\frac{5}{6} > \frac{5}{8} > \frac{2}{5} > \frac{3}{8}$.

I found a common denominator to compare all the fractions.

I will find the amount of water in each bucket first.

b) Bella collected $\frac{5}{6}$ of 4,800 ml.

4,800

800	800	800	800	800	800

$4{,}800 \div 6 = 800$

$800 \times 5 = 4{,}000$ ml

Olivia collected $\frac{3}{8}$ of 4,800 ml.

$4{,}800 \div 8 = 600$; $600 \times 3 = 1{,}800$ ml

$4{,}000$ ml $+ 1{,}800$ ml $= 5{,}800$ ml

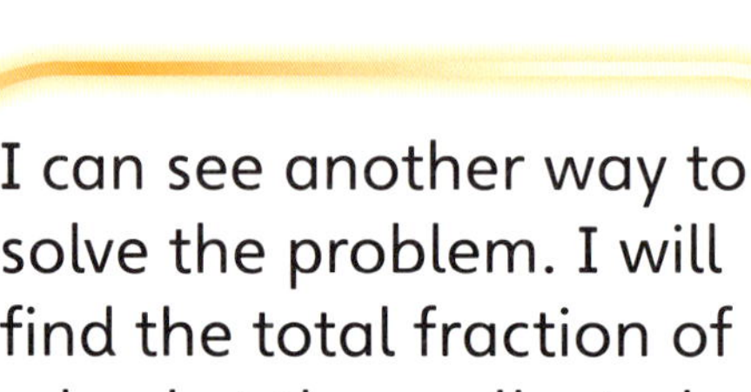

$\frac{5}{6} + \frac{3}{8} = \frac{20}{24} + \frac{9}{24} = \frac{29}{24} = 1\frac{5}{24}$

1 bucket = 4,800 ml

$\frac{5}{24}$ of 4,800 ml = 1,000 ml

$4{,}800$ ml $+ 1{,}000$ ml $= 5{,}800$ ml

Olivia and Bella collected 5,800 ml of water in total.

Think together

1 Bella collected more water than Mo, in her bucket.

What fraction of a bucket more did Bella collect?

$\frac{5}{6}$ Bella

$\frac{2}{5}$ Mo

2 In the next race, Mo collects $\frac{3}{4}$ of a bucket.

Danny collects half as much as Mo.

What fraction of a bucket does Danny collect?

3 Which shape has the greatest fraction shaded?

A

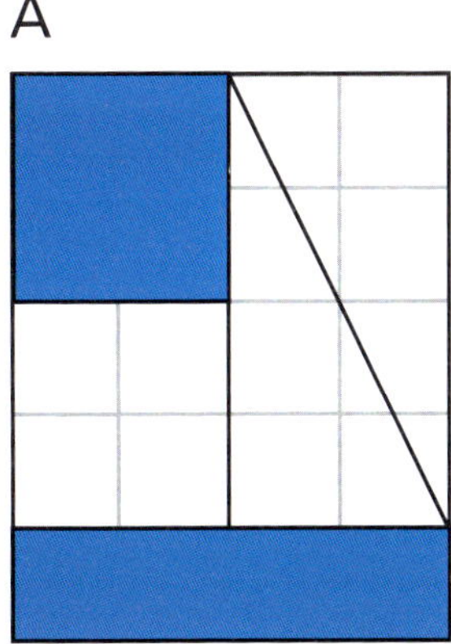

B

C

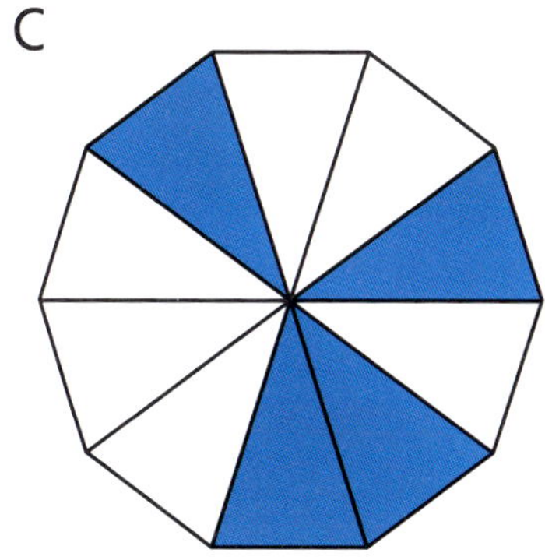

4 Olivia has some money to make lemonade for her friends.

She spends £2·20 on sugar and £2·80 on lemons.

She has $\frac{3}{5}$ of the money left.

How much money did she have to start with?

Think about how this problem can be represented using a bar model.

→ Practice book 6C p60

Problem solving – decimals

Discover

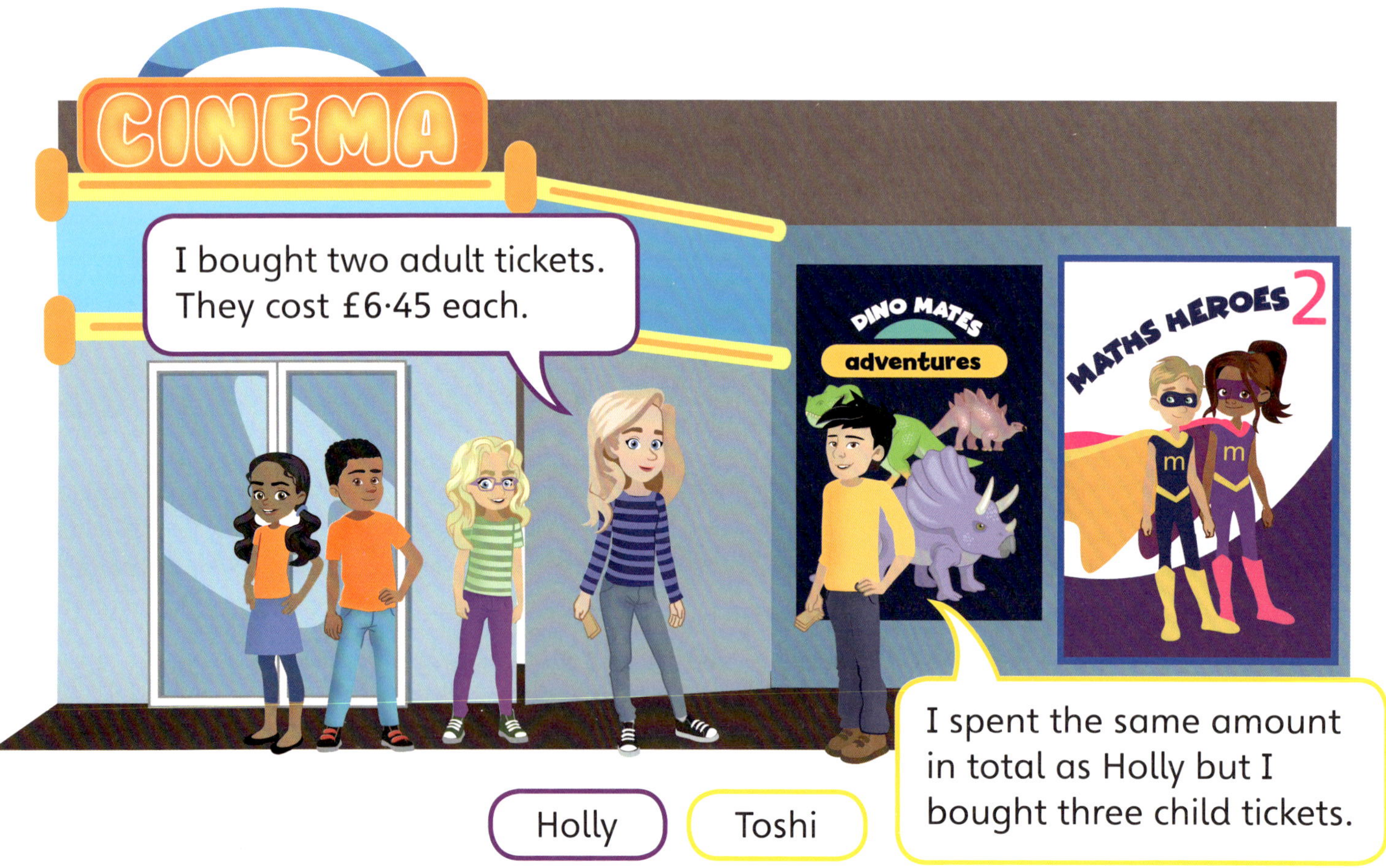

1 **a)** What is the price of one child ticket?

b) There are 48 seats in the front row of the cinema.

How much more money will the cinema take when the front row is filled with adults than when it is filled with children?

Share

a) Two adult tickets cost the same as three child tickets.

First calculate the cost of two adult tickets: £6·45 × 2 = £12·90

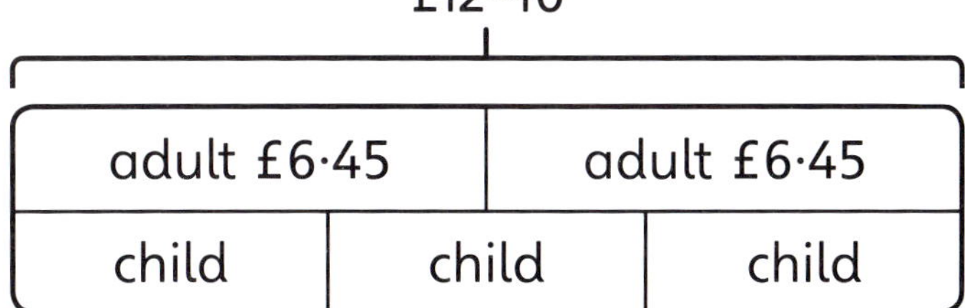

	0	4	·	3	0
3	1	^{1}2	·	9	0

Then find the cost of a child ticket: £12·90 ÷ 3 = £4·30

The price of one child ticket is £4·30.

b) Change the pounds and pence to pence before multiplying by 48.

adults

		6	4	5	
×			4	8	
	5	1 $_3$	6 $_4$	0	
2	5 $_1$	8 $_2$	0	0	
3	0	9	6	0	

children

		4	3	0
×			4	8
	3	4 $_2$	4	0
1	7	2 $_2$	0	0
2	0	6	4	0

When we convert back to pounds and pence, the two amounts are £309·60 and £206·40.

	H	T	O	·	Tth	Hth
	3	0	9	·	6	0
–	2	0	6	·	4	0
	1	0	3	·	2	0

I think I can solve this by finding the difference between the price of an adult ticket and a child ticket, and then multiplying it by 48.

The cinema takes £103·20 more when the front row is filled with adults.

Think together

1. The cinema sells cartons of juice.

   A box of 8 cartons has a total mass of 6·65 kg.

   The empty box has a mass of 0·41 kg.

   What is the mass of each carton?

I think there is more than one step to each of these problems. I will use bar models to help me.

2. Here are the dimensions of the seats and the aisle in the front row.

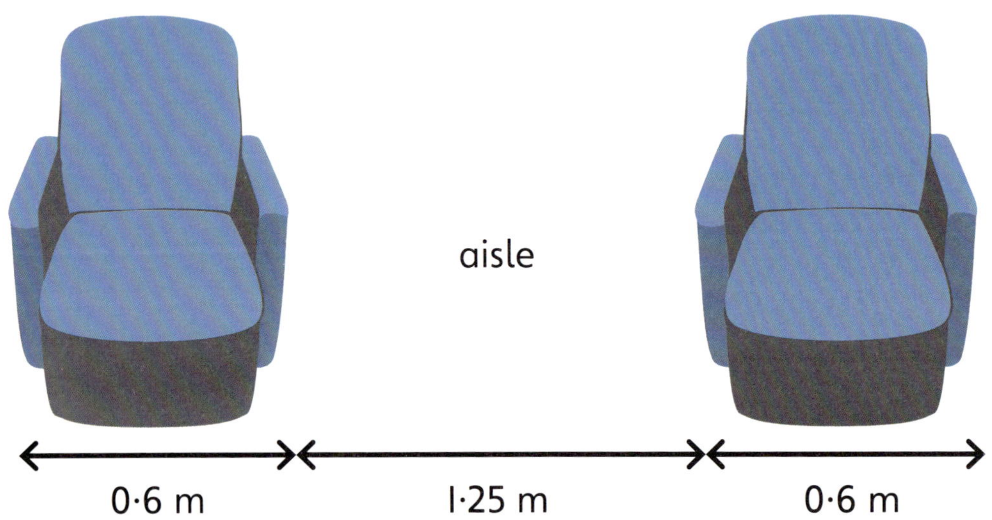

   The front row has 48 seats and 1 aisle.

   How long is the row?

3 Which of these numbers is closest to 0·4?

0·039 0·5 0·14 0·35 0·48

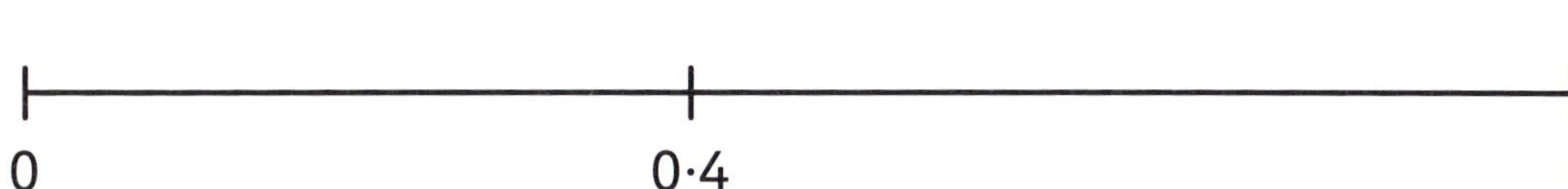

I am going to think about how close the numbers are to 0·4 on a number line.

4 The **sum** of two numbers is 7.

The **difference** between the two numbers is 0·7.

What are the two numbers?

The two numbers are ☐ and ☐.

I am going to draw a bar model to show the difference of 0·7 first.

→ Practice book 6C p63

Problem solving – percentages

Discover

1 **a)** How much does Jen pay for her computer?

b) What is the full price of Amal's television?

Share

a)

£450

10%	10%	10%	10%	10%	10%	10%	10%	10%	10%

price paid (first 8 parts) | discount (last 2 parts)

450 ÷ 10 = 45

10% of £450 is £45 so 20% is double this.

£45 × 2 = £90

£450 – £90 = £360

Jen pays £360 for her computer.

b)

25% is the same as $\frac{1}{4}$, so we can draw a bar model with 4 parts.

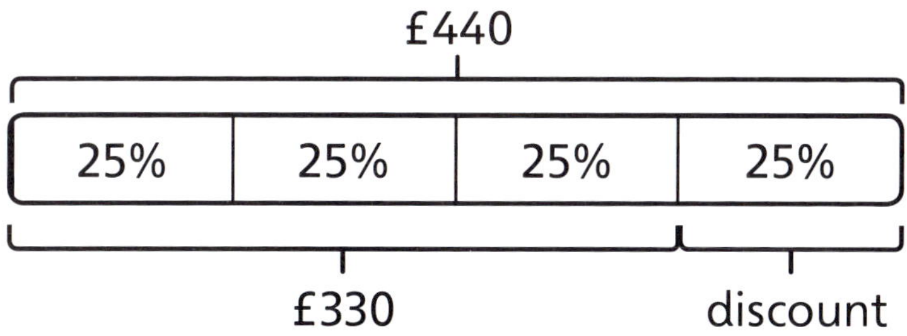

The value of 1 part (25%) is £330 ÷ 3 = £110.

The full price is 4 of these parts: £110 × 4 = £440.

The full price of Amal's television is £440.

Think together

1. Jen also buys a case for her new computer.

The case is reduced by 30%.

The price is now £42.

What was the full price of the computer case?

I need to think about the percentage of the full price that £42 represents.

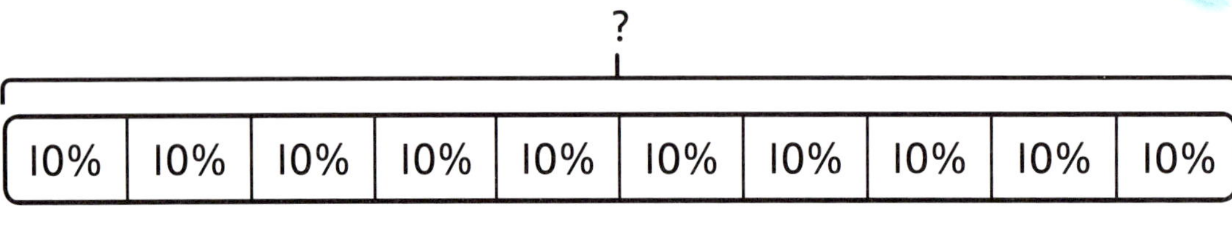

The full price of the computer case was £ ☐ .

2. The table shows the number of customers in the shop on the day of the sale.

Find the missing information.

	Adults	Children
Percentage (%) of total customers	60%	☐
Number of customers	☐	700

Remember that 100% represents all of the customers.

3 a) Which grid matches this description?

25% dotted blue, 40% striped green and 10% solid red

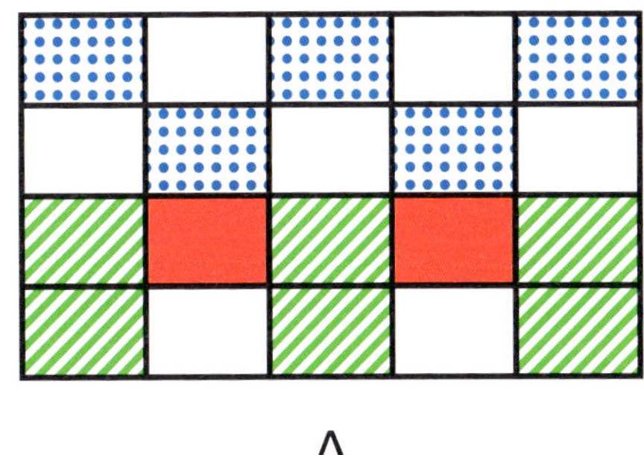

A

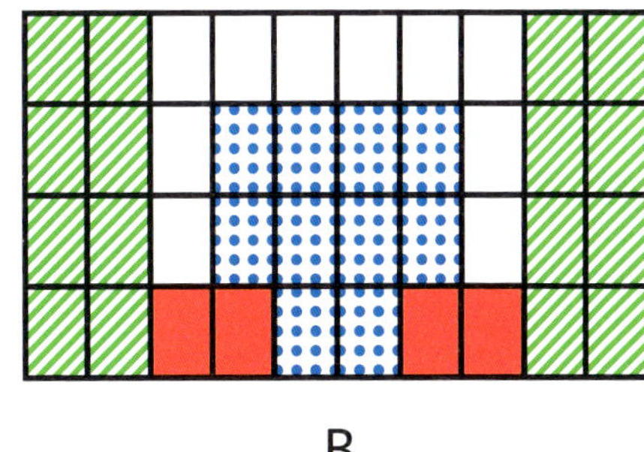

B

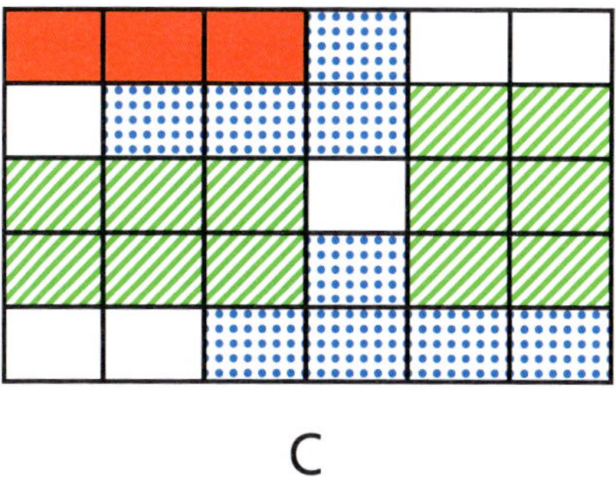

C

b) What percentage of the grid you identified in part **a)** is white?

CHALLENGE

4 The class is voting for Alex, Jamie or Lee to be on the School Council.

Alex: I got 35% of the vote.

Jamie: I got $\frac{2}{5}$ of the votes.

Lee: I got the rest of the votes.

What percentage of votes did the winner get?

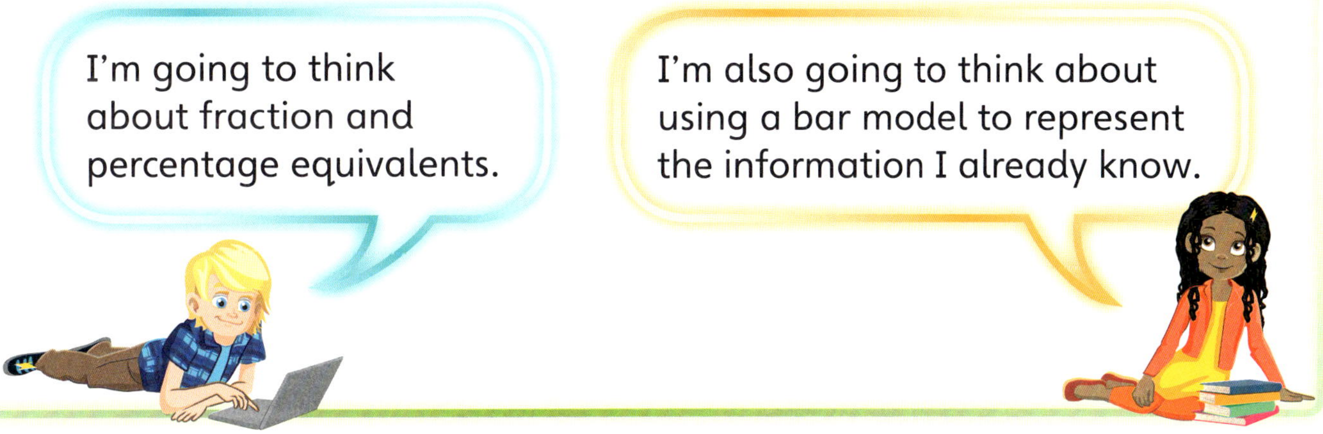

I'm going to think about fraction and percentage equivalents.

I'm also going to think about using a bar model to represent the information I already know.

→ Practice book 6C p66

Problem solving – ratio and proportion

Discover

1 **a)** Andy buys some packets of stickers.

He has 32 car stickers.

How many stickers does he have in total?

b) There are 50 more car stickers than train stickers in a box.

How many packets of stickers are in a box?

Share

a) Method 1:

Represent the problem using a bar model.

There are 4 car stickers for every 2 train stickers in a packet.

Andy has 32 car stickers.

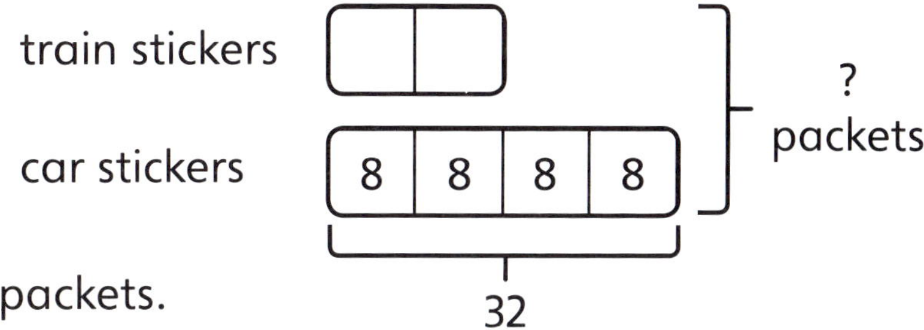

32 ÷ 4 = 8, so Andy buys 8 packets.

8 × 6 = 48, so Andy has 48 stickers in total.

Method 2:

1 packet	4 cars + 2 trains
2 packets	8 cars + 4 trains
4 packets	16 cars + 8 trains
8 packets	32 cars + 16 trains

32 + 16 = 48, so Andy has 48 stickers in total.

I can solve the problem another way using **scaling**.

b) This bar model shows that there are 50 more car stickers.

train stickers | | | ← 50 →

car stickers | 25 | 25 | 25 | 25 |

? packets

The extra 50 stickers are equal to 2 parts of the car stickers bar.

Each part represents 25 so there are 25 packets of stickers in each box.

Think together

1 a) Here is one of Andy's train stickers.

I cm on the picture represents 2·5 m in real life.

What is the length of the train in real life?

I know that I cm is 2·5 m so I can use this information to help me.

The train is ☐ m long in real life.

b) Another sticker to the same scale shows a train that is 20 metres long in real life. How many centimetres long is the sticker?

The sticker is ☐ cm long.

2 A recipe uses 4 spoons of honey for every 240 grams of fruit.

How many spoons of honey are needed for 600 grams of fruit?

I think I can use scaling to help me here.

☐ spoons of honey are needed for 600 g of fruit.

3 Here are two circles.

Write the ratio of diameter a to diameter b.

a : b = ☐ : ☐

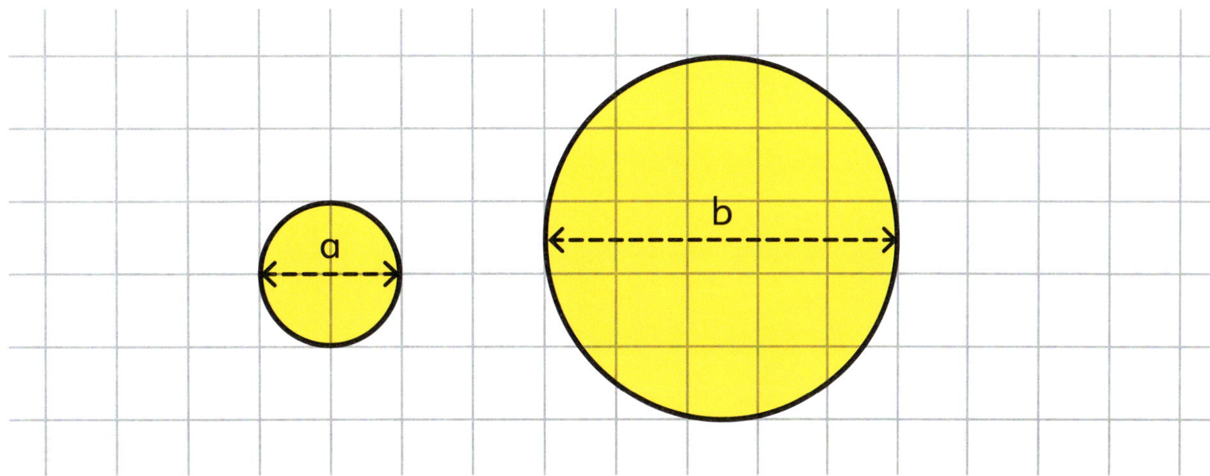

4 Sofia and Toshi lay a path that is 4·8 metres long.

They use 8 small rectangular paving slabs for every 3 large square slabs.

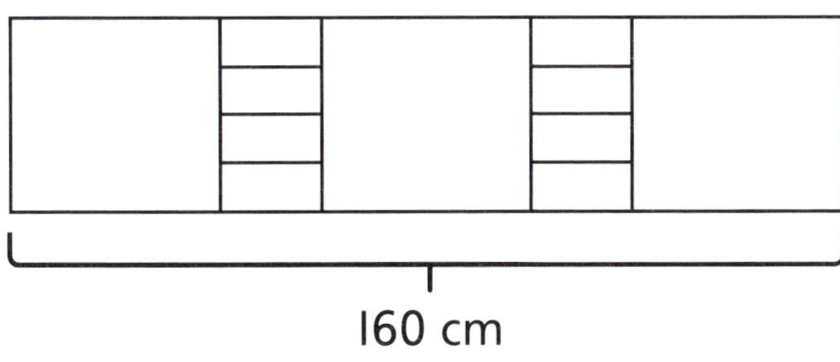

How many small rectangular slabs do they use?

How many large square slabs do they use?

→ Practice book 6C p69

Problem solving – time 1

Discover

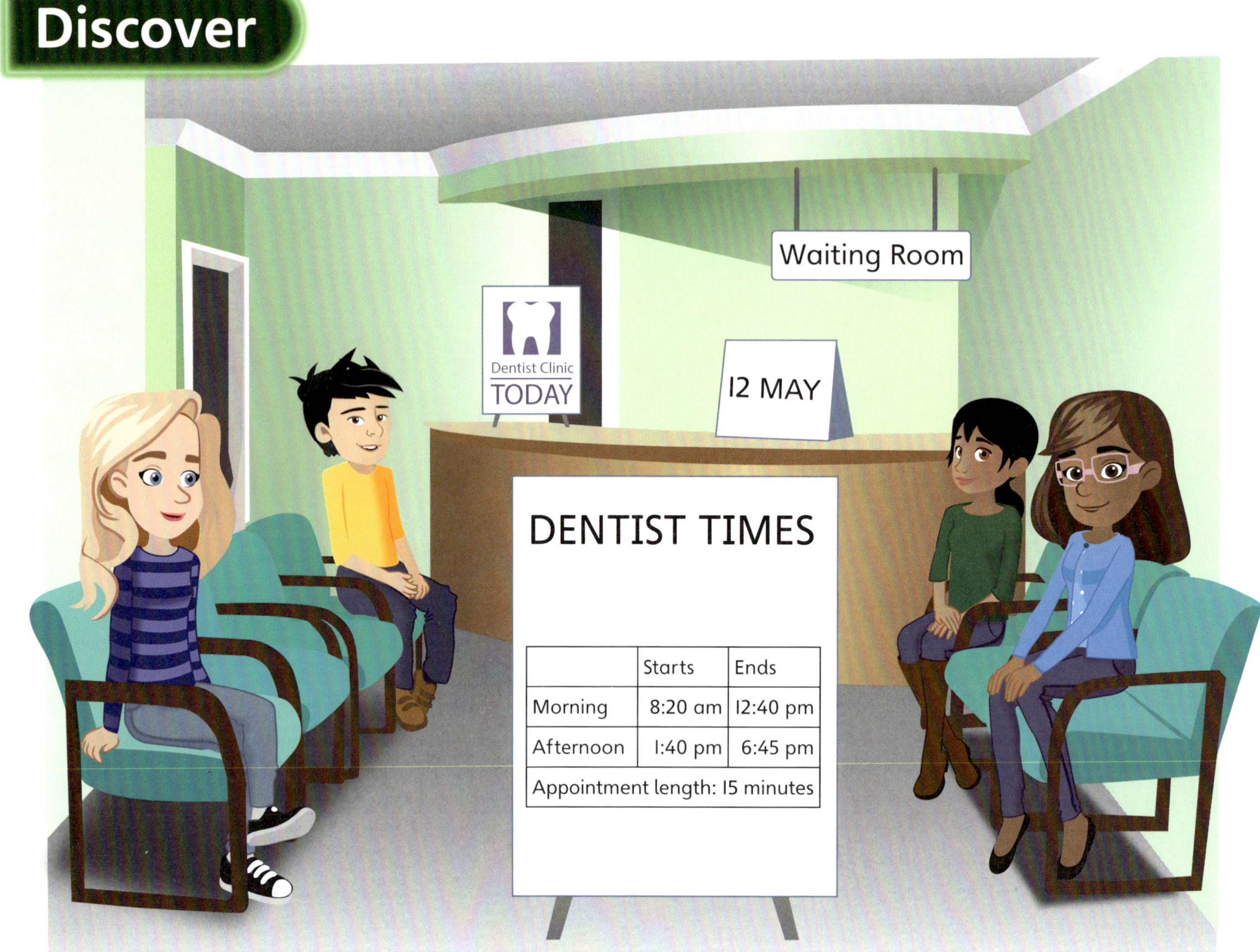

	Starts	Ends
Morning	8:20 am	12:40 pm
Afternoon	1:40 pm	6:45 pm
Appointment length: 15 minutes		

1 a) The dentist has a 20 minute break during the morning session and another 20 minute break in the afternoon.

How many more appointments can be made in the afternoon than in the morning?

b) There is a dentist clinic at the surgery every 28 days.

What was the date of the previous dentist clinic?

Share

a)

I'm going to use a time line to calculate the length of the morning session and the afternoon session. It's just like a number line.

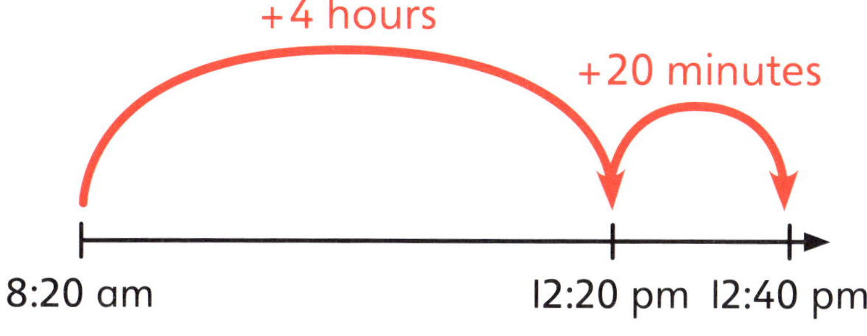

Subtract 20 minutes for breaks.

4 hours 20 minutes – 20 minutes

= 4 hours

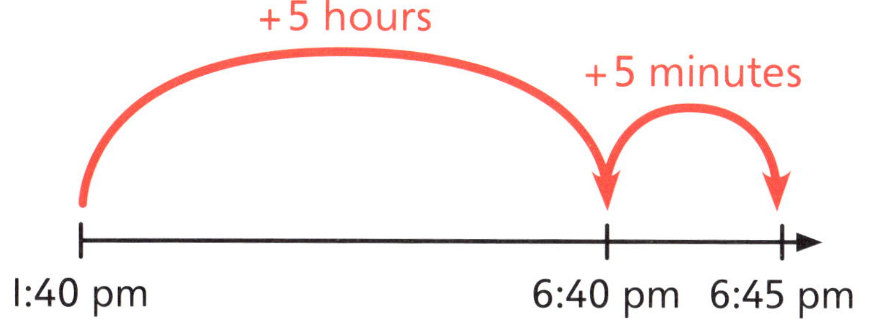

5 hours 5 minutes – 20 minutes

= 4 hours 45 minutes

The time available for appointments is 4 hours in the morning and 4 hours 45 minutes in the afternoon.

The afternoon session is 45 minutes longer. Appointments are 15 minutes.

45 minutes ÷ 15 minutes = 3, so 3 more appointments can be made in the afternoon than in the morning.

b) The previous dentist clinic was 28 days ago. This is equivalent to 4 weeks.

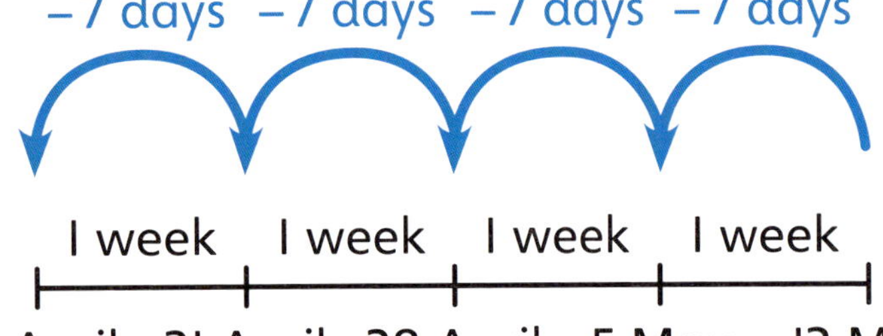

April						
Su	Mo	Tu	We	Th	Fr	Sa
		1	2	3	4	5
6	7	8	9	10	11	12
13	14	15	16	17	18	19
20	21	22	23	24	25	26
27	28	29	30			

May						
Su	Mo	Tu	We	Th	Fr	Sa
				1	2	3
4	5	6	7	8	9	10
11	12	13	14	15	16	17
18	19	20	21	22	23	24
25	26	27	28	29	30	31

The date of the previous dentist clinic was 14 April.

Remember that different months have a different number of days.

Think together

1 This time line shows some of the dentist's appointments on 12 May.

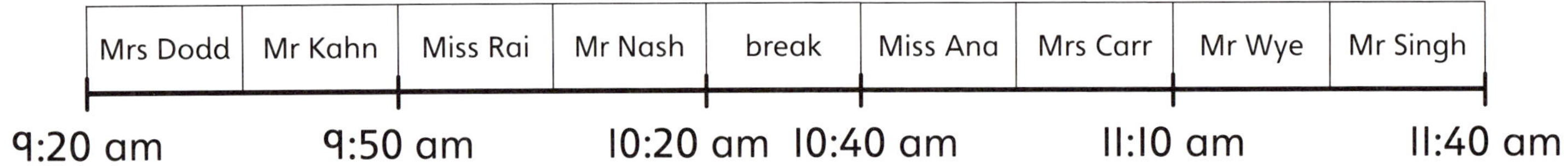

a) Mr Nash and Miss Ana arrive together 5 minutes before Mr Nash's appointment. They both leave at the end of Miss Ana's appointment.

How long do they spend at the surgery?

b) Mr Wye has to wait 25 minutes after his appointment for some medicine.

What time does he leave the surgery?

2. Max runs 15 laps of the park in $\frac{3}{4}$ hour.

   Jamilla starts running laps of the same park at 13:30. She completes 30 laps of the park at 14:56.

   Who runs faster?

3. A company spends £245 per month on electricity bills.

   How much do they spend in total from 1 January 2014 to 31 August 2017?

4. There is a bus to the city every 25 minutes. There is a bus to the seaside every 45 minutes.

   The buses start running at 08:00.

   At what time will a bus to the city and a bus to the seaside next depart together?

I wonder if the buses depart together at other times during the day.

→ Practice book 6C p72

Problem solving – time 2

Discover

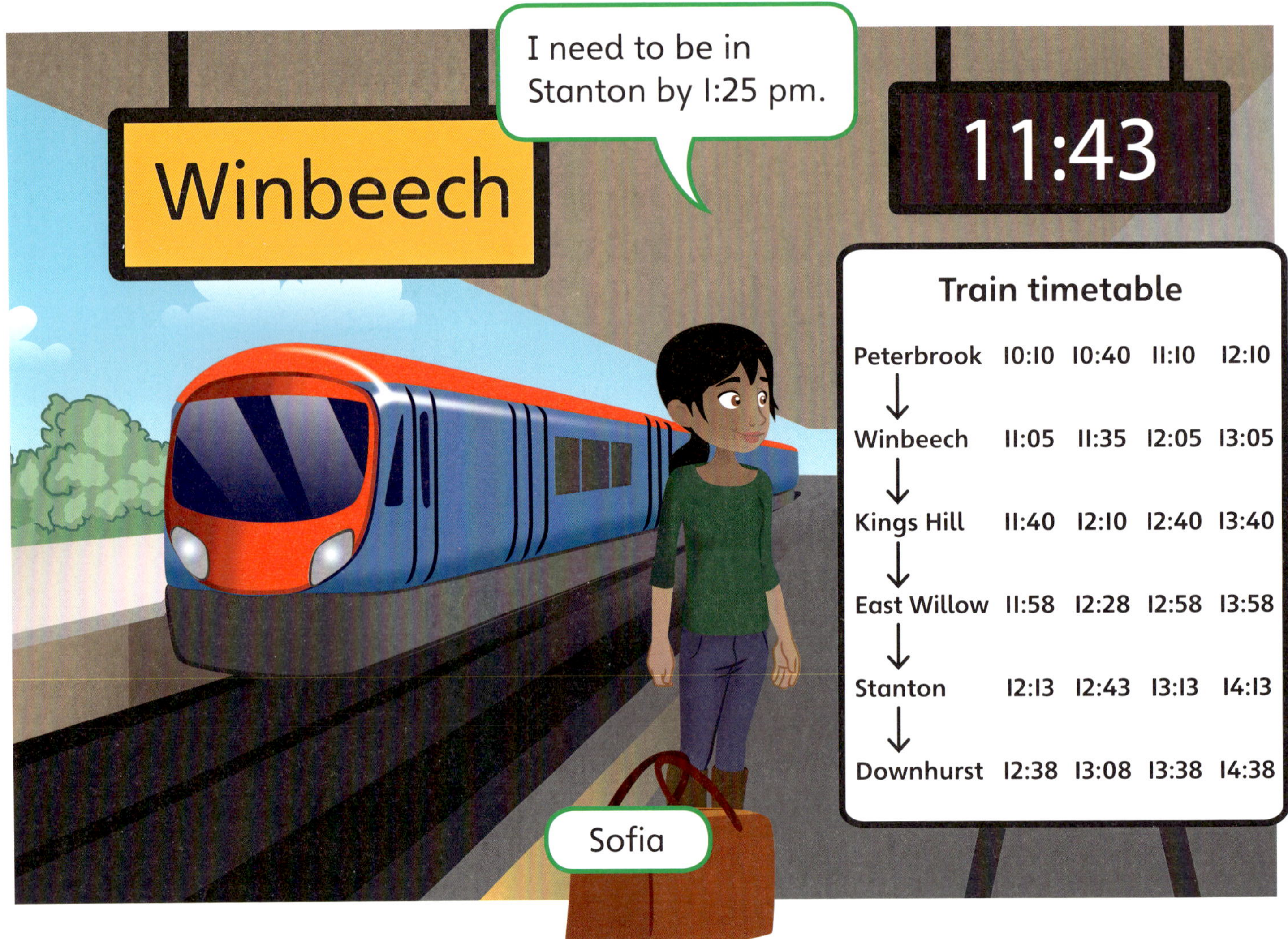

Train timetable

Peterbrook	10:10	10:40	11:10	12:10
↓ Winbeech	11:05	11:35	12:05	13:05
↓ Kings Hill	11:40	12:10	12:40	13:40
↓ East Willow	11:58	12:28	12:58	13:58
↓ Stanton	12:13	12:43	13:13	14:13
↓ Downhurst	12:38	13:08	13:38	14:38

1 a) How many minutes will Sofia have to wait for her train?

b) The same journey by bus takes double the time.

The bus arrives in Stanton at 13:10.

What time does it leave Winbeech?

Share

a) Sofia needs to be in Stanton by 1:25 pm.

This is 13:25 using the 24-hour clock.

She can take the 12:05 from Winbeech, arriving at 13:13.

The time now is 11:43.

Use a time line to check how long she must wait.

The timetable uses the 24-hour clock. I need to convert 1:25 pm to a 24-hour time first.

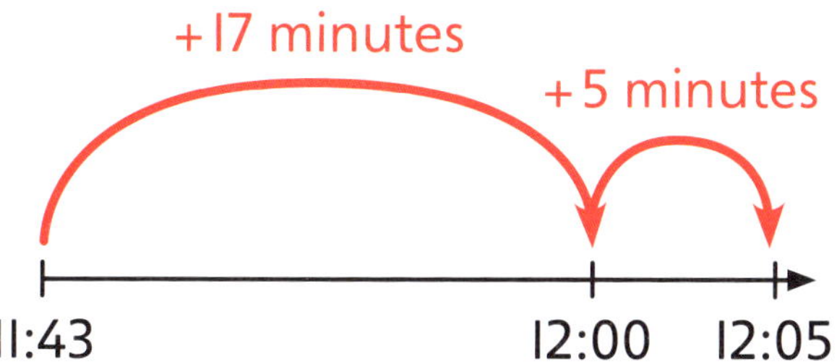

Sofia will have to wait 22 minutes for her train.

b) The bus journey takes double the time of the train journey.

The train journey is 1 hour 8 minutes so the bus journey is 2 hours 16 minutes.

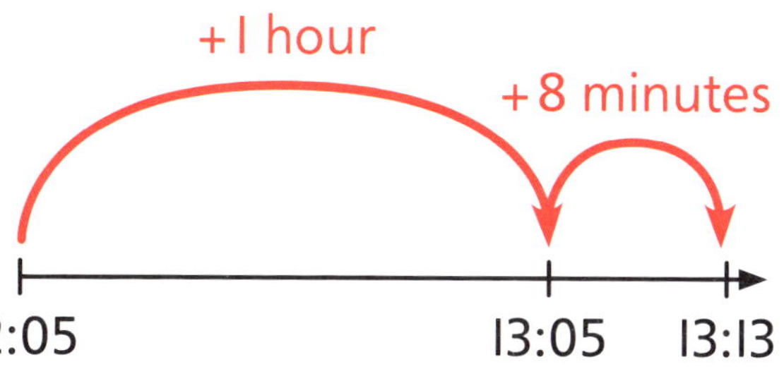

The bus arrives in Stanton at 13:10.

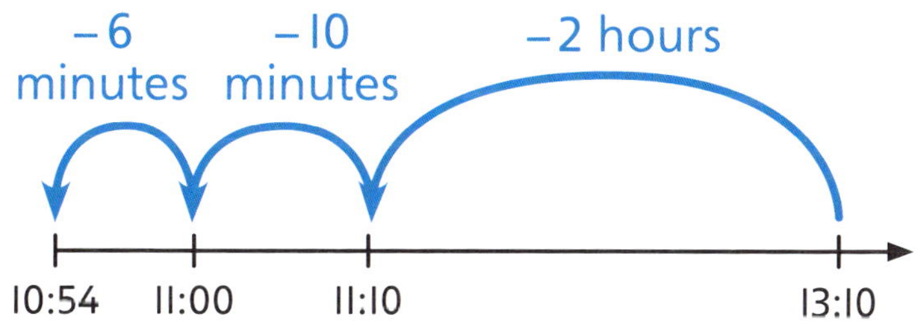

I can use a time line to subtract 2 hours 16 minutes to find out the time the bus leaves Winbeech.

The bus leaves Winbeech at 10:54.

Think together

1 Sofia meets Jen at the sports centre in Stanton to play badminton.

The cost of hiring the court is £2·95 per 20 minutes.

The cost of hiring a racquet is £2·60 each.

Sofia and Jen play from 14:00 to 15:40.

How much do they pay together in total?

There are several steps to these problems. I must check that I have answered each step.

2 Here is the timetable showing the use of the badminton courts each weekend.

Times	Saturday	Sunday
08:30–10:30	lessons	for hire
10:30–12:00	for hire	lessons
12:00–14:15	competition	competition
14:15–16:00	for hire	lessons
16:00–17:30	lessons	for hire
17:30–20:45	for hire	closed

a) What is the total number of hours for which the courts are used for lessons?

b) The courts are available for hire on both days.

For how much longer are they available on Saturday?

3 The time graph shows the number of visitors to the sports centre one Saturday morning.

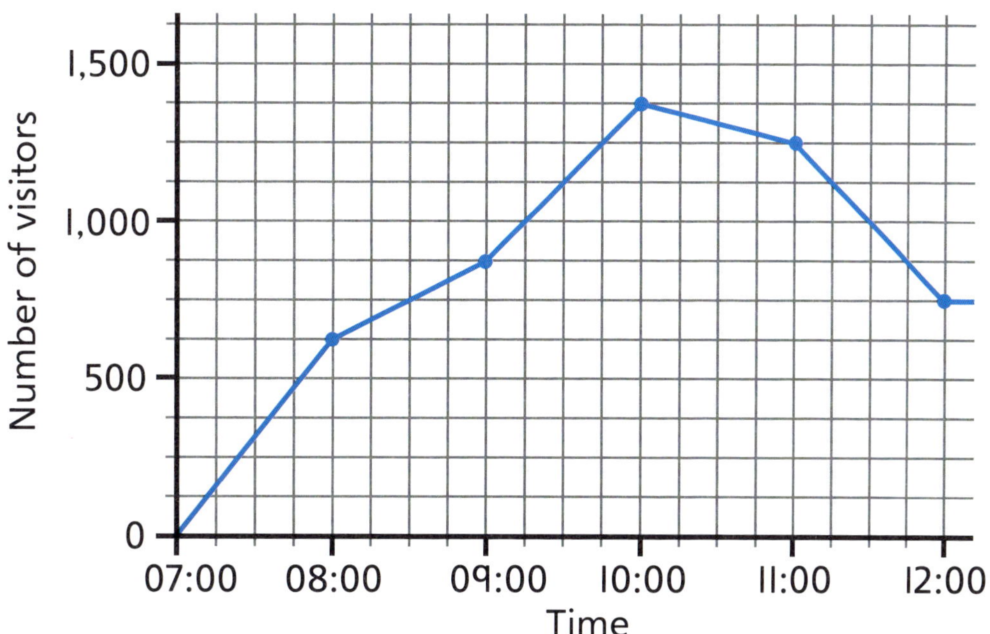

a) At what times were there 750 visitors?

b) For how many minutes were there 1,000 or more visitors at the sports centre?

CHALLENGE

4 There is a swimming pool at the sports centre.

The pool is 35 metres long and 16 metres wide.

Holly swims 18 lengths in 45 minutes.

Toshi swims 80 widths in $1\frac{1}{2}$ hours.

Who is the faster swimmer?

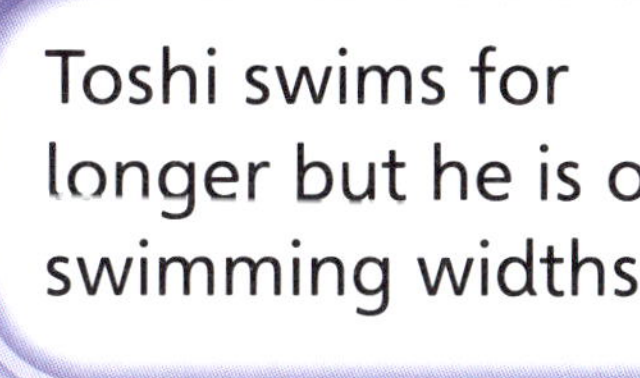

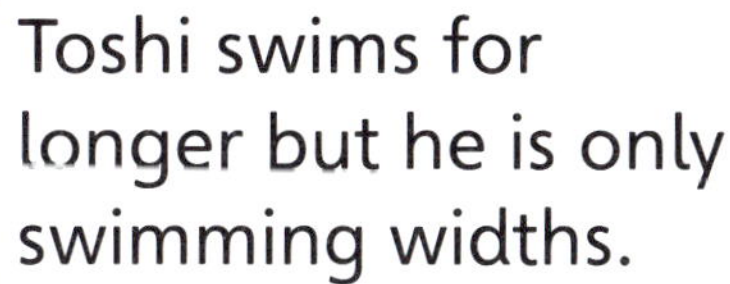

→ Practice book 6C p75

Problem solving – position and direction

Discover

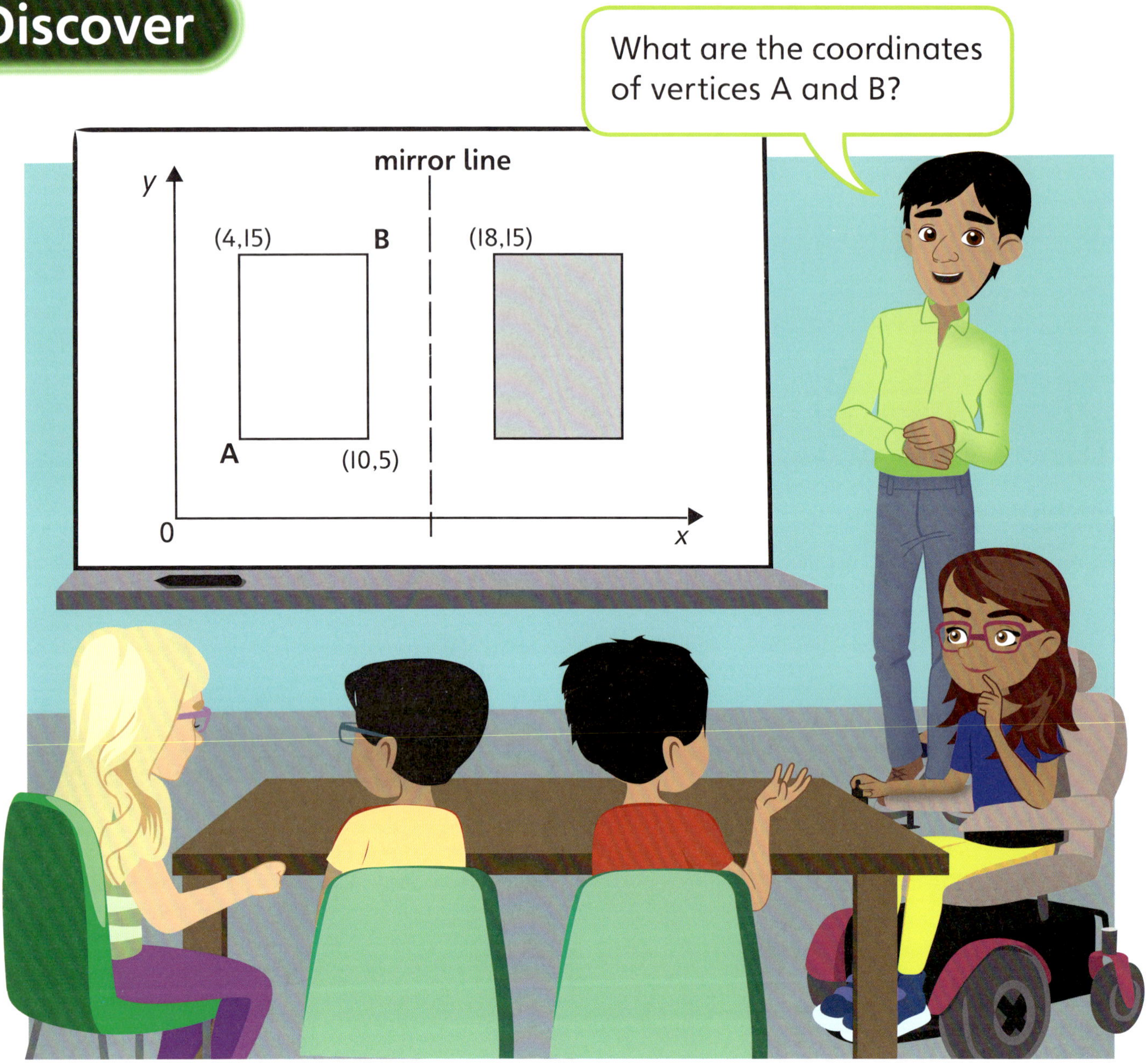

1 **a)** Give the coordinates of vertices A and B.

b) The rectangle is reflected in a mirror line. One vertex is at (18,15).

What are the coordinates of the other three vertices?

Share

a) The coordinates of two vertices are (4,15) and (10,5).

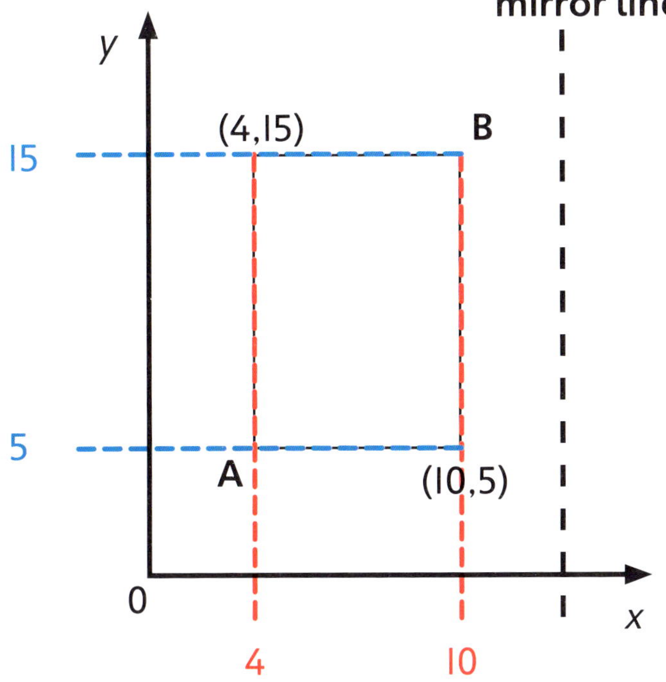

I can use what I know about the structure of the coordinate grid.

Vertex A is (4,5).

Vertex B is (10,15).

b)

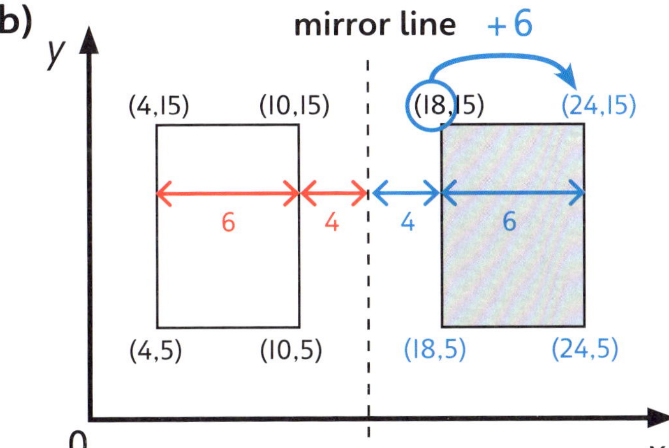

Each rectangle is 6 units wide.

From (10,15) to (18,15) there is a distance of 8 units. Each rectangle must be 4 units from the mirror line.

The coordinates of the reflected vertex B are (18,15). Add 6 to the *x*-coordinate to locate another vertex at (24,15).

I know that a reflected shape is the same size as the original shape.

Work out the other reflected vertices in the same way. They are (18,5) and (24,5).

Think together

1 An isosceles triangle is reflected in the *y*-axis.

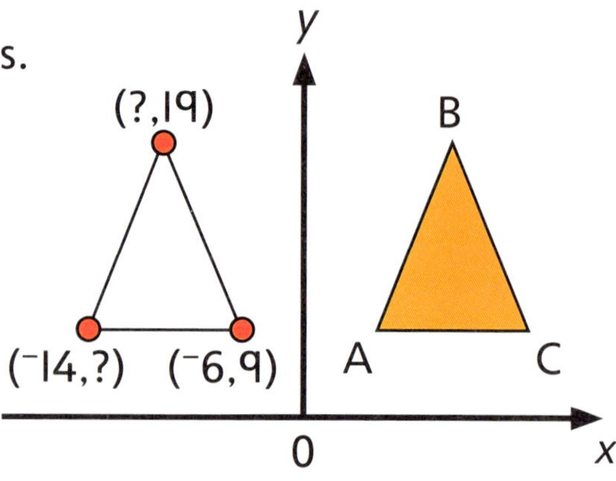

a) One of the vertices of the original triangle is (⁻6,9).

What are the coordinates of the other two vertices?

The other two vertices are (⁻14, ☐) and (☐,19).

b) What are the coordinates of the reflected triangle, ABC?

A (☐,☐) B (☐,☐) C (☐,☐)

2 Points N, P, S and T are an equal distance from each other.

What are the coordinates of points P and T?

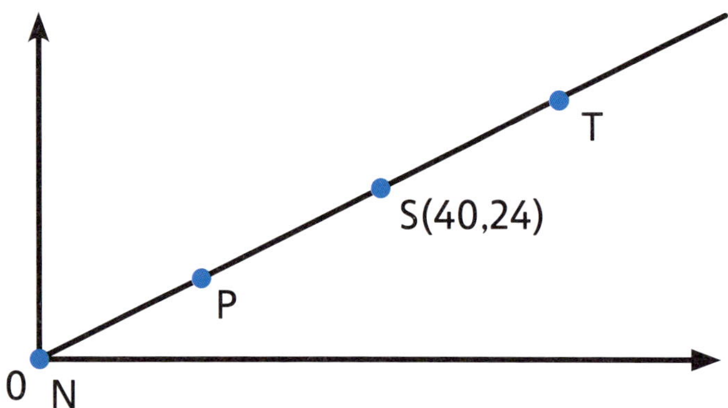

P (☐,☐)

T (☐,☐)

3 Jamie draws two sides of a parallelogram.

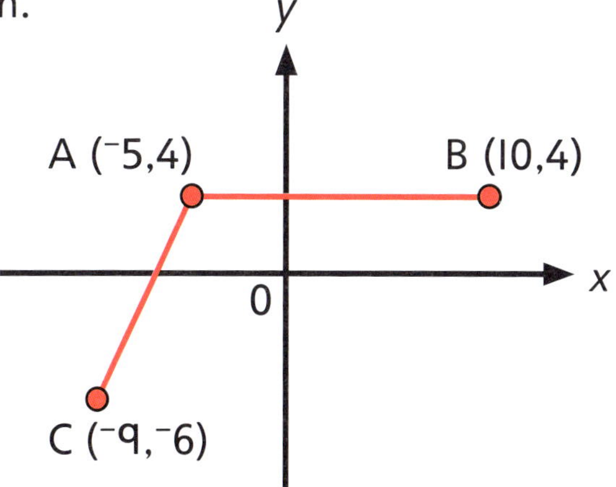

a) Where should she plot the fourth vertex, D, to complete the parallelogram?

b) The shape is translated 5 units right and 4 units up.

What are the new coordinates of vertex C?

4 The length of a side of a square is 5 units.

The coordinates of one vertex are (10,10).

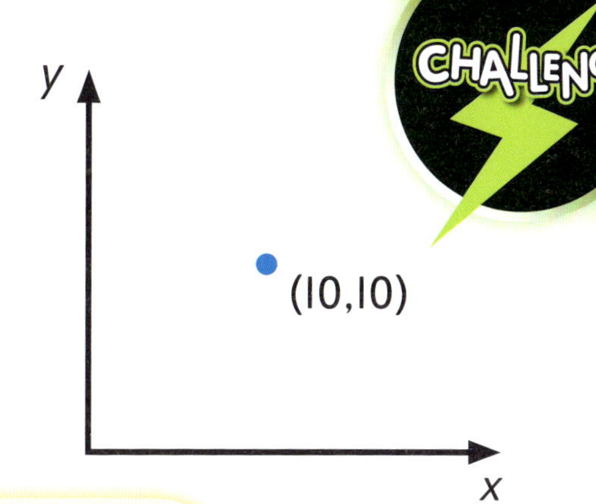

a) What are the possible coordinates of the other three vertices?

Find at least two different solutions.

I think there are four possible squares so I need to think about all of them.

b) The coordinates (8,12) will be inside only one of the squares.

Explain why Max is correct.

→ Practice book 6C p78

Problem solving – properties of shapes 1

Discover

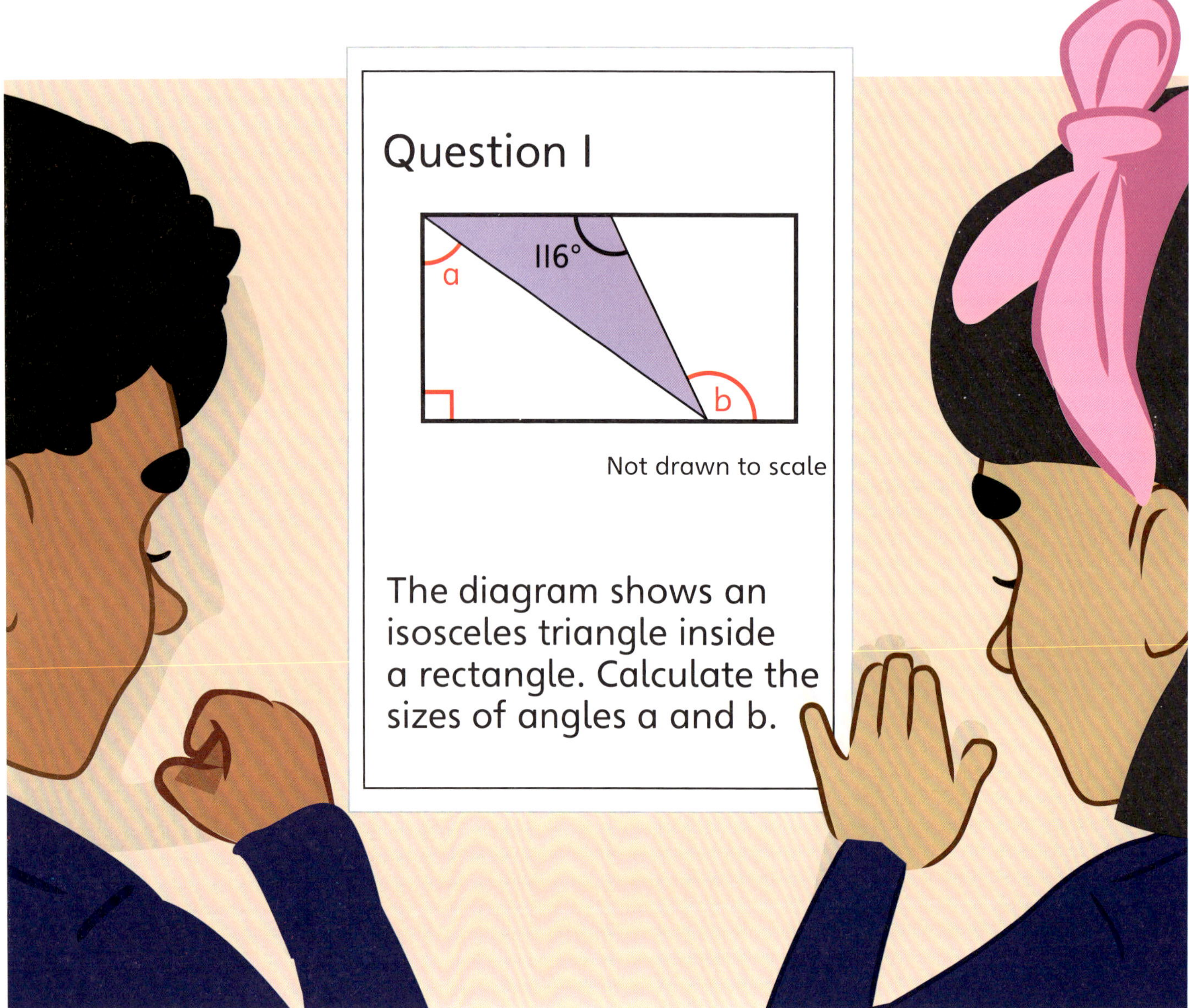

1 **a)** Calculate the size of angle a.

b) Now use what you know to calculate angle b.

Share

a) I am going to write all the information I know on the diagram.

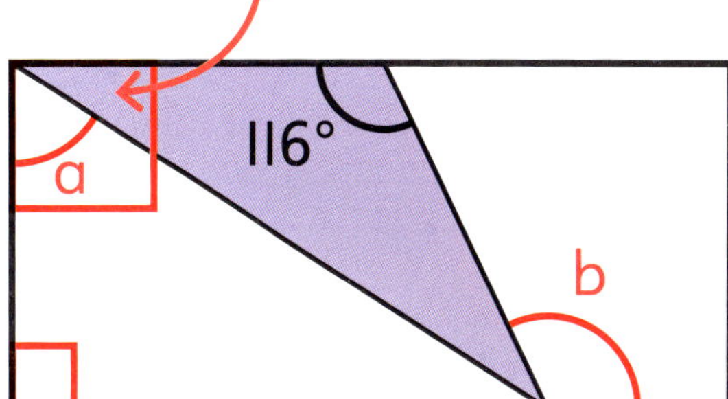

We can calculate the size of each of the equal angles in the isosceles triangle:

(180° – 116°) ÷ 2 = 32°

Angle a is part of a right angle, 90°.

angle a = 90° – 32°, so angle a is 58°.

b) We know two of the angles in the right-angled triangle.

We can work out the third angle:
180° – 90° – 58° = 32°

Angle b is one of three angles on a straight line.

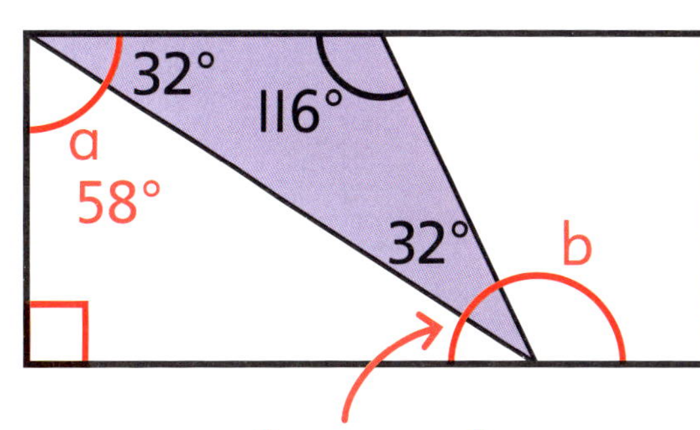

Remember that angles on a straight line add up to 180°.

We now know that 32° + 32° + b = 180°.

So, 180 – 64 = 116.

Angle b is 116°.

Think together

1 This diagram includes an isosceles triangle.

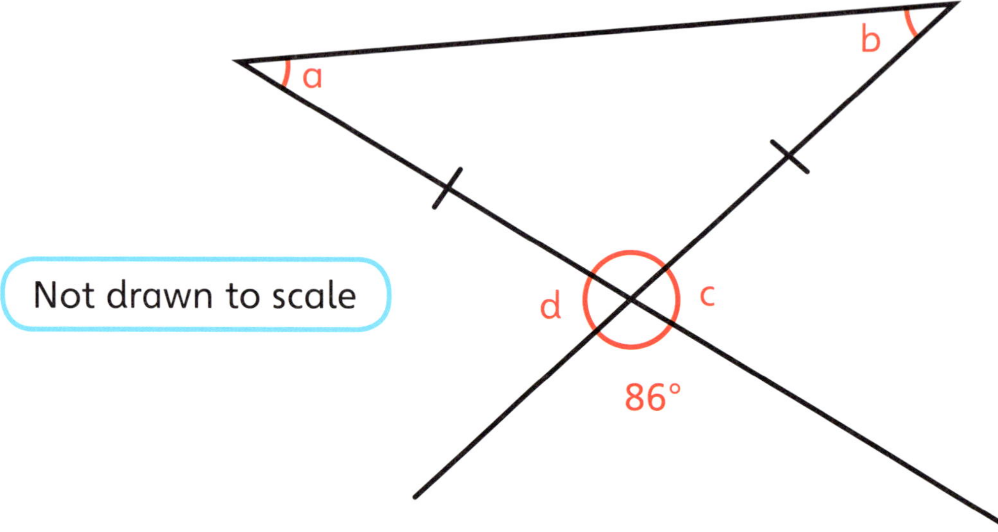

a) What are the sizes of angles a and b?

Angles a and b are both ☐°.

b) What are the sizes of angles c and d?

Angles c and d are both ☐°

2 Here is a scalene triangle.

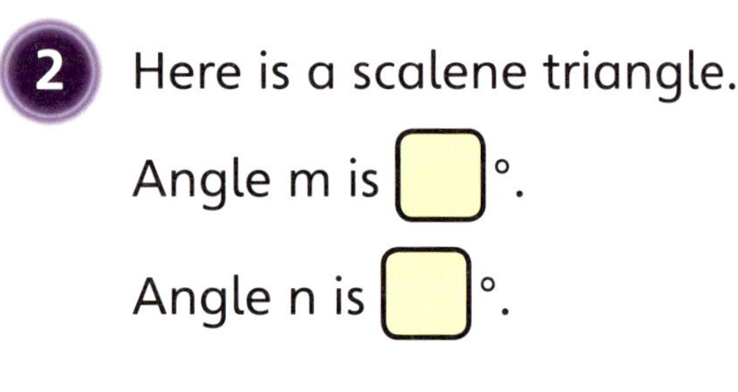

Angle m is ☐°.

Angle n is ☐°.

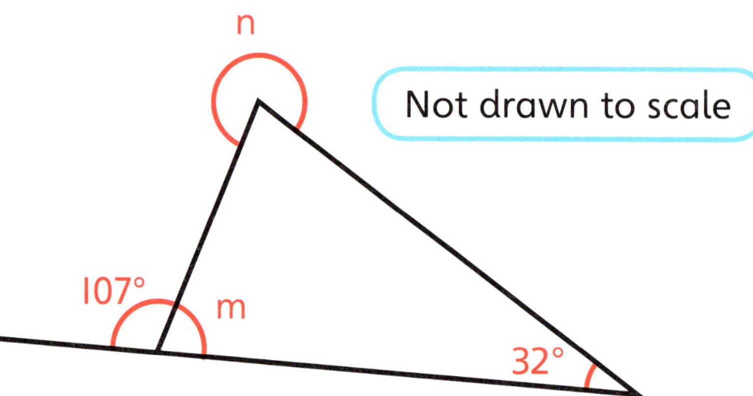

Remember that angles that meet at a point add up to 360°.

3 Three angles meet at a point.

Angle a is obtuse. It is half the size of angle b.

Angle c is acute. It is 15° smaller than a right angle.

What is the size of each angle?

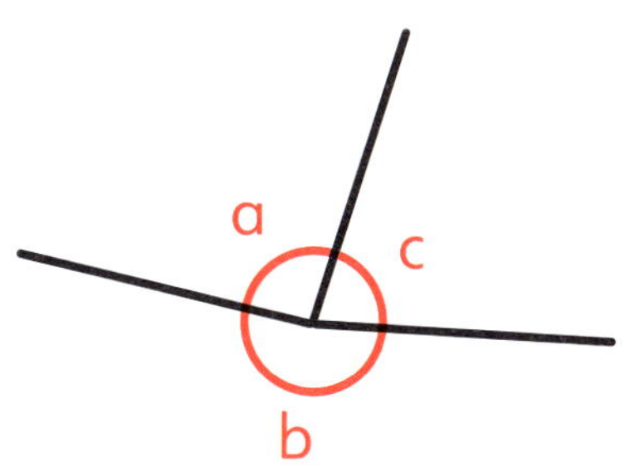

4 Work out the size of angles x, y and z.

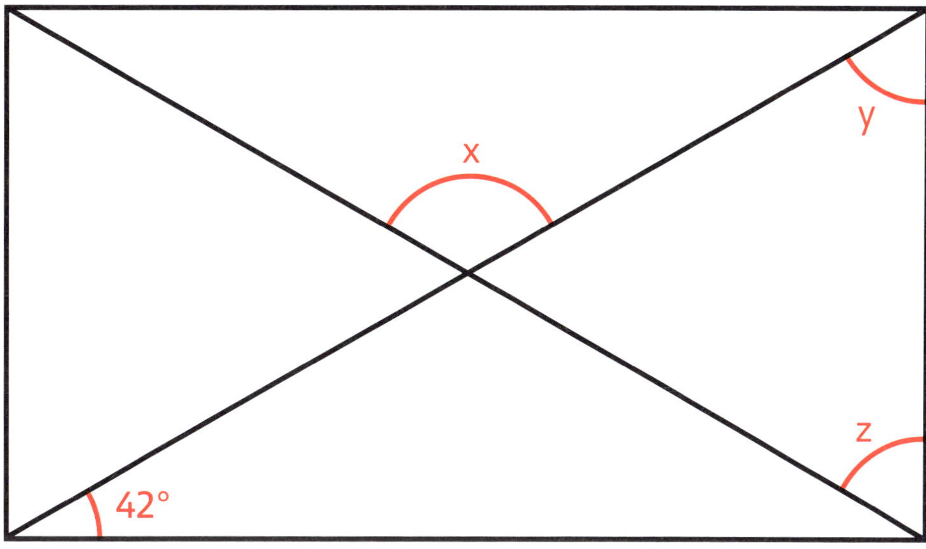

Not drawn to scale

I'm going to need to work out the size of some of the other angles before I can work out the size of angles x, y and z.

→ Practice book 6C p81

Problem solving – properties of shapes 2

Discover

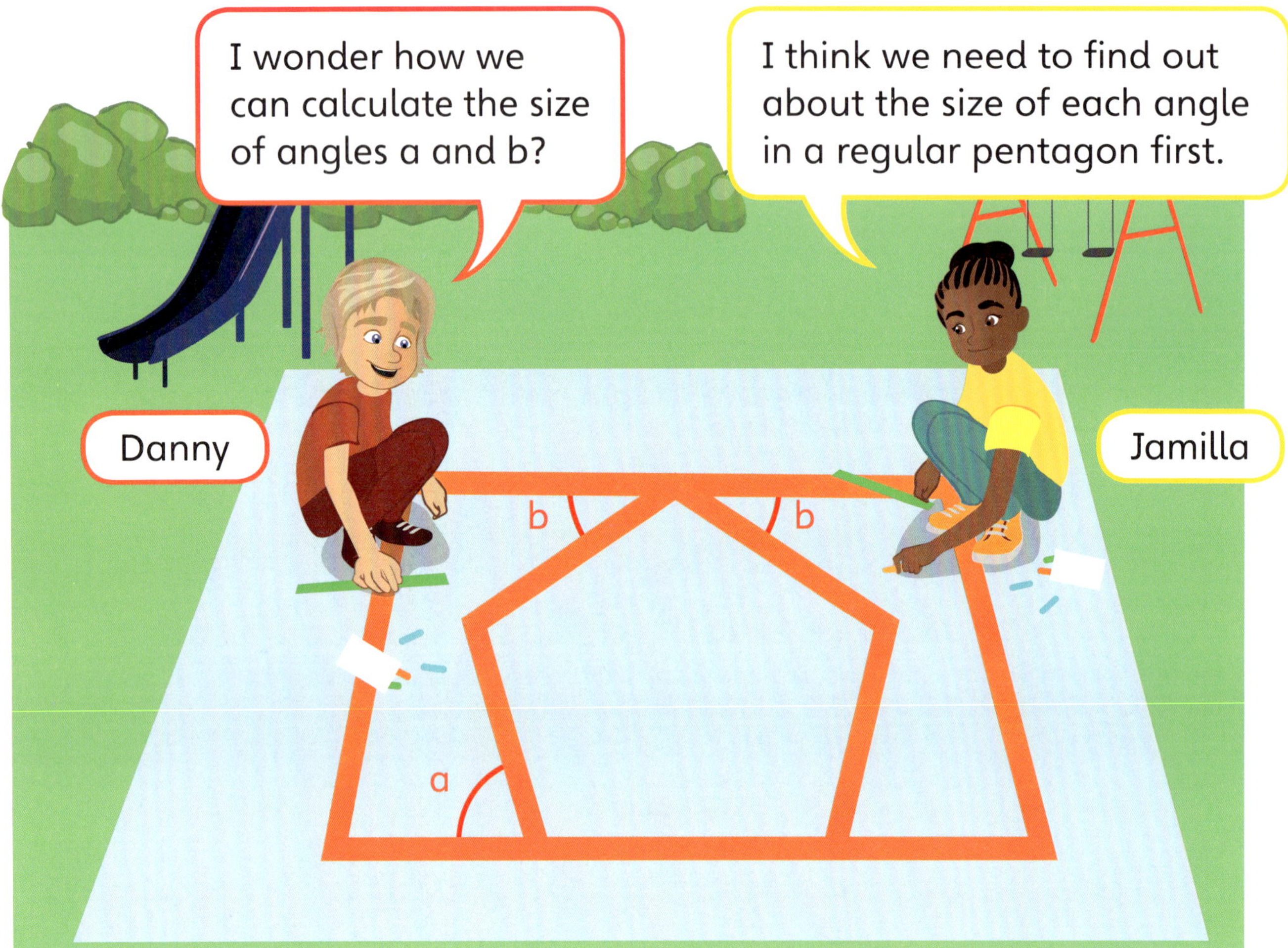

1 **a)** What is the size of each angle in a regular pentagon?

b) Calculate the sizes of angles a and b.

Share

a)

I know that I can split a regular polygon into triangles. The sum of the angles in each triangle is 180°.

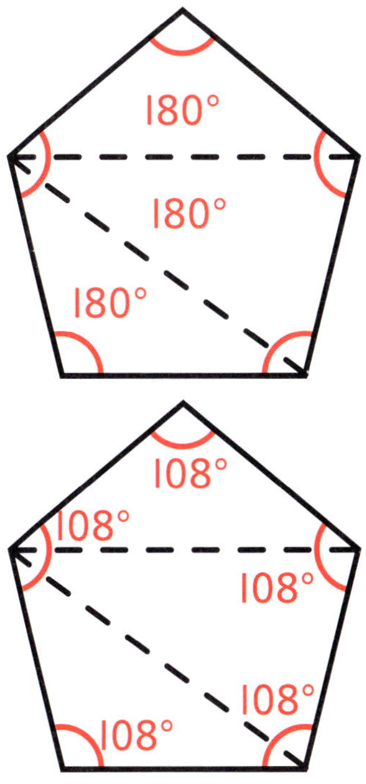

There are 3 triangles inside this pentagon.

180° × 3 = 540°

The interior angles in the pentagon total 540°.

So each angle is 540° ÷ 5 = 108°.

b) Label other angles that will help.

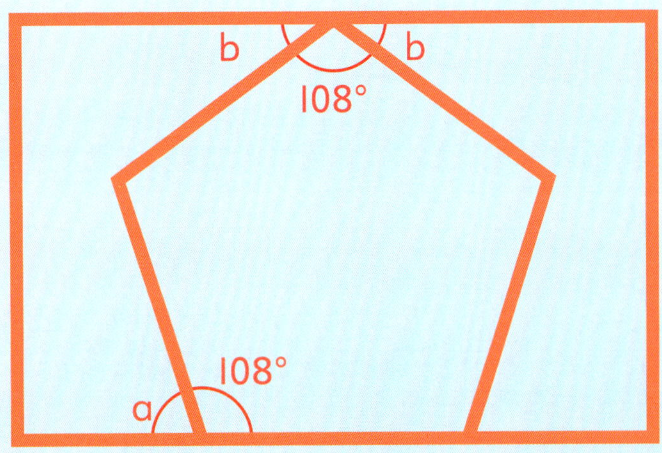

I have noticed that angle a and one of the angles in the pentagon are on a straight line.

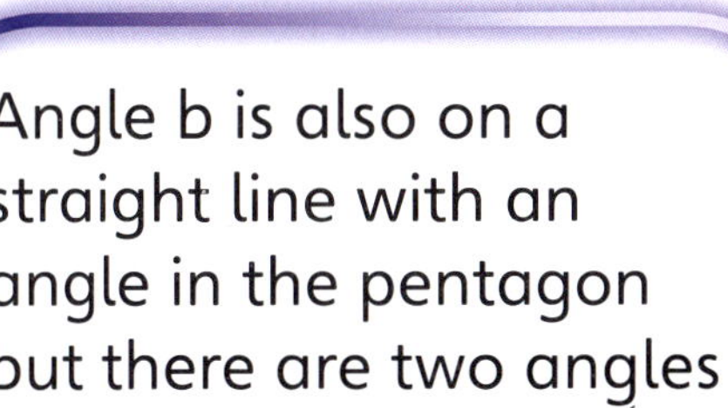

Angle b is also on a straight line with an angle in the pentagon but there are two angles labelled b.

Angle a is 72° because 180° – 108° = 72°.

Angle b must be 72° ÷ 2 = 36° because there are two angles of the same size.

36° + 36° + 108° = 180°

Think together

1. Danny and Jamilla now draw a regular hexagon inside a rectangle.

   Calculate the sizes of angles x and y.

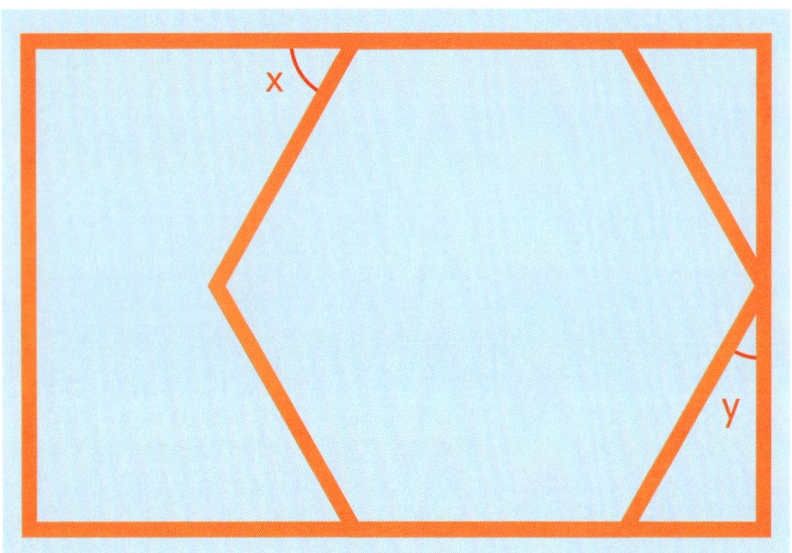

2. What is the size of angle a in this irregular pentagon?

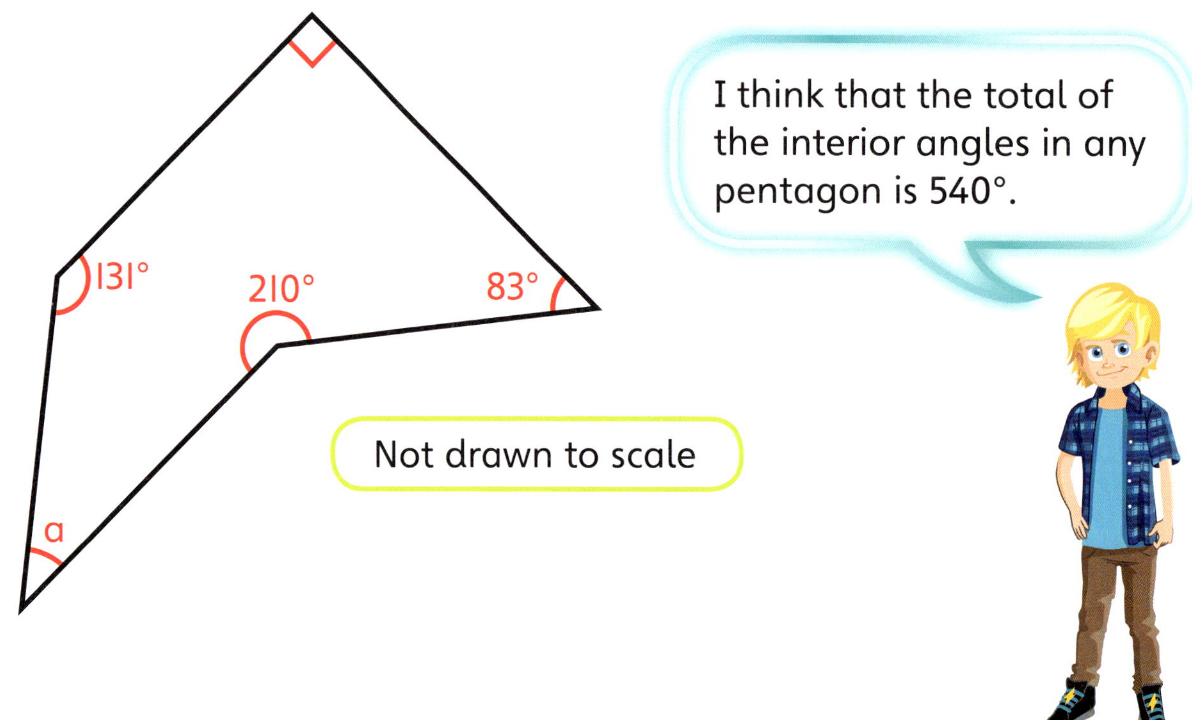

3 Here are two quadrilaterals.

Explain how you know that angle a in each quadrilateral is 50°.

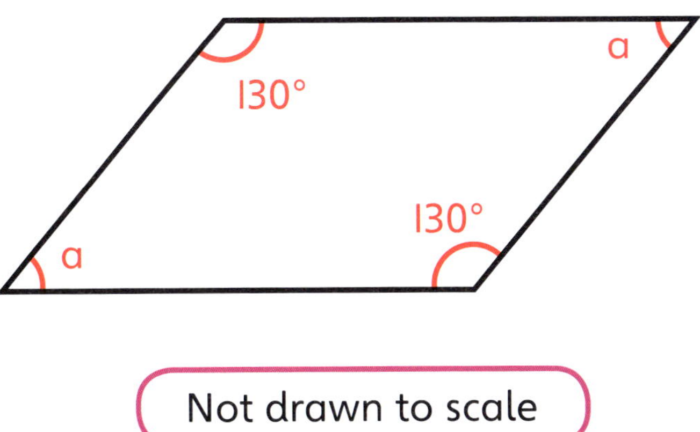

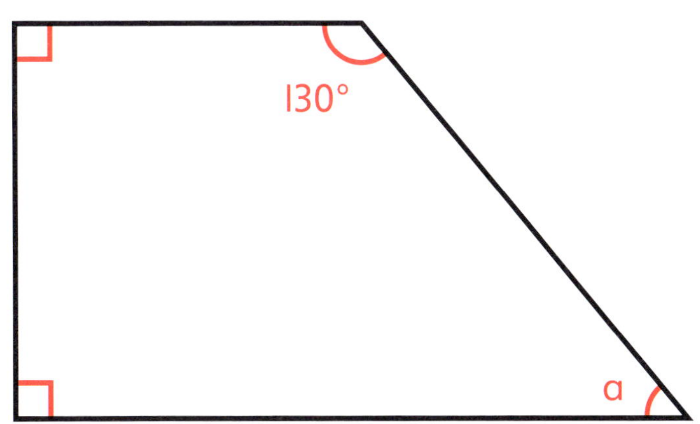

Not drawn to scale

4 This diagram shows a regular pentagon joined to an equilateral triangle.

Work out the size of angle a.

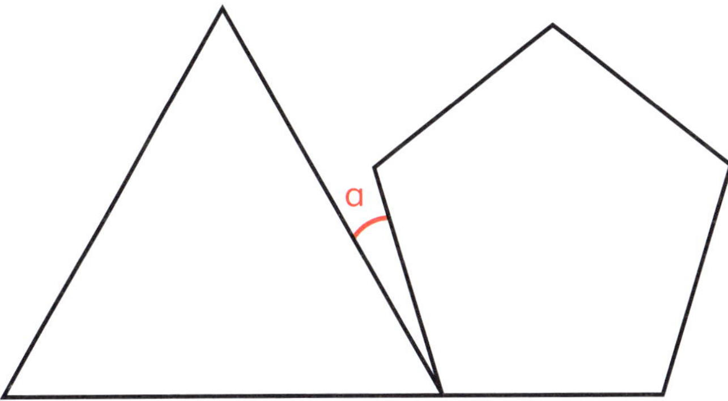

I can see that the shapes meet on a straight line.

I am going to use what I know about the sizes of angles in an equilateral triangle and a regular pentagon.

→ Practice book 6C p84

End of unit check

1 Put the numbers in order, starting with the smallest.

A	B	C	D	E
148,500	98,4000	184,500	200,795	89,750

One has been done for you.

smallest		A		largest
______	______	A	______	______

2 The temperature falls by 12°. What is the new temperature?

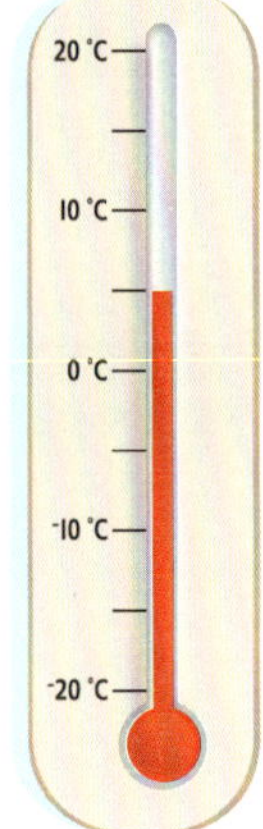

3 Find the size of angles x and y.

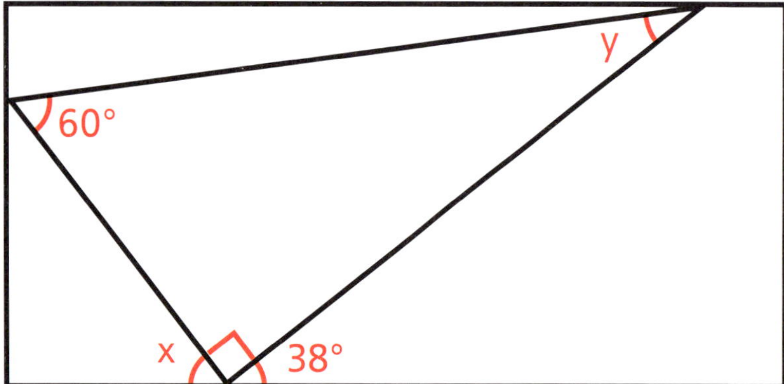

4 The total value of four cars in a car showroom is £98,700.

Here are three of the cars.

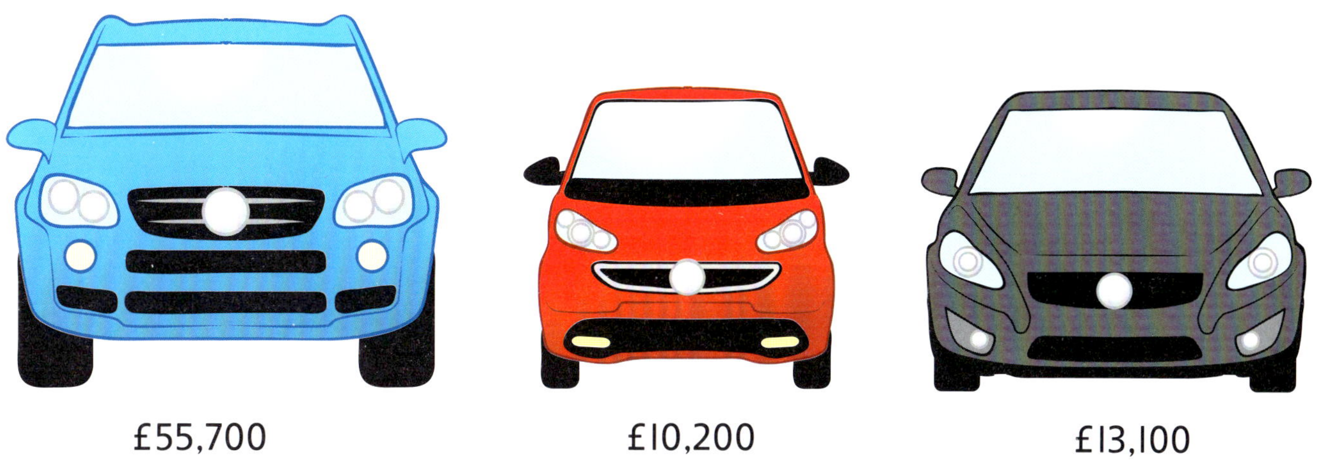

What is the price of the fourth car? What method will you use to calculate this?

5 

What fraction of the whole bar is not shaded?

6 Three identical squares and two identical triangles are placed in a line.

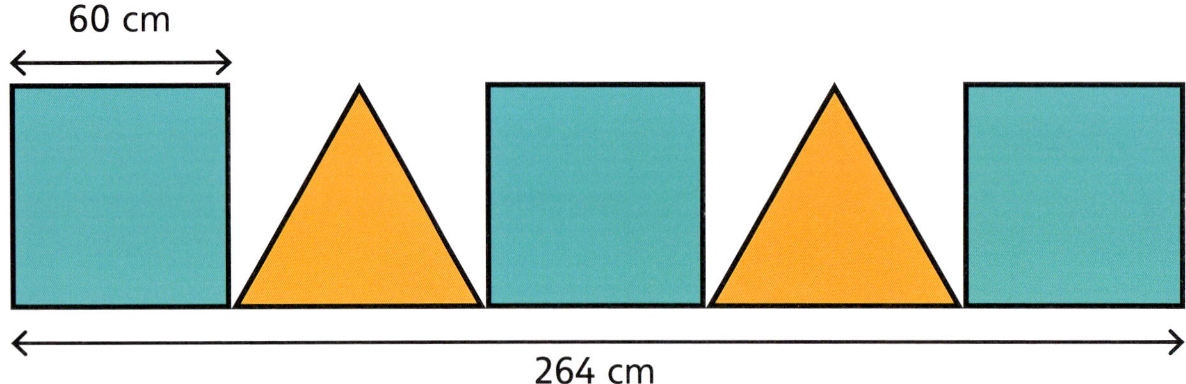

What is the length of the base of one triangle? What method will you use to calculate this?

7 A school is raising money to buy library books.

Complete the table to show the money collected.

	Class 1	Class 2	Class 3	Total
Cake sale	£27·50		£32·29	
Fun walk	£53·80	£45·20		£164
				£264·50

8 Jamie buys 800 g of fruit.

25% of the fruit are strawberries.

35% of the fruit are cherries.

The rest are raspberries.

How many grams of raspberries does Jamie buy? Show your method.

9 On a bookshelf, there are 3 picture books for every 2 story books.

Altogether, there are 12 story books.

How many books are on the shelf?

10 The clocks show the time that Max leaves home and the time he arrives at the swimming pool.

leaves home

pm

arrives at swimming pool

How long is Max's journey from home to the swimming pool?

→ Practice book 6C p87

Unit 15
Statistics

In this unit we will ...

- Learn to calculate the mean of a set of data
- Use the mean to find missing data
- Read and interpret pie charts using fractions
- Read and interpret pie charts using percentages
- Interpret and create line graphs

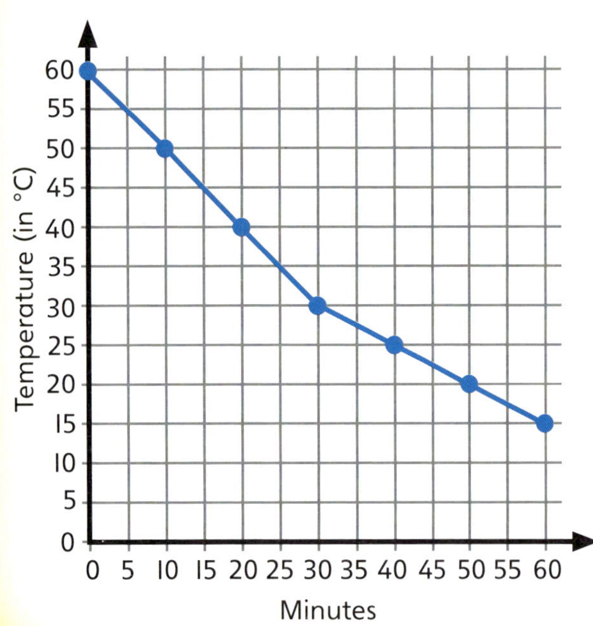

We will be interpreting line graphs.

Here is a line graph that shows the temperature of a hot chocolate drink that was left to cool.

What was the temperature of the hot chocolate after ten minutes?

We will need some maths words.
Which ones do you recognise?

mean **average**

pie chart **segment** **line graph**

bar chart **percentage**

fraction **data**

We need to know that the angles around a point add up to 360°. Calculate the missing angle.

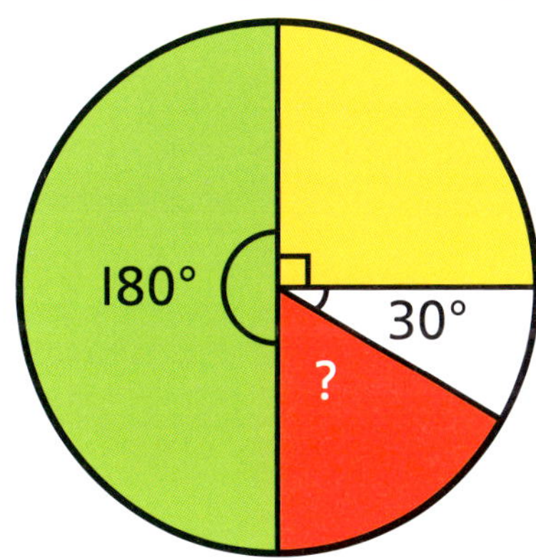

The mean 1

Discover

1 a) What is the average number of marshmallows on a stick?

b) The children find six more marshmallows in the packet.

What would be the average number on a stick now?

Share

a)

Lexi

Olivia

Kate

7 + 2 = 9

8 + 1 = 9

12 – 3 = 9

If every child had the same number of marshmallows, they would each have 9.

The mean is 9. The mean (average) number of marshmallows on a stick is 9.

b) Now there are 33 marshmallows in total.

Method 1

Share 33 marshmallows between the 3 children.

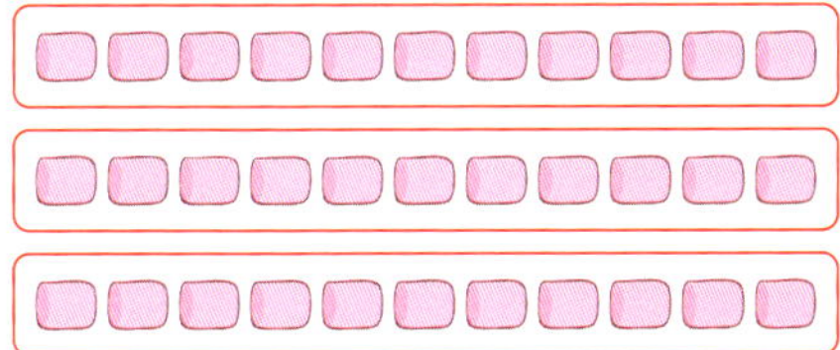

33 ÷ 3 = 11

Method 2

Share the extra 6 marshmallows between the 3 children. Each child gets 2 more.

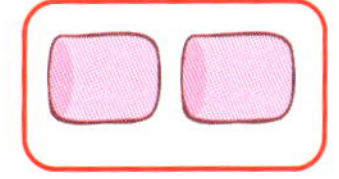
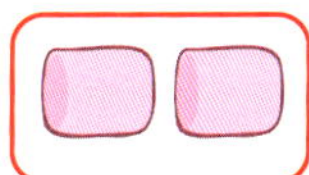
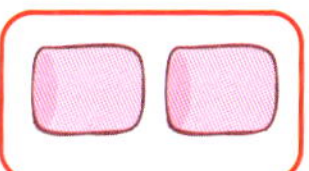

9 + 2 = 11

The mean (average) number of marshmallows on a stick would be 11.

Think together

1. Bella joins the other children. She has only 1 marshmallow.

   What is the mean number of marshmallows per child?

2. What is the mean number of cubes in each group of towers?

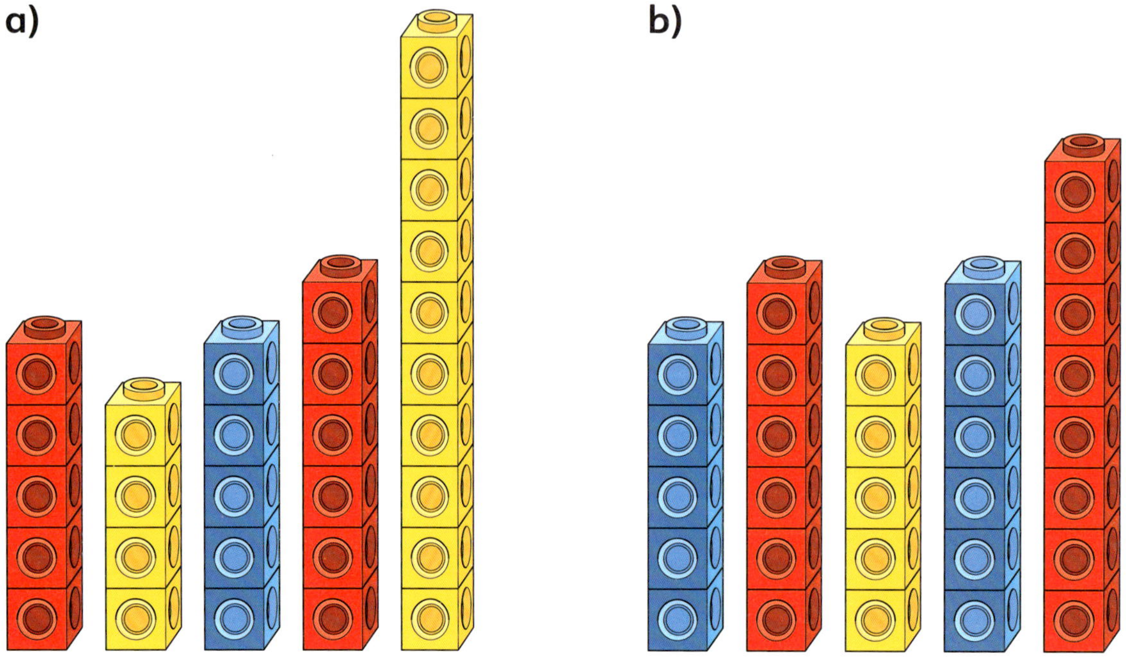

What do you notice? Can you explain?

3 Isla and Aki have found the mean of the numbers 8, 4 and 9.

a) Discuss the similarities and differences between their methods. Do they both work all the time?

I made towers and rearranged the cubes to make equal heights.

Aki

Each new tower is 7 cubes high.

The mean of 8, 4 and 9 is 7.

I worked out the total. I shared this into 3 equal groups because there were 3 numbers.

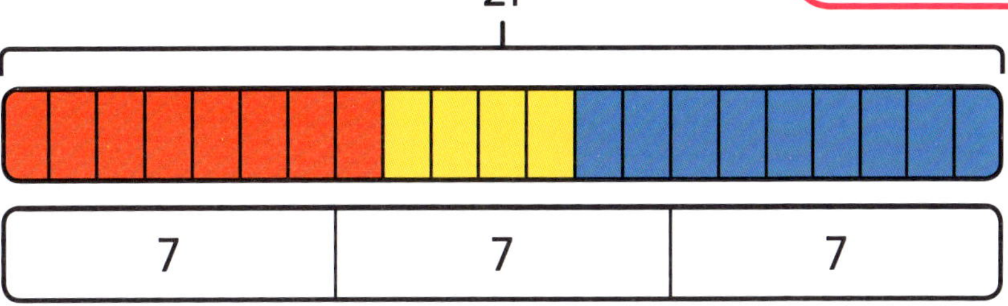

Isla

$8 + 4 + 9 = 21$

$21 \div 3 = 7$

The mean of 8, 4 and 9 is 7.

b) Which method would you use to find the mean height of these children? Why?

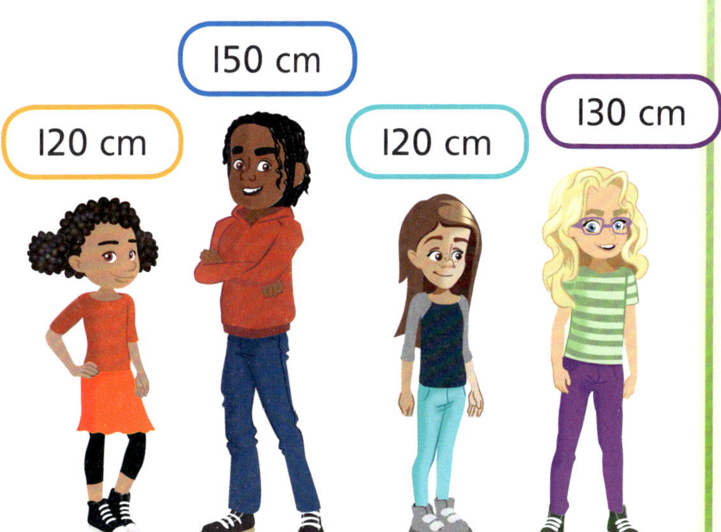

→ Practice book 6C p90

The mean 2

Discover

1 **a)** Who had the highest mean score?

b) What other ways could you compare the skaters' scores?

Share

a) The skaters received a different number of scores.

Ambika

Finding the mean is a useful way to compare groups of different sizes.

5 + 6 + 5 + 4 + 10 = 30

The total is 30, and the number of scores is 5.

30 ÷ 5 = 6

The mean score is 6.

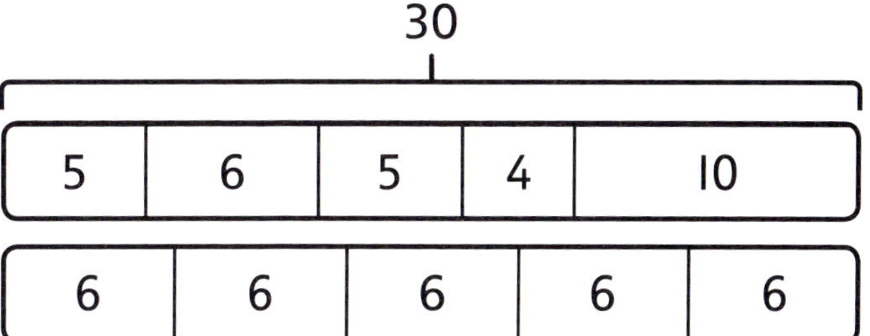

Jamie

6 + 8 + 6 + 6 = 26

The total is 26, and the number of scores is 4.

$26 \div 4 = 6\frac{2}{4} = 6{\cdot}5$

The mean score is 6·5.

26

6	8	6	6
6·5	6·5	6·5	6·5

I don't think the mean has to be a whole number.

Jamie had the highest mean score.

b) There are other ways to compare the scores.

Ambika received the highest mark, but also the lowest mark.	Jamie was more consistent. The judges all gave similar marks.
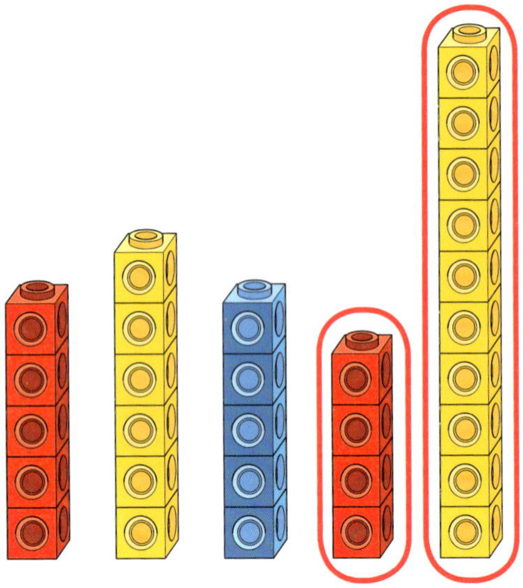	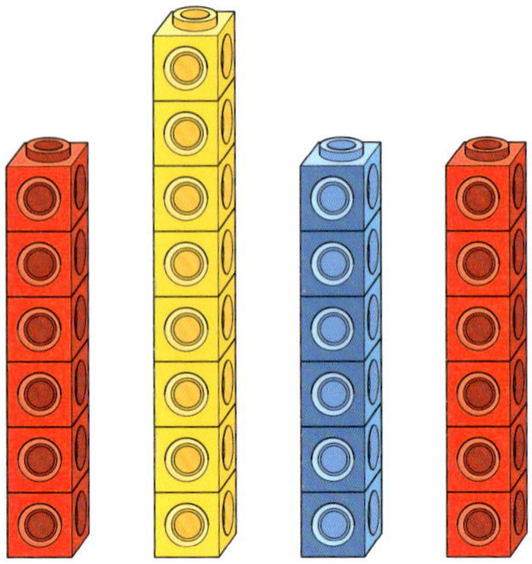
Ambika's most common mark was 5. 5 6 5 4 10	Jamie's most common mark was 6. 6 8 6 6

Think together

1 Compare the mean scores of these skaters.

Aki				Lee					
6	7	7	8	6	4	7	8	2	6

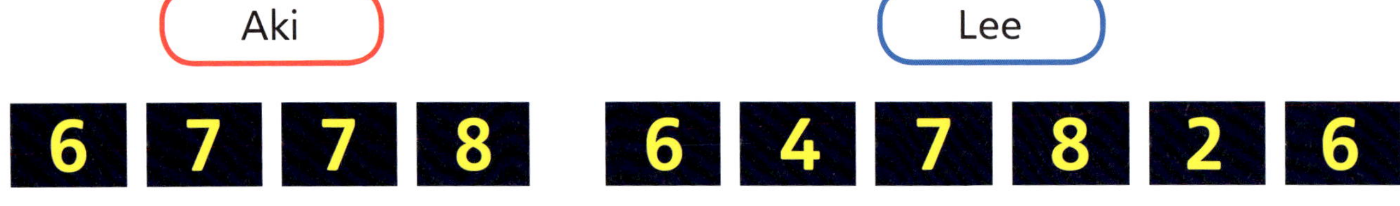

2 What is the mean height of each athlete's jumps?

	Emma	Lee	Luis
Jump 1	1·4 m	1·55 m	2 m
Jump 2	2·1 m	1·1 m	1·2 m
Jump 3	1 m	1·1 m	No jump due to injury

3 Find the mean of each set of numbers. Explain what you notice.

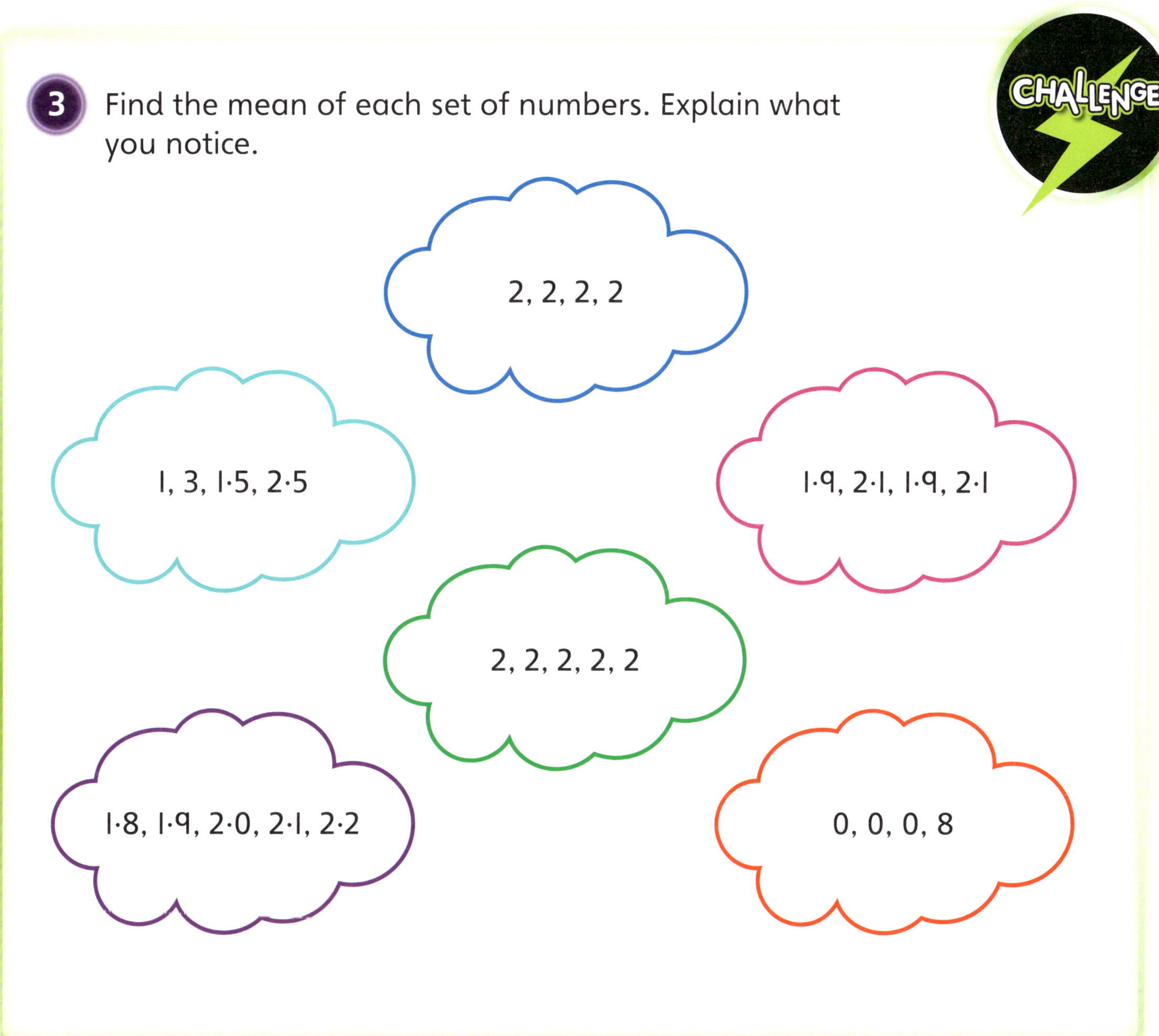

→ Practice book 6C p93

The mean 3

Discover

1 **a)** What is the length of the fifth snake?

b) One more corn snake is born. The mean length increases by 1 cm.

What is the length of the new snake?

Share

a) There are 5 snakes in total, with a mean length of 20 cm.

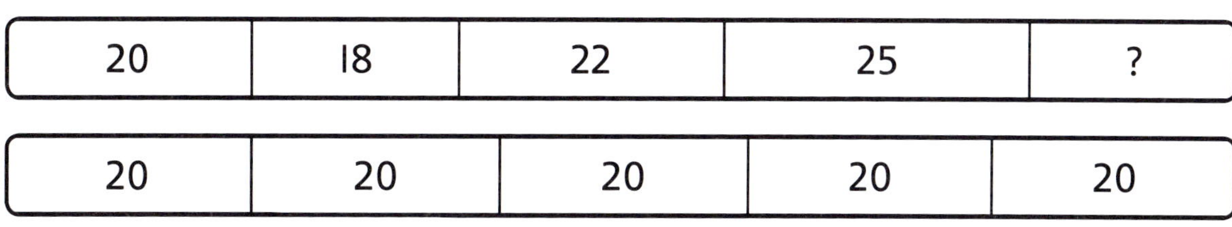

20	18	22	25	?
20	20	20	20	20

$20 + 18 + 22 + 25 + ? = 20 \times 5$

$85 + ? = 100$

The fifth snake must be 15 cm long.

b) Now there are 6 snakes.

If the mean was still 20 cm, then the new snake would also be 20 cm long.

The new mean is actually 21 cm, so there are 6 additional centimetres.

20	20	20	20	20	← 26 →
21	21	21	21	21	21

$6 \times 21 = 126$

$126 - 100 = 26$

The new snake is 26 cm long.

Think together

1 The mean height of six towers is 4. What is the height of the sixth tower?

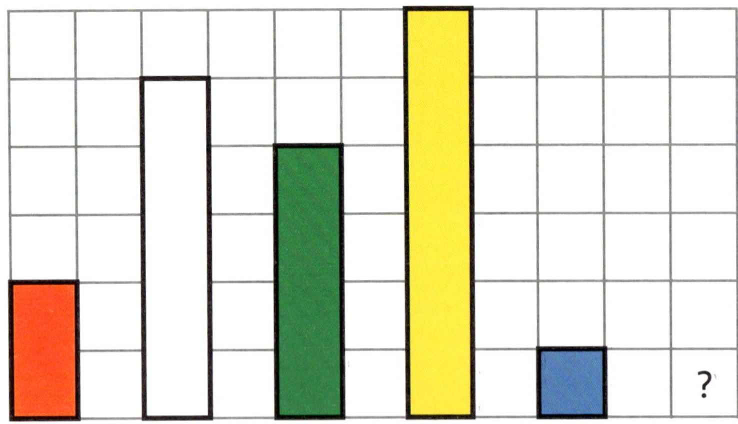

2 The mean weight of these adult snakes is 1·5 kg. What is the weight of the last snake?

1·1 kg	1·7 kg	2·1 kg	? kg

Four people are thinking of numbers. What are the numbers?

I am thinking of three numbers. The mean is 11.

I wonder whether there is more than one solution.

I will choose one number to be 11, and then pick two other numbers to balance the mean.

I am thinking of five numbers. The mean is 10.

I am thinking of five numbers. The mean is 10, but none of the numbers is 10.

I am thinking of four numbers. The difference between the biggest and the smallest number is 4. The mean is 10.

→ Practice book 6C p96

Introducing pie charts

Discover

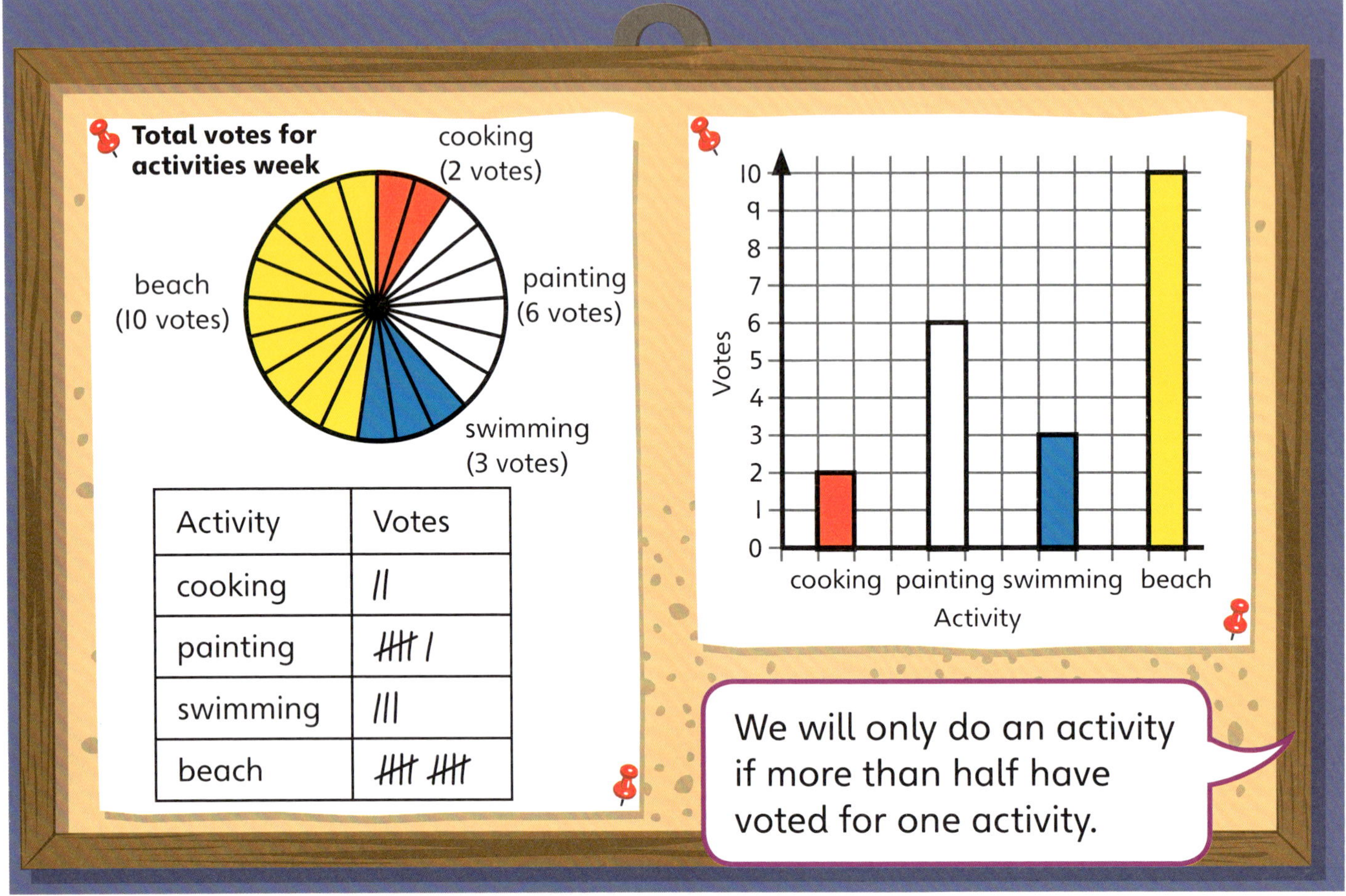

Activity	Votes
cooking	//
painting	卌 /
swimming	///
beach	卌 卌

1 **a)** Which chart shows the most clearly whether an activity received more than half the votes?

b) Compare the three ways of presenting the results.

What are the advantages and disadvantages of each chart?

Share

The pie chart is split into **segments** to show how each part fits into the whole. The whole circle represents **all** the results.

a) This type of chart is called a **pie chart**.

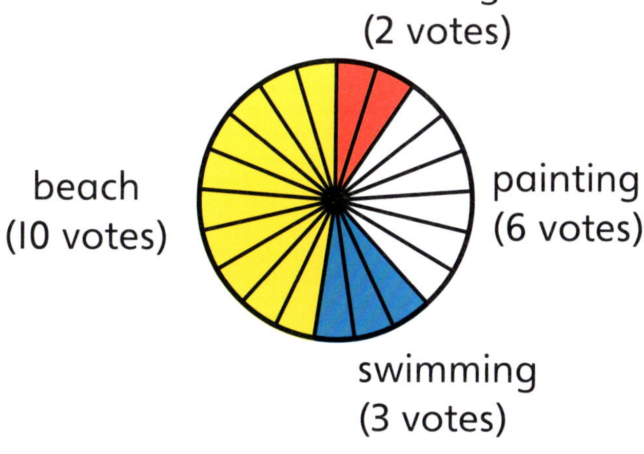

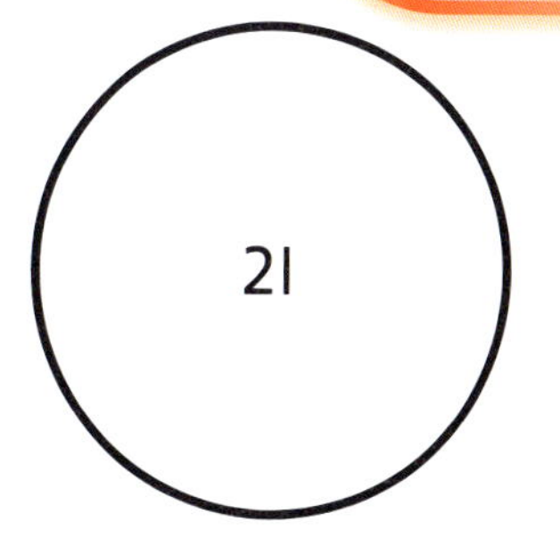

The pie chart shows the most clearly that no activity received half the votes.

b) Each type of chart shows the same information, but presents it differently.

	Tally chart	Bar chart	Pie chart
Advantages	Can fill it in while you collect data. Easy to draw Easy to see 5s	Easy to compare which is most and least. Can use the scale to work out how much more or less.	Very easy to compare the parts with the whole.
Disadvantages	Have to count to compare. Does not show the whole clearly.	Does not show the whole clearly.	Not always easy to compare the parts. Can be difficult to draw accurately.

Think together

1 Which section of the pie chart represents each activity?

cricket	|||
cycling	卌 |||
swimming	||
football	卌 卌 ||||

Tally chart

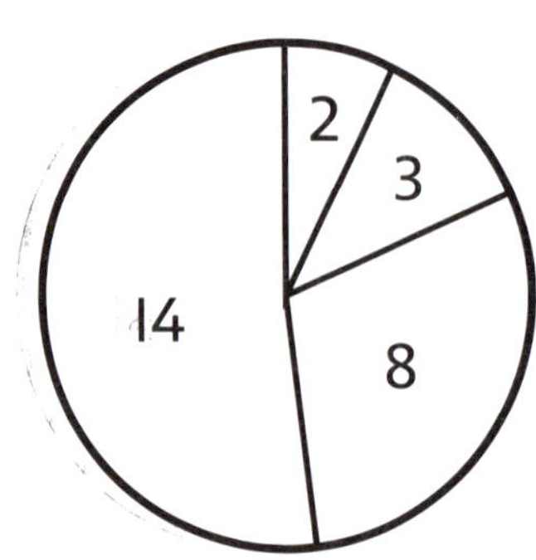

Pie chart

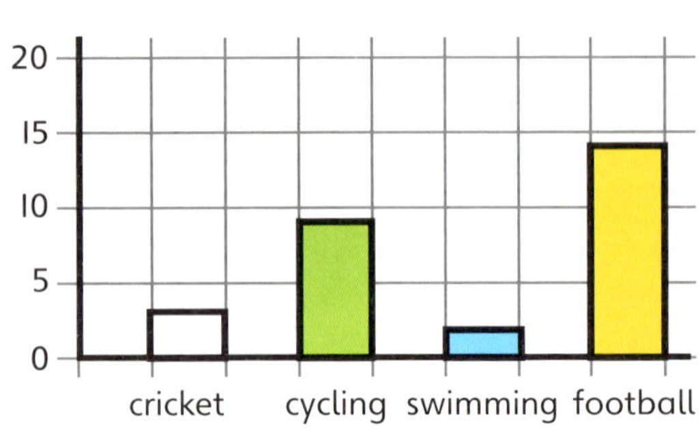

Bar chart

2 Below are three charts showing the medals that the British team won at the Olympic Games in 2016. Choose a chart to answer each question.

gold	卌 卌 卌 卌 卌 ||
silver	卌 卌 卌 卌 |||
bronze	卌 卌 卌 ||

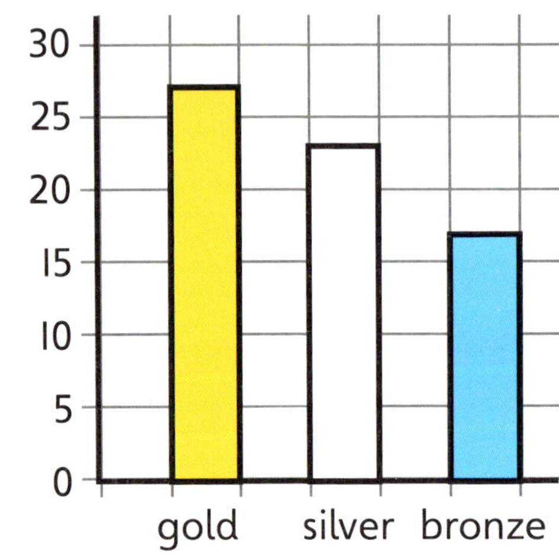

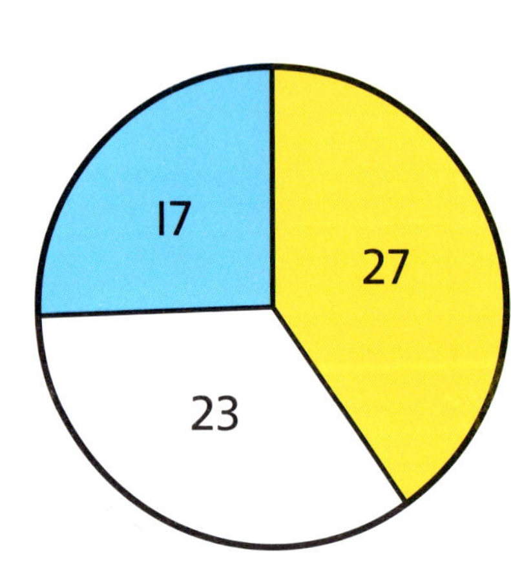

a) How many more gold medals than silver medals did the team win?

b) Which colour medal was approximately a quarter of the total?

c) How many medals were won in total?

3 Max spins a spinner 30 times and records the results in a tally chart.

Animal	Frequency
cat	~~||||~~ ~~||||~~ ||||
bird	~~||||~~ ~~||||~~ |
fish	~~||||~~

Which pie chart most closely matches the results?

A

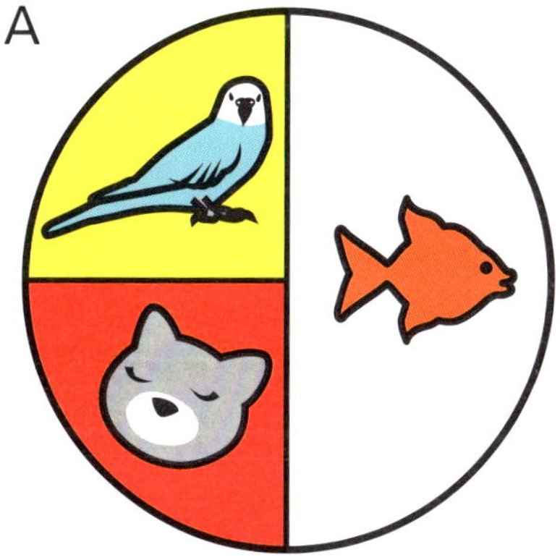

B

C

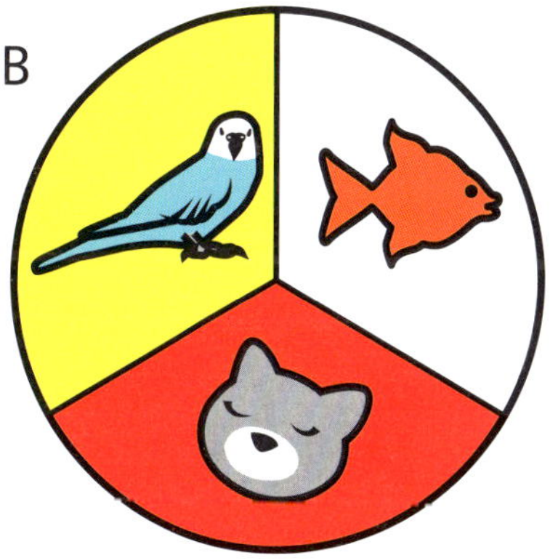

D

I will try to explain why the other pie charts do not match the results.

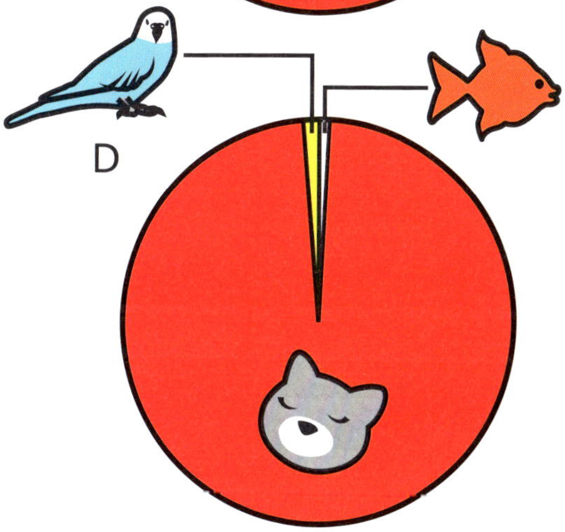

→ Practice book 6C p99

Reading and interpreting pie charts

Discover

1 **a)** How could you represent the children at the fancy dress party with a pie chart?

b) One superhero, one cat and two pirates leave early. What would the pie chart look like now?

What is the same and what is different about the two pie charts?

Share

a)

Costume	Number
superhero	𝍸
princess	|
cat	|||
pirate	|||

I will use the pie chart to represent the different types of costume shown on this tally chart.

The pie must be divided into 12 equal segments. Each segment represents one child.

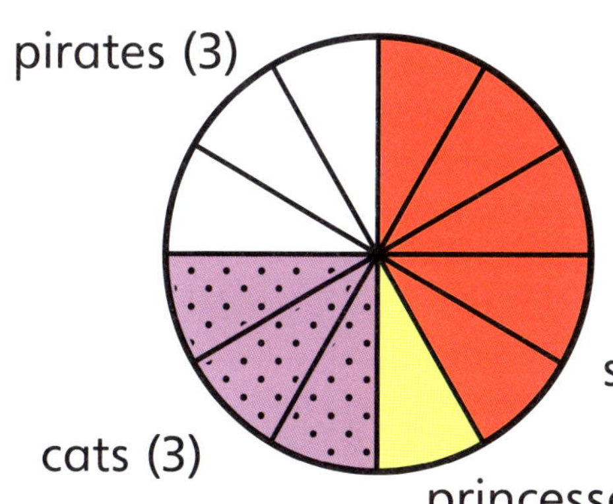

There are 5 superhero segments, because there are 5 superheroes.

b) Now there are only 8 children left at the party, so there will only be 8 segments in the pie chart.

Each segment now takes up more of the chart.

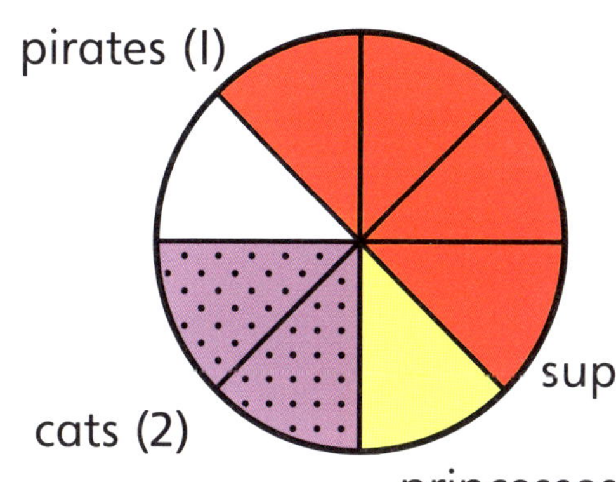

I noticed that the section for cat costumes is the same size on both pie charts. I wonder why.

Think together

1 Some children have voted for their favourite party games. Each segment represents one child.

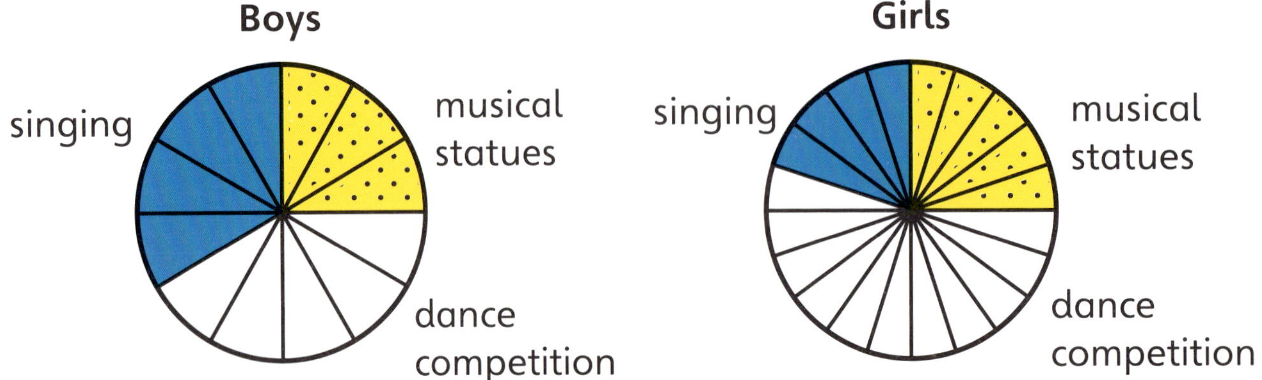

Look at the information in the pie charts then read the statements below. Do you agree with the statements?

Singing is more popular amongst boys than girls.

The same number of boys and girls like musical statues.

2 Before a party, some children voted for their favourite type of music.

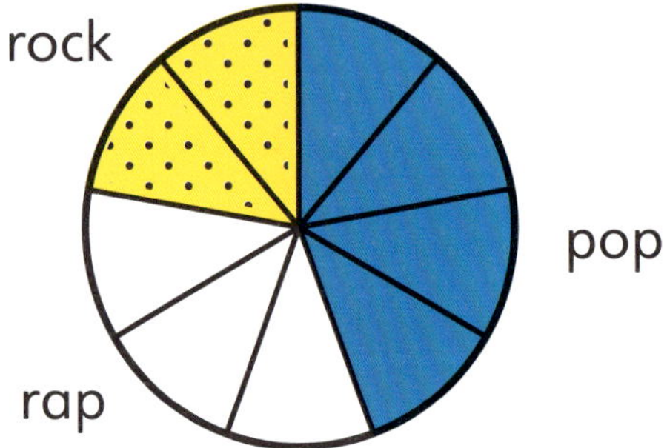

At the party four more children voted.

What did these children vote?

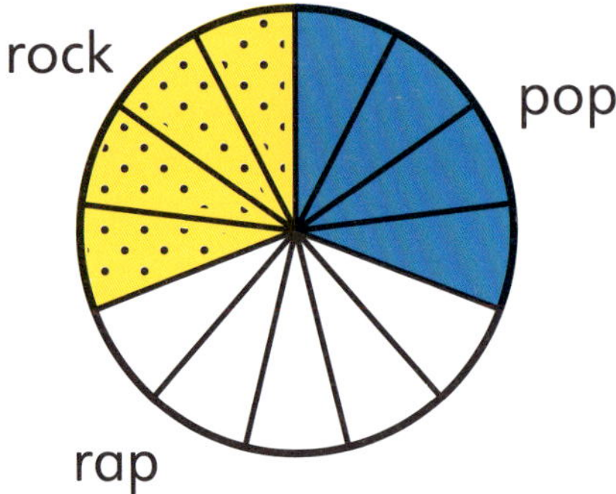

3 24 people entered a talent show. The pie chart shows what they performed.

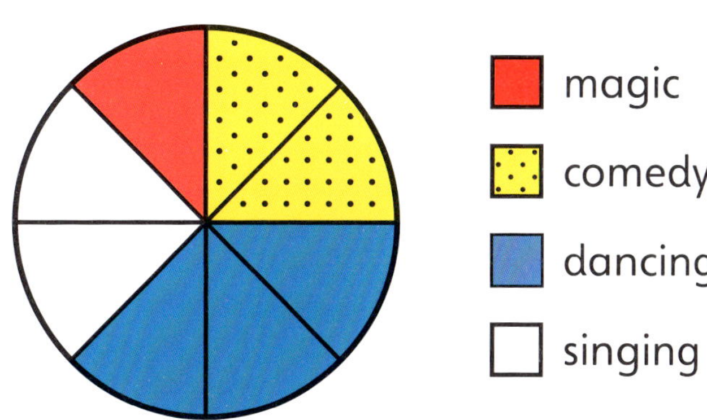

a) How many more people danced than performed magic?

How many people did not sing?

b) Here is a chart showing the information for a different talent show.

Sketch a pie chart that you could use to represent this information.

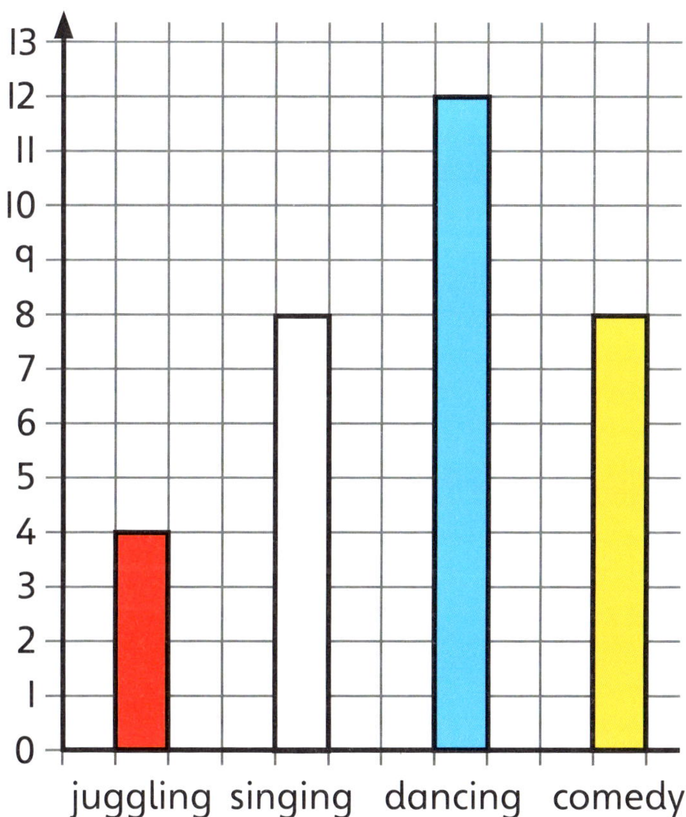

I will see if I can use each segment in my pie chart to represent more than one person.

→ Practice book 6C p102

Fractions and pie charts 1

Discover

1 a) For what fraction of the day does Emily sleep?

b) Max says: 'I think she spends $\frac{1}{3}$ of each day just eating!'

Is he correct?

Share

a) There are 24 segments in the pie chart. Each segment represents one hour out of 24.

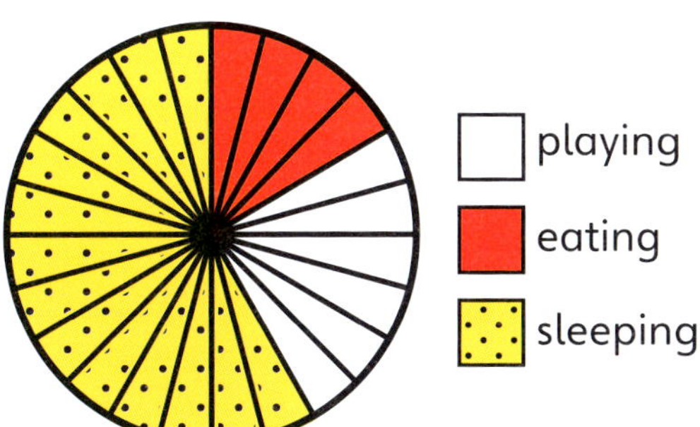

14 segments out of 24 are dotted.

$\frac{14}{24} = \frac{7}{12}$

Emily sleeps for $\frac{7}{12}$ of each day.

b) 24 divided by 3 is 8.

So $\frac{1}{3}$ of the chart would be 8 segments out of 24.

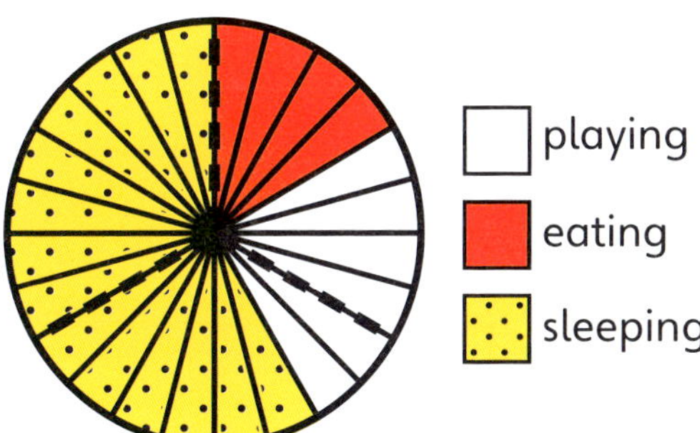

Max is not correct. Emily spends $\frac{4}{24}$ of the day eating.

$\frac{4}{24} = \frac{1}{6}$

Think together

1 Emily is now 2 years old. The pie chart shows how her day is divided. Complete the information.

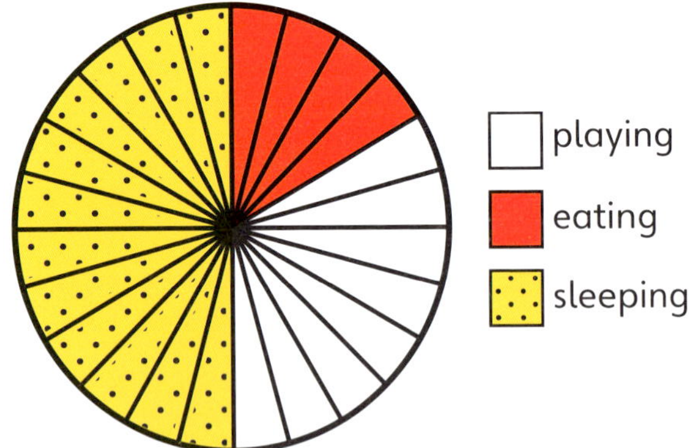

$\frac{1}{2}$ of Emily's time is spent ______________ .

______________ of Emily's time is spent eating.

______________ of Emily's time is spent playing.

2 Emily is now 6 years old. The table shows how she spends her time. Discuss how you would fill in the pie chart and fraction statements based on this information.

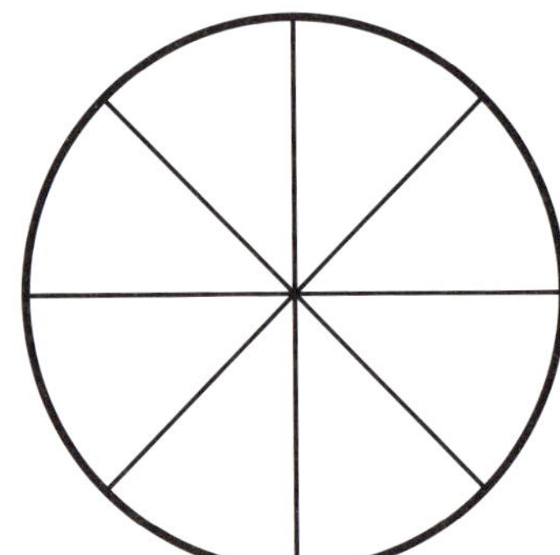

Sleeping	Eating	Playing	School
9 hours	3 hours	6 hours	6 hours

$\frac{1}{8}$ of Emily's time is spent ______________ .

$\frac{3}{8}$ of her time is spent ______________ .

$\frac{1}{4}$ of her time is spent ______________ .

3 **a)** 80 adults were asked what they do when a computer stops working.

Estimate the fractions for each action.

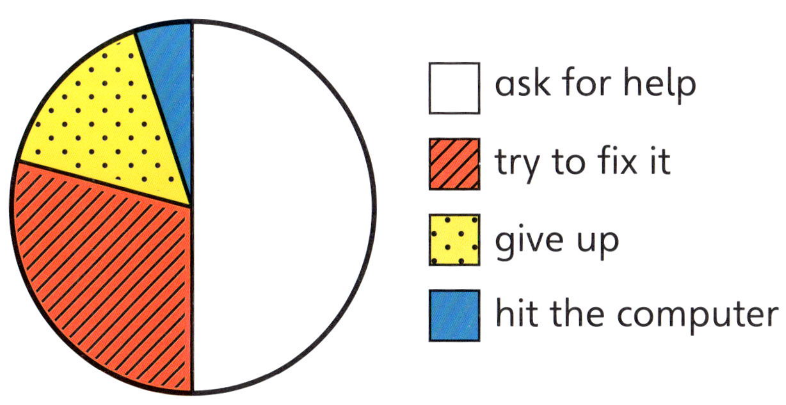

I will check that my fractions add up to 1.

What other information can you get from the pie chart?

b) This pie chart shows how 30 children answered the question.

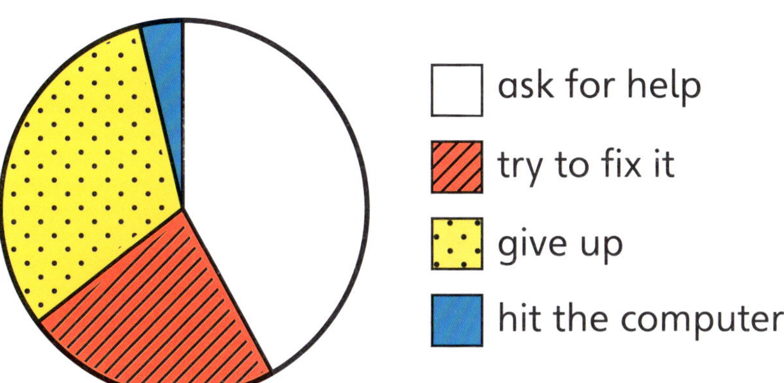

More children than adults said they would give up. Do you agree?

→ Practice book 6C p105

Fractions and pie charts 2

Discover

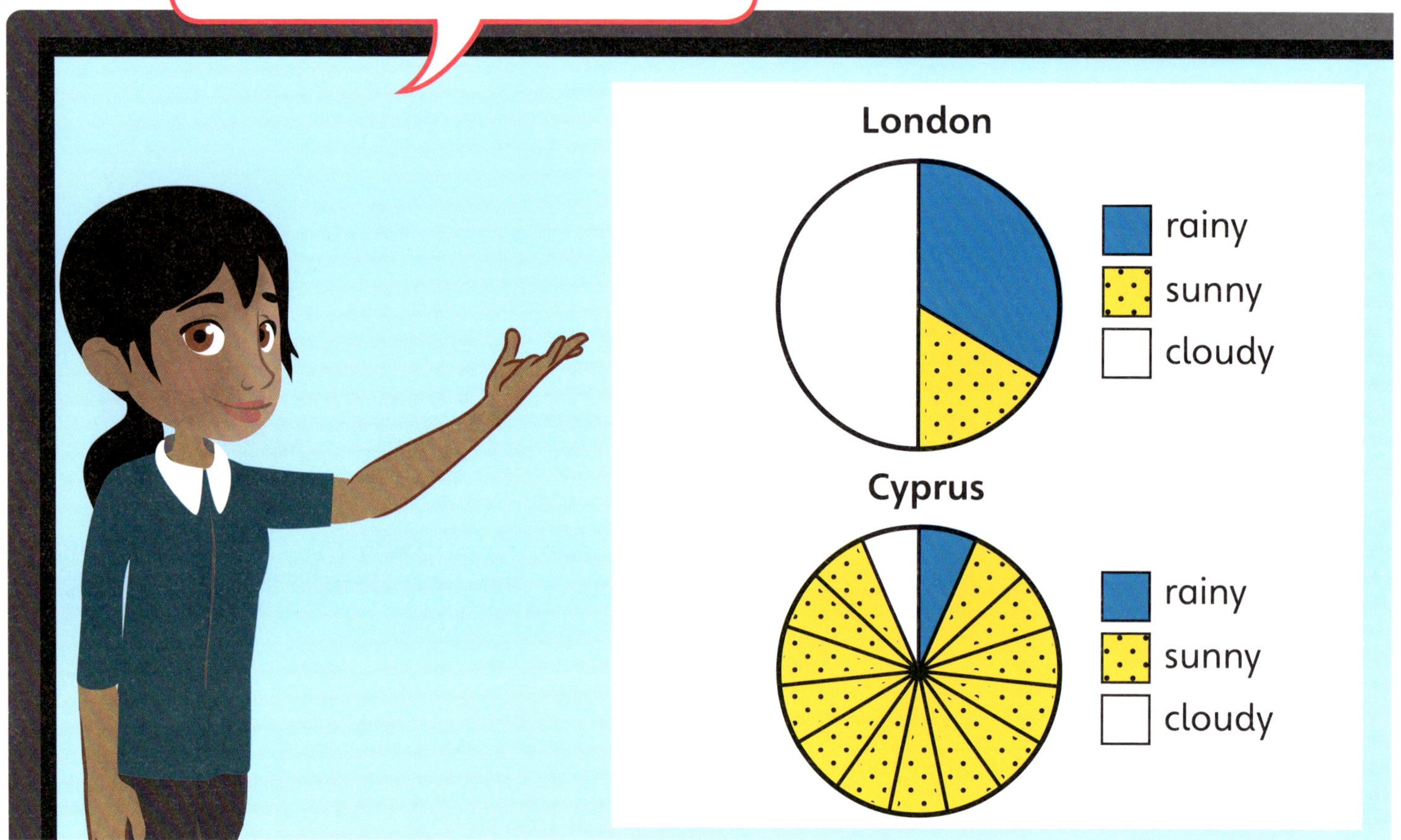

1 a) In London $\frac{1}{3}$ of the month of April was rainy.

How many days were sunny?

b) How many sunny days were there in Cyprus in April?

Share

a) There are 30 days in April.

Method 1

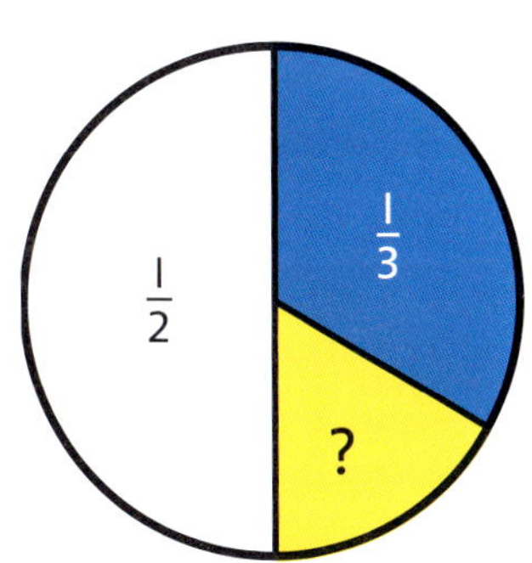

I found the remaining days.

$\frac{1}{3}$ of the days are rainy.

$\frac{1}{3}$ of 30 is 10.

$\frac{1}{2}$ of the days are cloudy.

$\frac{1}{2}$ of 30 is 15.

30 – 10 – 15 = 5.

So there were 5 sunny days.

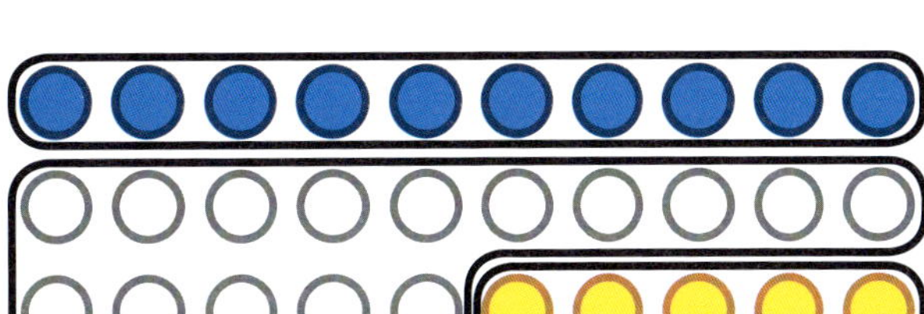

Method 2

I found the remaining fraction.

$\frac{1}{2} + \frac{1}{3} + ? = 1$

$\frac{3}{6} + \frac{2}{6} + ? = 1$

$\frac{1}{2}$	$\frac{1}{3}$	?

$\frac{1}{6}$ of the days are sunny.

$\frac{1}{6}$ of 30 is 5.

b) There are 15 segments in the pie chart.

$\frac{2}{15}$ of the days were not sunny.

$\frac{1}{15}$ of 30 = 30 ÷ 15 = 2

$\frac{2}{15}$ of 30 = 2 × 2 = 4

4 out of 30 days were not sunny.

So 26 days were sunny.

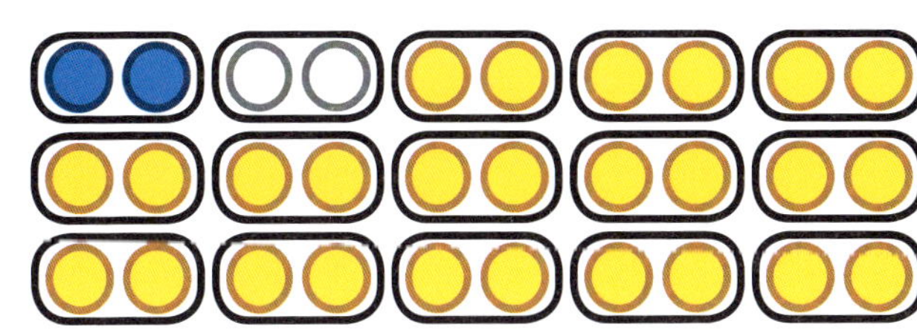

Think together

1 Max has been finding out the favourite food of the class. 4 more children like strawberries than like popcorn. Complete the statements.

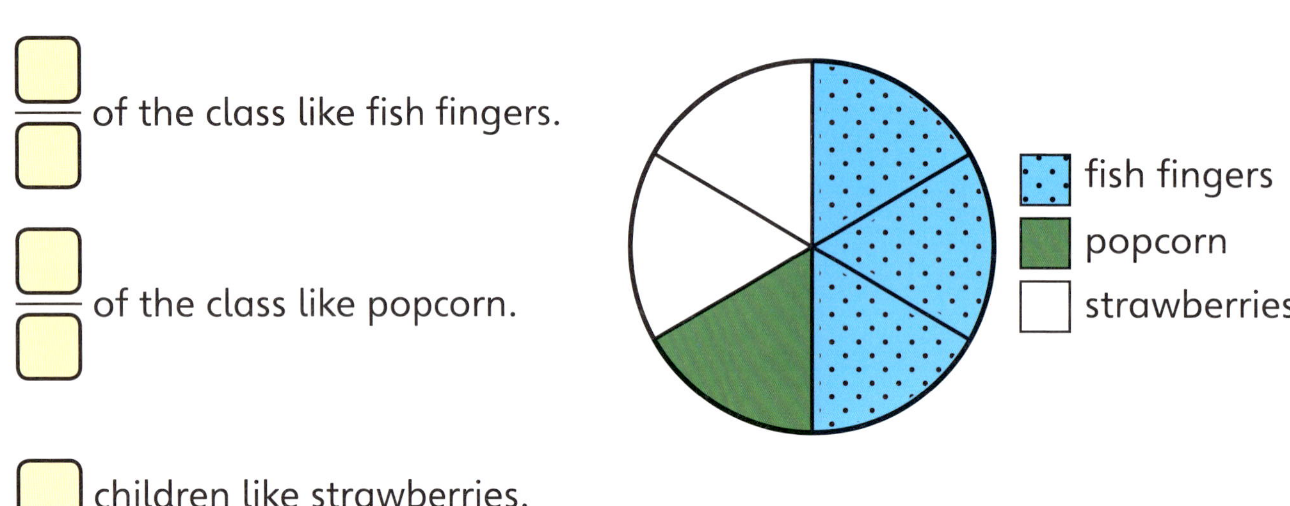

2 Isla investigated which school holiday was the favourite in the school. 45 children said the summer holidays. How many children said Christmas?

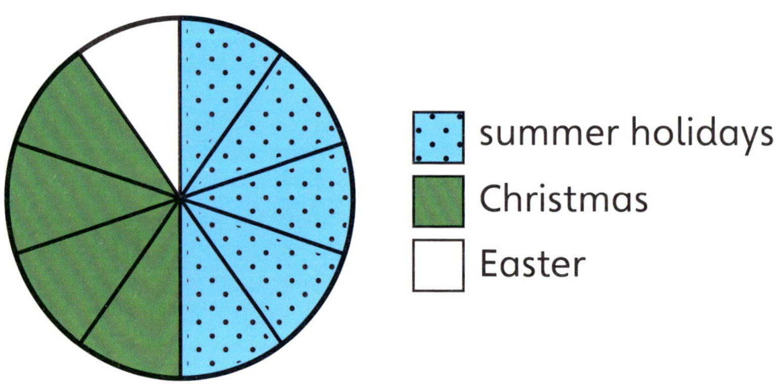

3 a) Classes 5 and 6 collected waste to recycle.

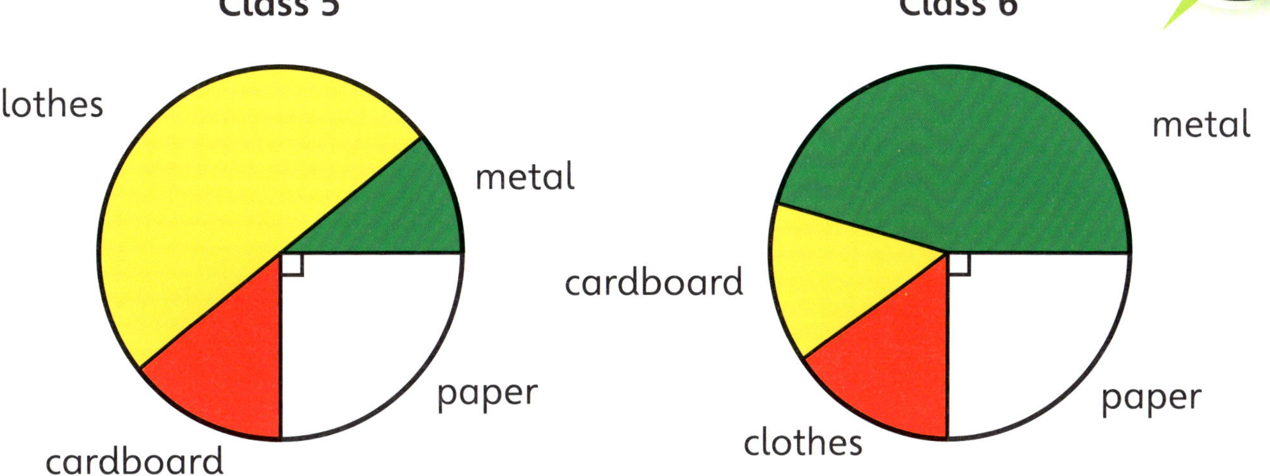

Class 5 collected 20 kg of waste in total.
Class 6 collected 10 kg of metal.

Which class collected more paper?

One section has a right angle sign. I can use this to work out the exact fraction of that part.

b) Class 4 also collected waste.

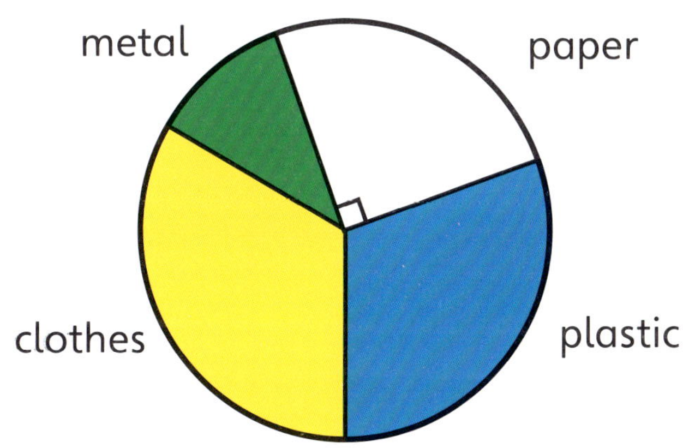

They collected 3·5 kg of metal. Estimate the weight of clothes.

→ Practice book 6C p108

Percentages and pie charts

Discover

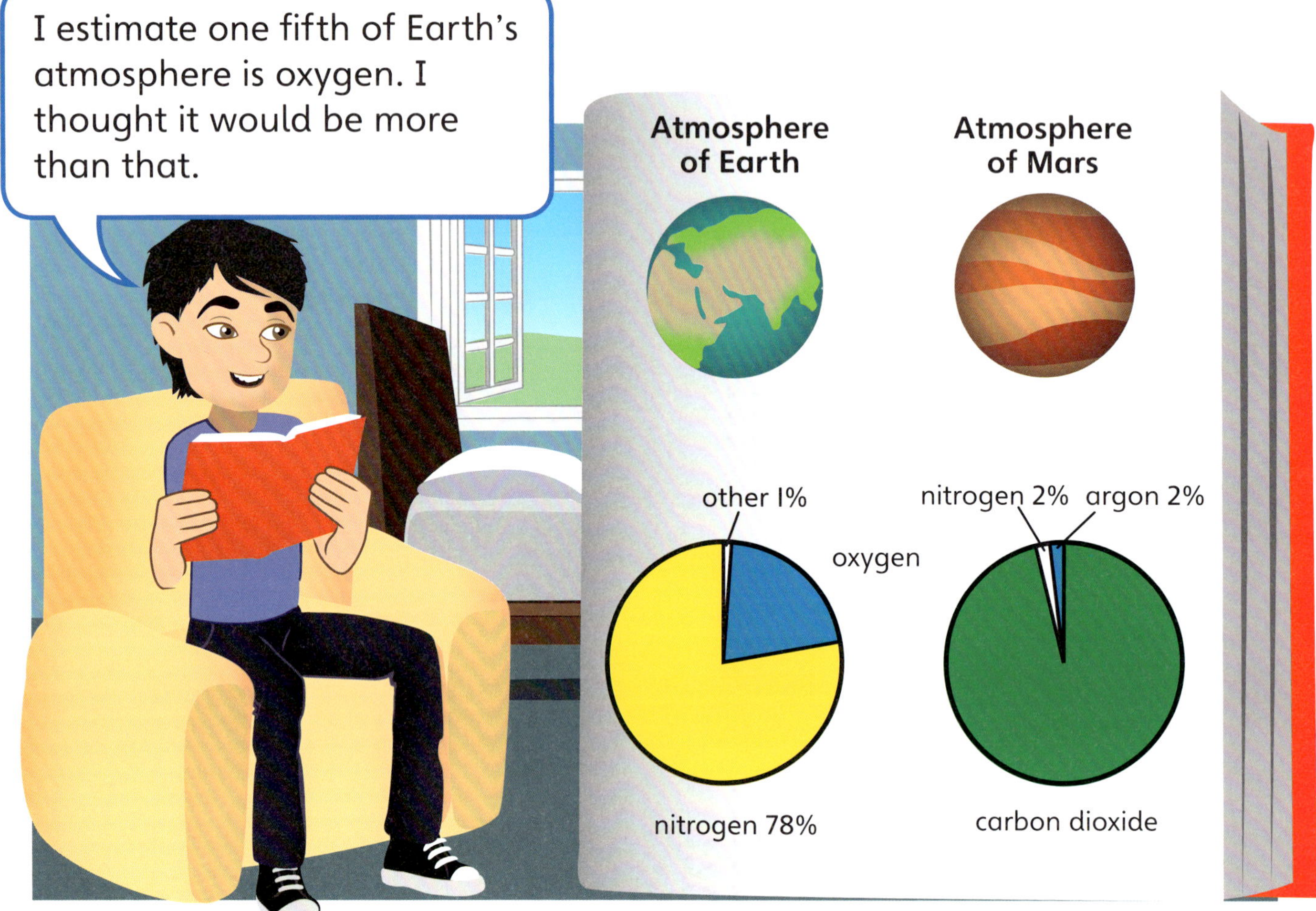

1 **a)** What fraction of the atmosphere of Mars is nitrogen, argon and carbon dioxide?

b) How accurate is Aki's estimate for Earth's atmosphere?

Share

a) 2% of the atmosphere of Mars is nitrogen and 2% is argon.

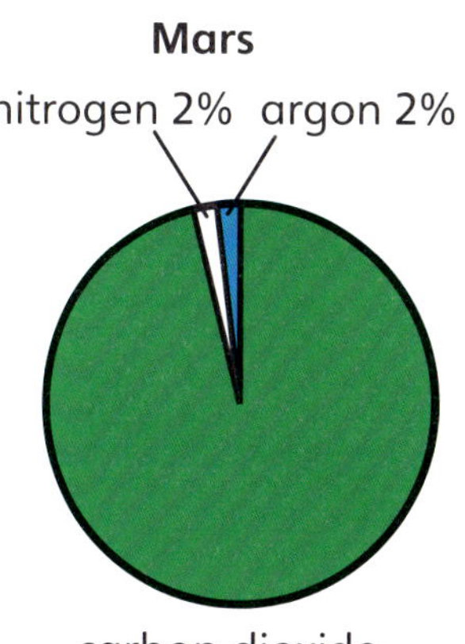

$2\% = \frac{2}{100} = \frac{1}{50}$

So $\frac{1}{50}$ of the atmosphere is argon and $\frac{1}{50}$ is nitrogen.

That means $\frac{48}{50}$ must be carbon dioxide.

$100\% - 2\% - 2\% = 96\%$

$96\% = \frac{96}{100} = \frac{48}{50} = \frac{24}{25}$

I checked using the percentages.

b) The whole pie chart represents 100%.

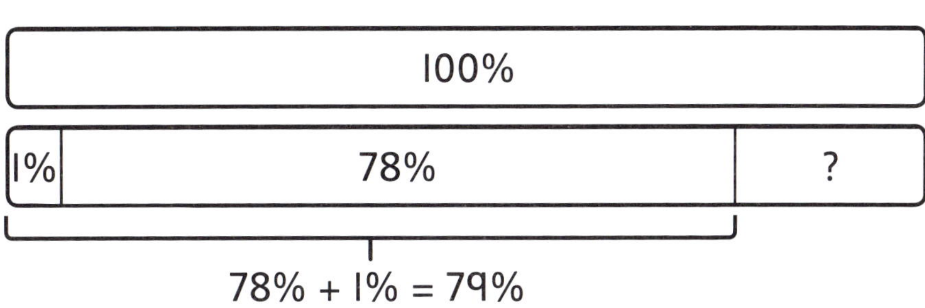

$100 - 79 = 21$

The section for oxygen must represent 21%.

Aki estimates $\frac{1}{5}$.

$\frac{1}{5} = \frac{20}{100} = 20\%$.

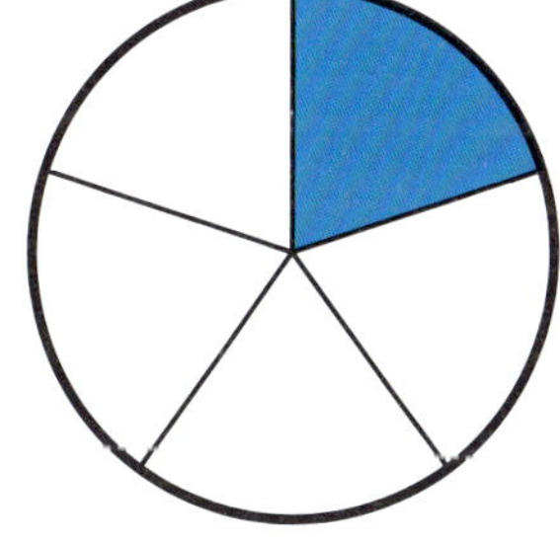

Aki's estimate is just 1% too small.

An estimate within 1% of the real value is very accurate.

Think together

1 This pie chart shows what percentage of Earth's surface is covered by the different features. What are the percentages shown for each section of the pie chart?

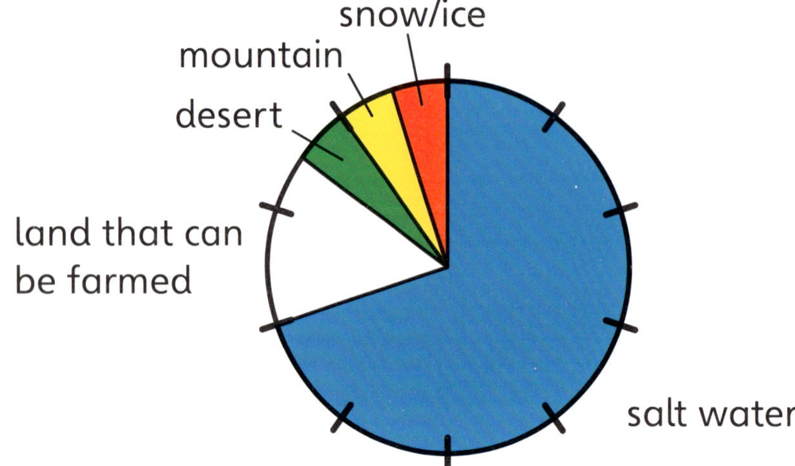

2 Andy produced this pie chart to show what he ate during the week.

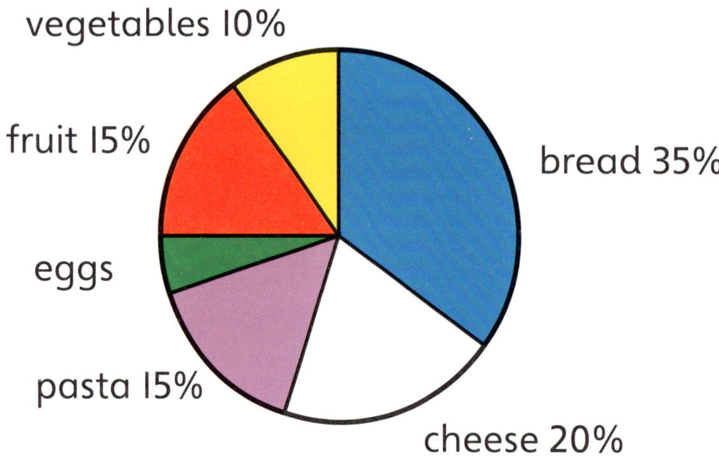

Which statements match the pie chart?

More than one third of his food was bread.

Out of every 250 g, 50 g was cheese.

$\frac{1}{3}$ of of his food was fruit and vegetables.

He ate three times as much pasta as eggs.

3 Some people were asked what exercise they liked doing best.

a) What percentage of the people preferred jogging?

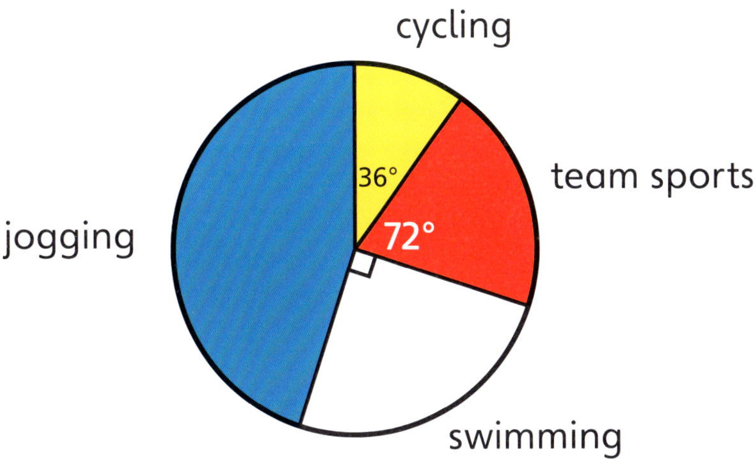

It looks like just less than half the people preferred jogging. I will guess 40%.

I think there is a way to use the angles to be exact. I know 100% would be 360°. So I can work out what 36° must be.

b) 240 people preferred swimming. How many liked team sports?

→ Practice book 6C p111

Interpreting line graphs

Discover

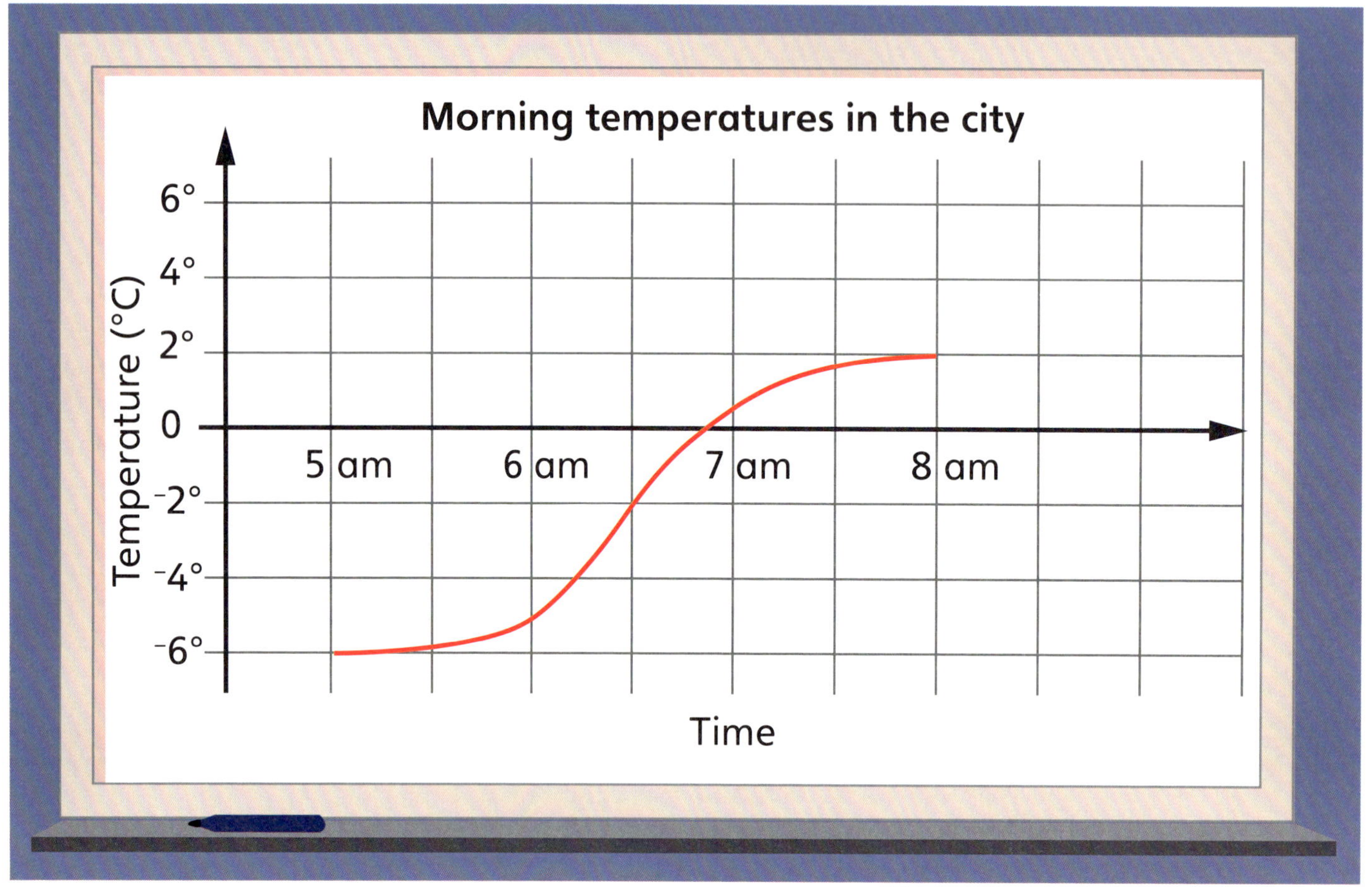

1 a) How much did the temperature increase between 6 am and 6:30 am?

b) Estimate at what time the temperature reached 1 °C.

Share

This graph shows temperatures above and below zero. There are values above and below the x-axis.

a)

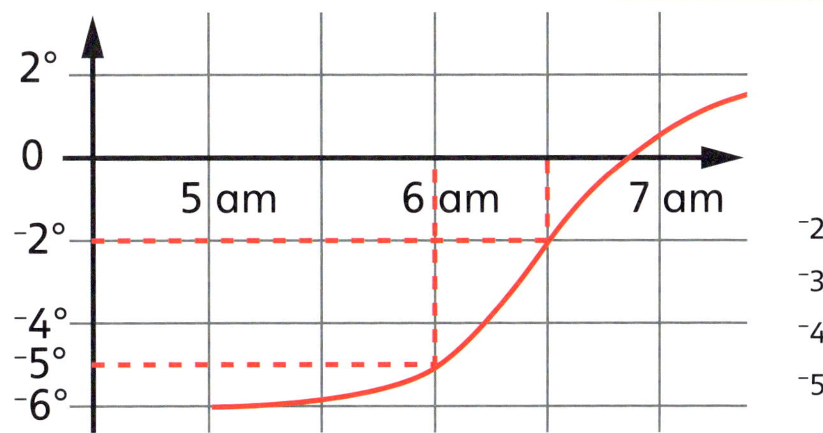

-2°
-3°
-4°
-5°

The temperature at 6 am was ⁻5 °C.

The temperature at 6:30 am was ⁻2 °C.

The temperature increased by 3 °C.

b)

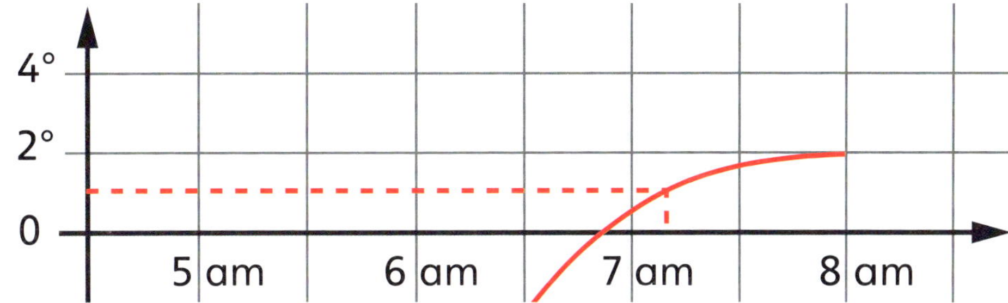

The temperature was 1 °C between 7 and 7:30 am.

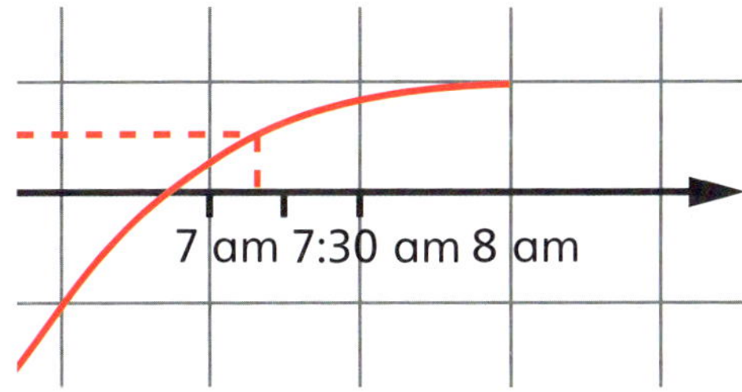

It was 1 °C just before 7:15 am. A reasonable estimate would be 7:10 am.

Think together

1 This graph shows the height at which a balloon floated between 13:00 and 17:00. How long did the balloon remain above 500 m?

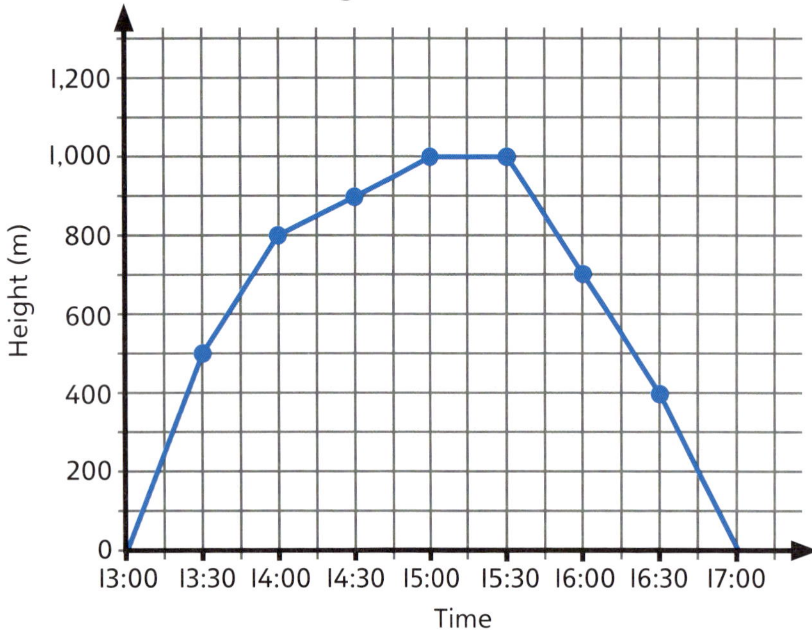

2 Below is a patient's temperature graph. Use the graph to complete the values in the table. Estimate the temperatures as accurately as you can.

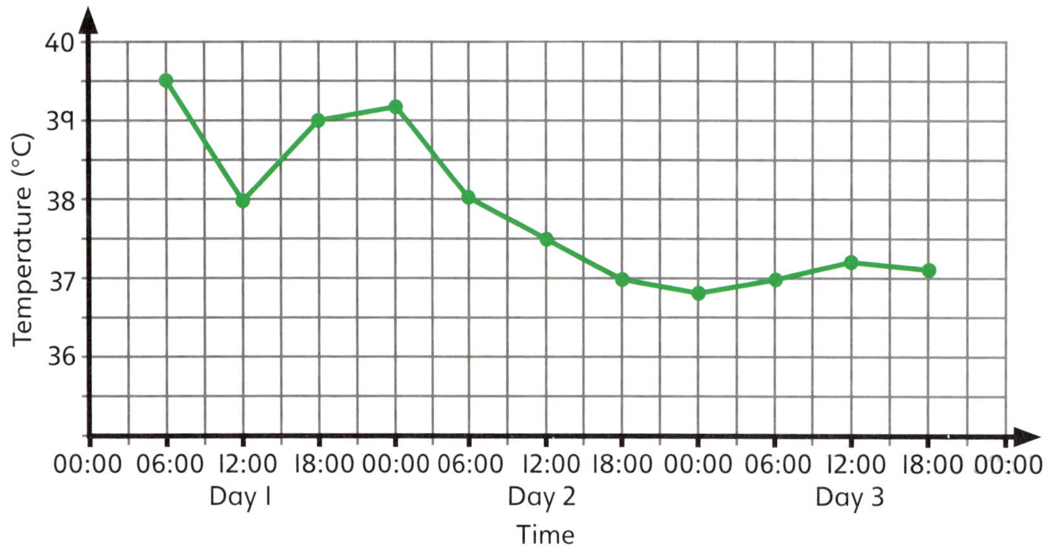

Time	9:00 – Day 1	9:00 – Day 2	9:00 – Day 3
Temperature			

CHALLENGE

3 **a)** This graph shows the distance Aki walks as he goes to the shop and then back home.

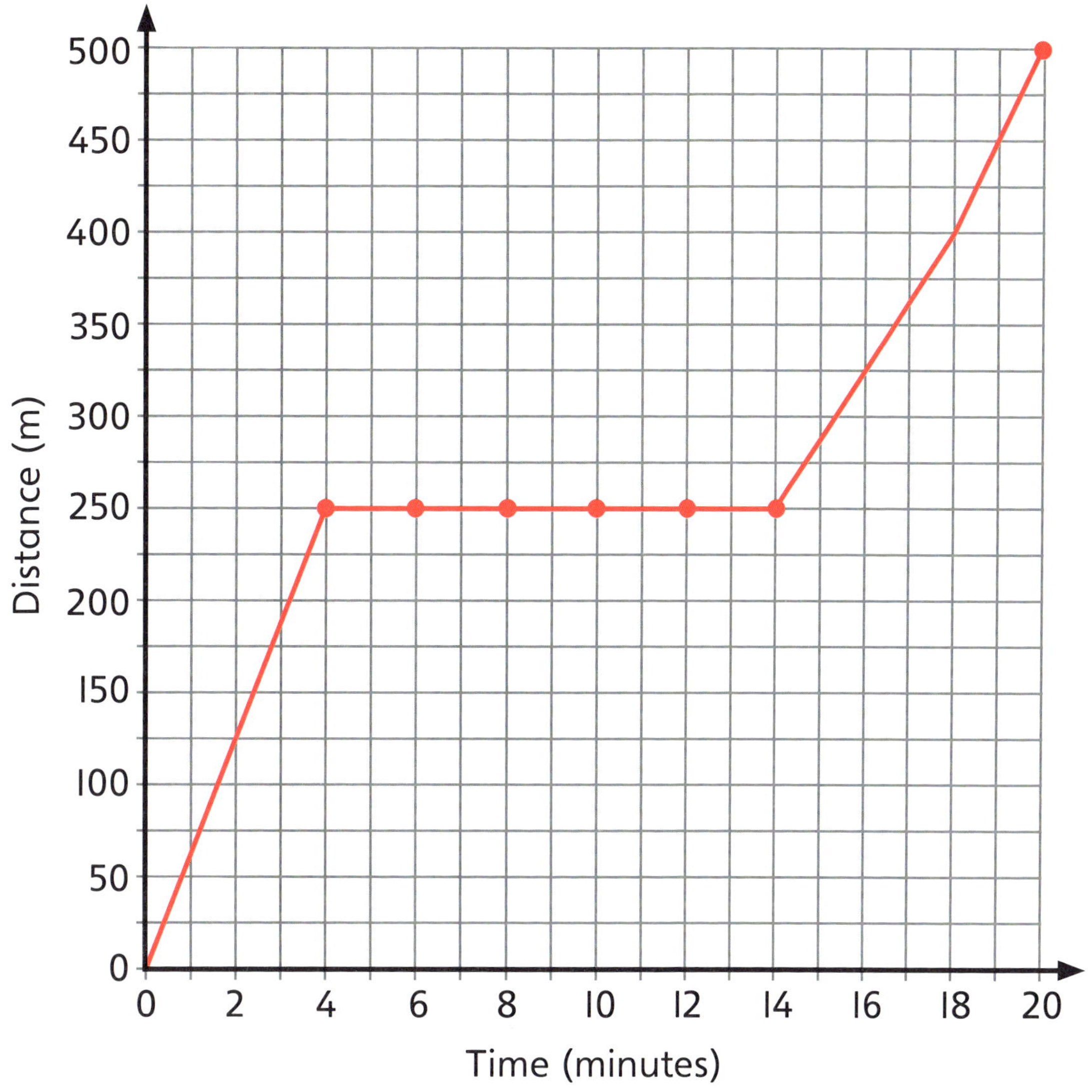

How long does it take Aki to reach the shop? How can you tell?

How long does Aki stay in the shop?

How far is the shop from his home?

b) Andy says: 'I think the graph is incorrect. The last part of the graph should return to 0 km by the end of his journey.'

Explain Andy's mistake.

→ Practice book 6C p114

Constructing line graphs

Discover

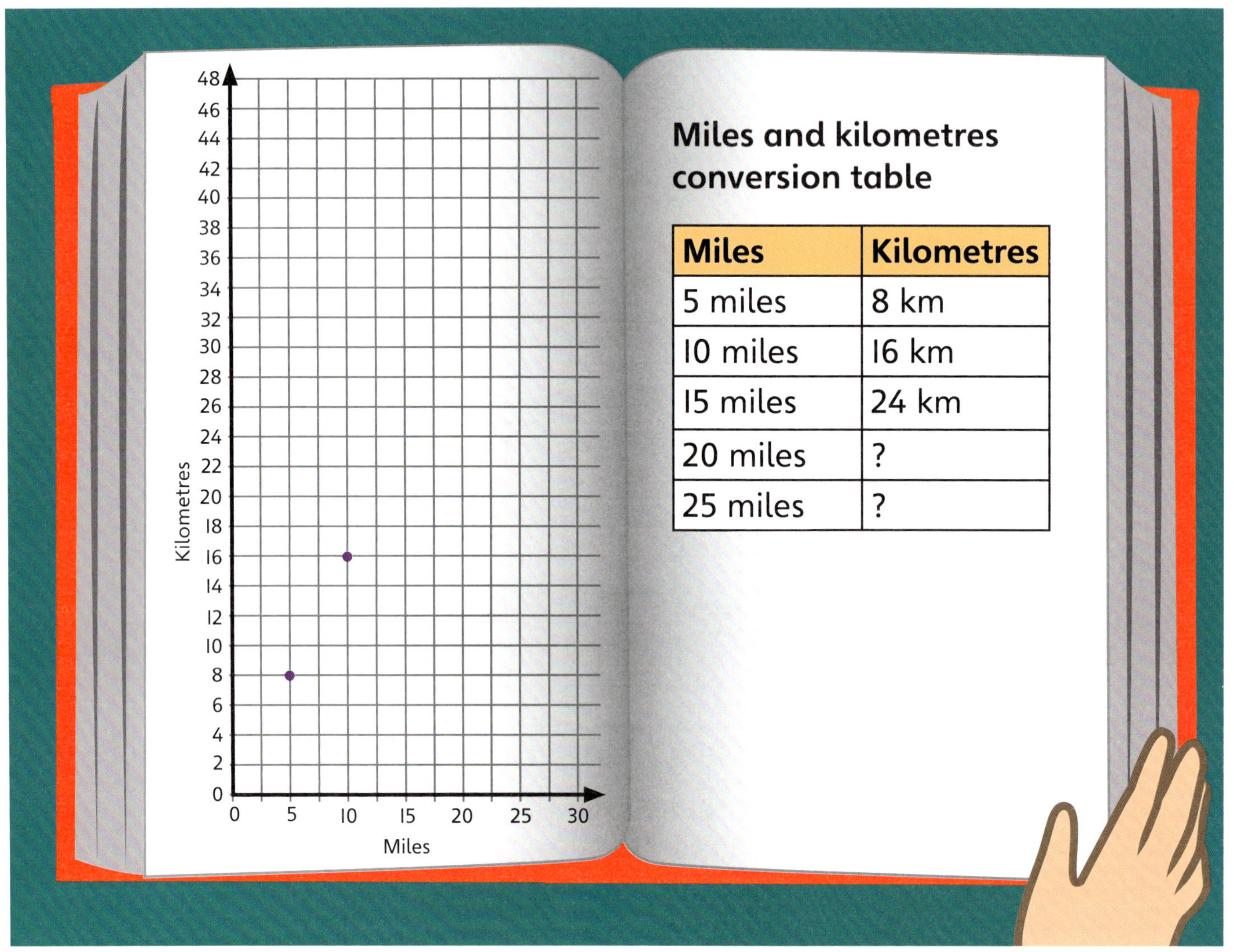

Miles and kilometres conversion table

Miles	Kilometres
5 miles	8 km
10 miles	16 km
15 miles	24 km
20 miles	?
25 miles	?

1 **a)** Show where the next points would go on the graph and complete the missing values in the table.

b) How many miles convert to 44 km?

Share

a) The next point on the graph shows that 15 miles convert to 24 km.

I noticed the points lie in a straight line.

Miles	Kilometres
5 miles	8 km
10 miles	16 km
15 miles	24 km
20 miles	32 km
25 miles	40 km

The graph converts miles and kilometres. It is a straight line because there are 5 miles for every 8 km.

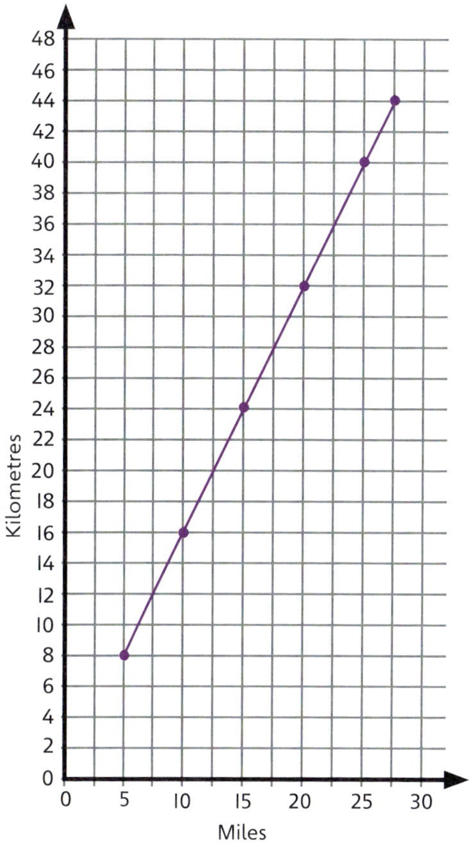

b) 44 km is halfway between 40 and 48 km.

27·5 miles is halfway between 25 and 30 miles.

So 27.5 miles convert to 44 km.

Miles	Kilometres
25 miles	40 km
27·5 miles	44 km
30 miles	48 km

Think together

1 This graph shows the conversion of miles and kilometres. Use the information on the graph to complete the conversions.

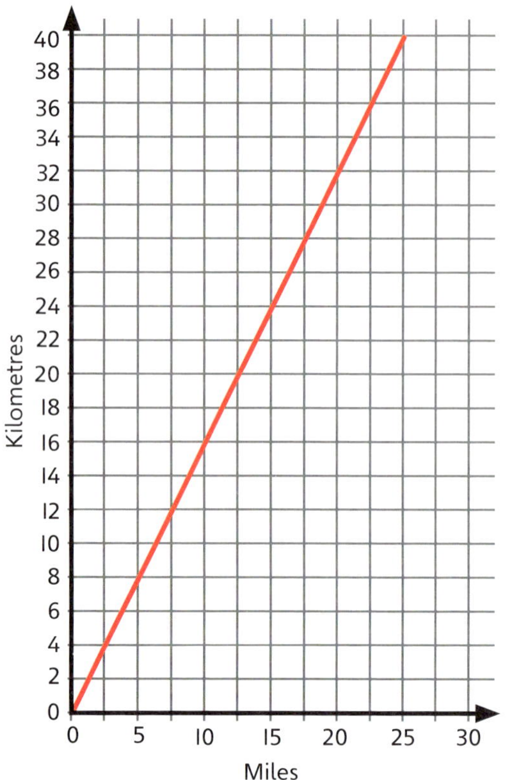

10 miles is equivalent to ☐ kilometres.

20 kilometres is equivalent to ☐ miles.

There are ☐ metres in one mile.

2 This graph shows the length of a shadow of a tree at different times of the day.

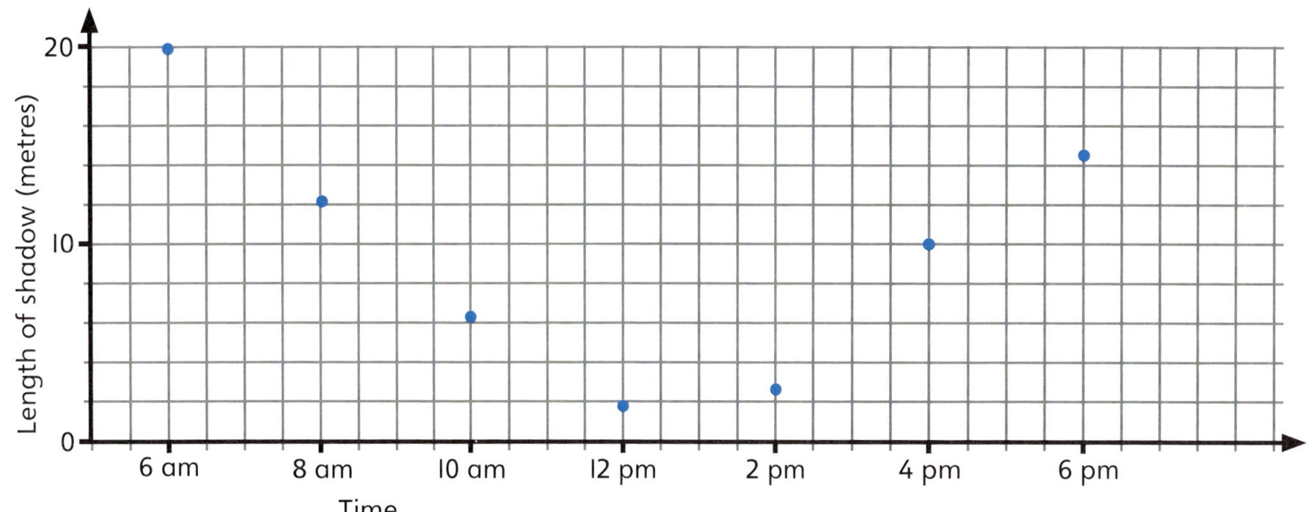

When was the shadow 10 m long?

Use this graph to predict the height of the shadow at 8 pm.

3 Use the figures in the table to draw a conversion line graph for inches to millimetres.

Inches and millimetres conversion table					
Inches	10	20	30		
Millimetres	254	508	762		

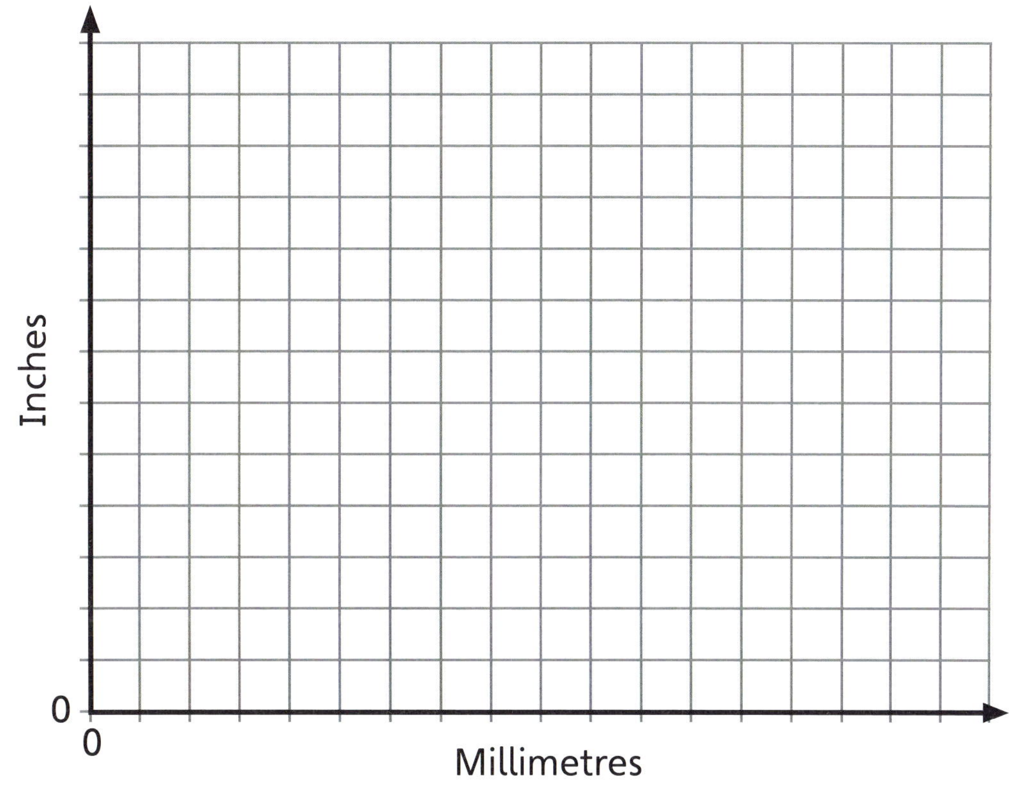

Use the graph to find the following approximate conversions.

25 inches = ☐ mm 1 m = ☐ inches

800 mm = ☐ inches 6 ft = ☐ m

15 inches = ☐ cm

→ Practice book 6C p117

End of unit check

1 What is the mean height of these towers?

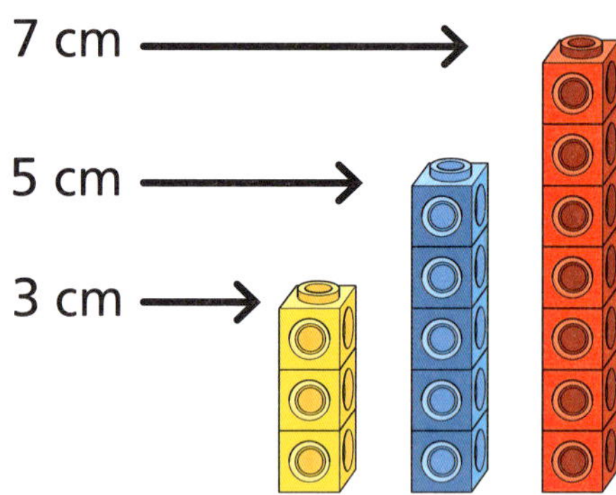

A 15 cm B 5 cm C 7 cm D 3 cm

2 The mean of the numbers on these cards is 10. What is the number on the final card?

9 | 11 | ?

A 10 B 15·5 C 2·55 D 14·5

3 What fraction of children prefer fish and chips?

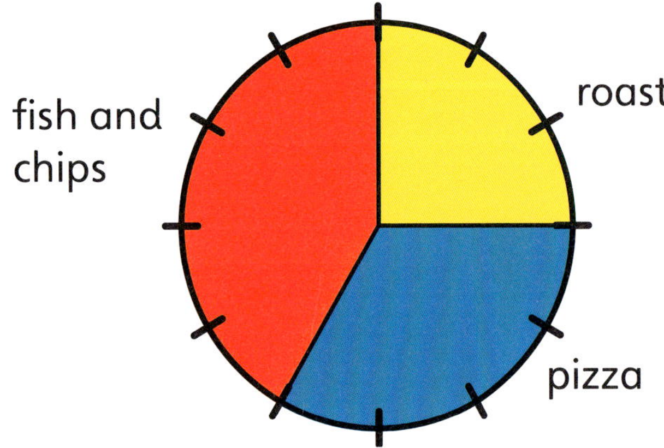

A $\frac{1}{3}$ B $\frac{5}{12}$ C 5 D $\frac{1}{4}$

4 Children have been voting for whether they would like to keep school uniform or not. Which statement is accurate?

Years 1 and 2
30 children

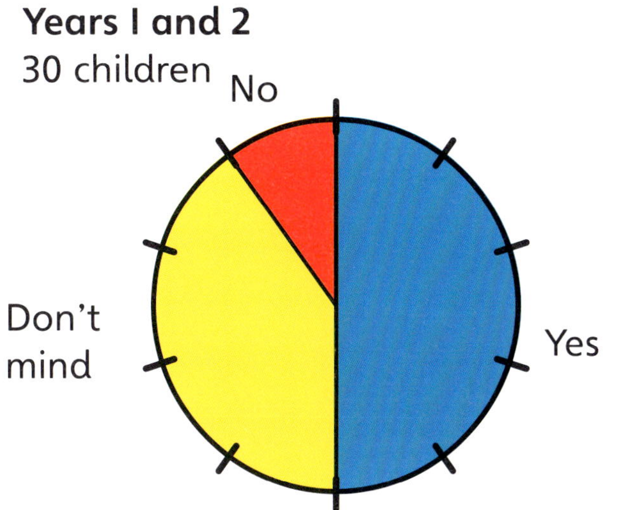

Years 3, 4, 5, 6
50 children

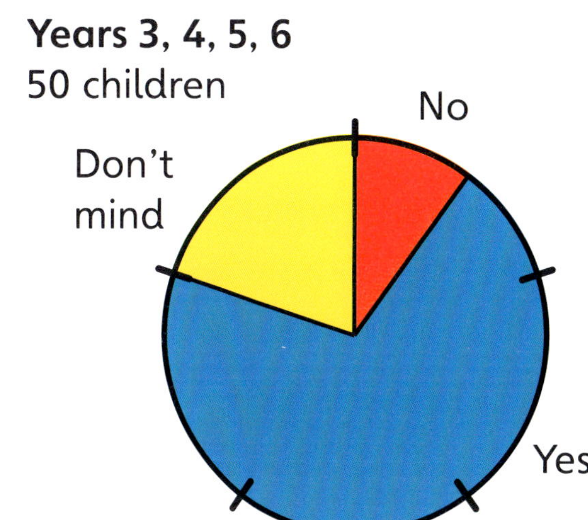

A The same number of children voted 'No' in both groups.

B 70% of all the children voted 'Don't mind'.

C $\frac{3}{5}$ of children in Years 3, 4, 5 and 6 voted 'Yes'.

D 8 out of all the children voted 'No'.

5 How far did the motorcyclist travel between 9:45 and 10:15?

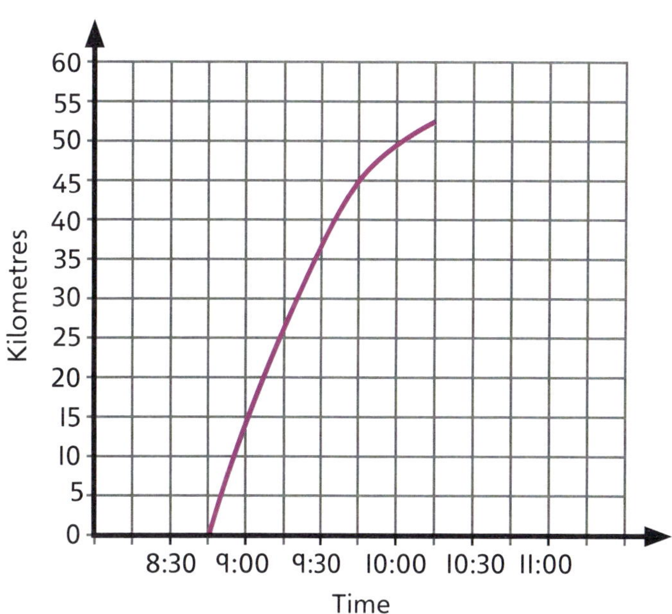

→ Practice book 6C p120

We have learnt so many things!

I think there are even
more things to learn.

I enjoyed solving
problems.

I am looking forward to learning more next year.

What have we learnt?

Can you do all these things?

- Measure angles with a protractor
- Calculate angles in shapes
- Draw nets for different shapes
- Find the mean of a group of numbers
- Create and interpret pie charts
- Interpret and construct line graphs

You now know lots about fractions, decimals and percentages, operations and measurement, geometry and algebra, ratio and proportion and statistics. Good luck with your next steps in maths!